Essential Yellowstone

A LANDSCAPE OF
MEMORY AND WONDER

MICHAEL J. YOCHIM

RIVERBEND
PUBLISHING

Essential Yellowstone: A Landscape of Memory and Wonder
Copyright © 2019 by Michael J. Yochim
Published by Riverbend Publishing, Helena, Montana

ISBN 13: 978-1-60639-120-4

Printed in the United States of America.

1 2 3 4 5 6 7 8 9 0 VP 25 24 23 22 21 20 19

Design by Sarah Cauble, www.sarahcauble.com

Riverbend Publishing
P.O. Box 5833
Helena, MT 59604
1-866-787-2363
www.riverbendpublishing.com

To the rangers and other staff members of the National Park Service,
its concessioners, and the many other organizations working
to protect the wonders of the Greater Yellowstone Ecosystem:
may you always succeed in your efforts.

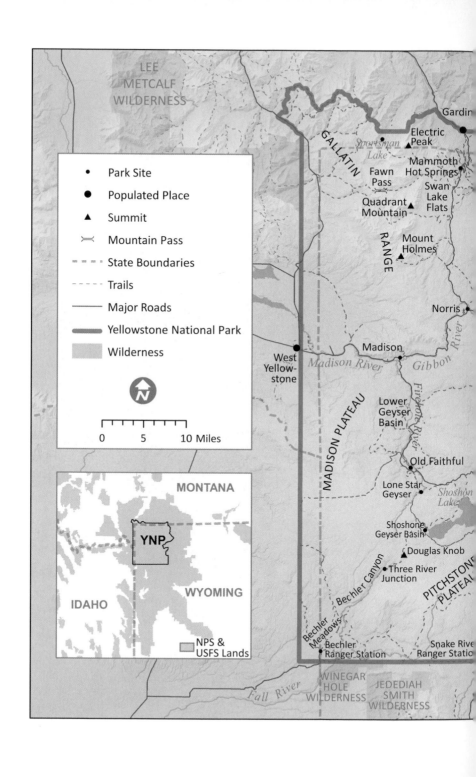

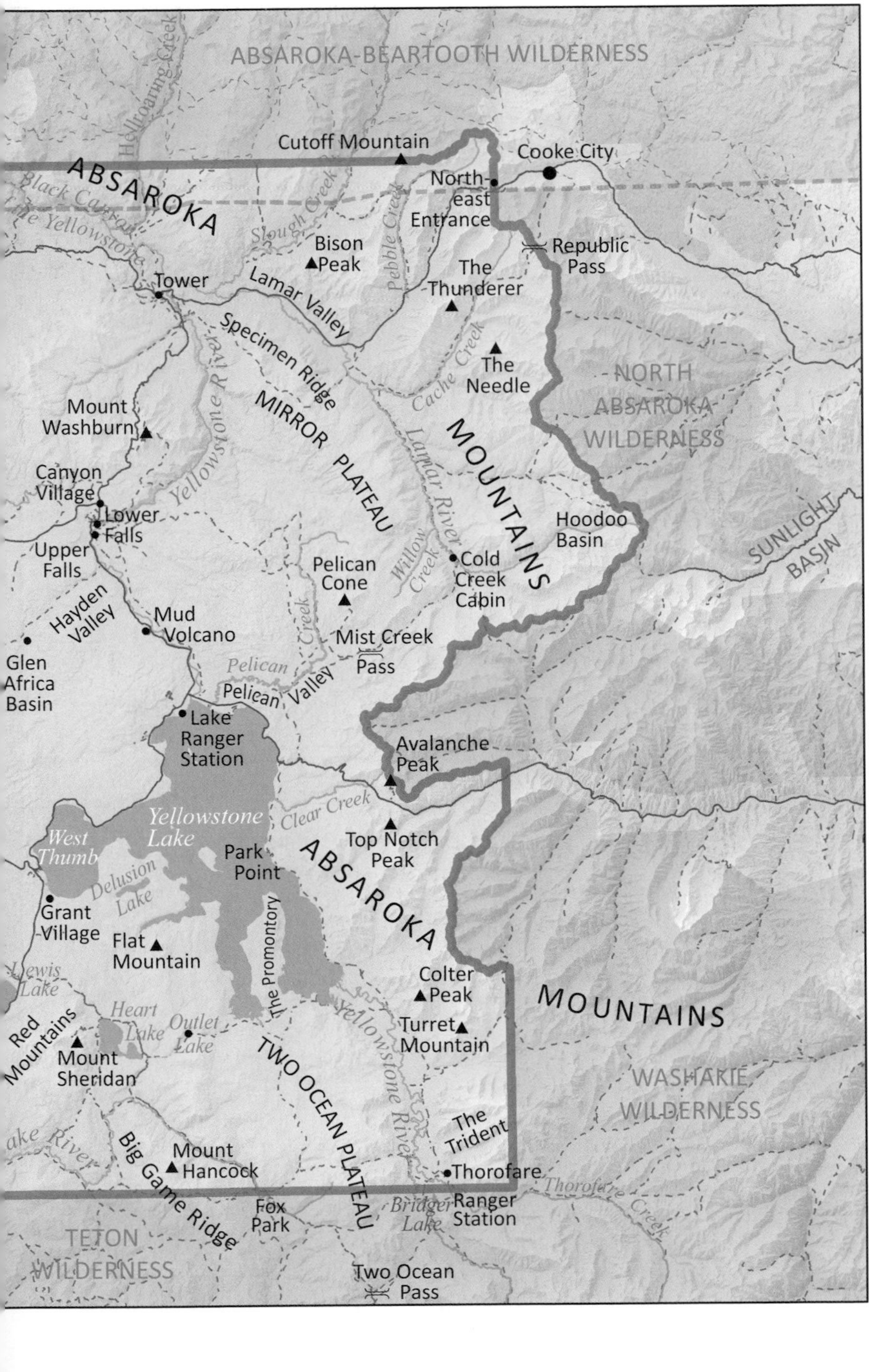
ABSAROKA-BEARTOOTH WILDERNESS
Hellroaring Creek
Cutoff Mountain
Cooke City
ABSAROKA
Black Canyon of the Yellowstone
Slough Creek
Pebble Creek
Northeast Entrance
Bison Peak
Republic Pass
Tower
Lamar Valley
The Thunderer
Specimen Ridge
The Needle
Cache Creek
NORTH ABSAROKA WILDERNESS
Mount Washburn
Yellowstone River
MIRROR PLATEAU
Lamar River
MOUNTAINS
Canyon Village
Lower Falls
Upper Falls
Hoodoo Basin
SUNLIGHT BASIN
Pelican Cone
Willow Creek
Cold Creek Cabin
Hayden Valley
Mud Volcano
Creek
Mist Creek Pass
Glen Africa Basin
Pelican Creek
Pelican Valley
Lake Ranger Station
Avalanche Peak
Yellowstone Lake
West Thumb
Clear Creek
Top Notch Peak
Park Point
ABSAROKA
Delusion Lake
Grant Village
Flat Mountain
The Promontory
Lewis Lake
Colter Peak
MOUNTAINS
Red Mountains
Heart Lake
Outlet Lake
Turret Mountain
Mount Sheridan
TWO OCEAN PLATEAU
Yellowstone River
WASHAKIE WILDERNESS
Snake River
Big Game Ridge
Mount Hancock
The Trident
Thorofare
Thorofare Creek
Fox Park
Bridger Lake
Ranger Station
TETON WILDERNESS
Two Ocean Pass

Contents

Introduction

Along the high ridge
we freeze and fall silent —
a griz with two cubs.
—David Kirtley

The Red Sea parted again for Moses in 1998 in Yellowstone National Park, with a grizzly bear playing the role of the prophet. It was early morning, and I had just picked up a busload of eager visitors for an all-day tour of the park. Driving through Hayden Valley, we were enjoying the valley's grasslands made green in the summer sun when we approached a line of cars parked alongside the road. In Yellowstone, that usually means people have sighted an animal; in Hayden Valley at that time of day and with no bison near the road, it was probably a bear. This one was easy to spot, walking through the sagebrush on the other side of the Yellowstone River, which the road parallels. I found a spot for the bus in a pullout just past the bear and let out my excited passengers. They walked down the small hill we had parked on and joined the other bear watchers lining the edge of the road. About a hundred people were there—a small bear-jam by Yellowstone standards—with another dozen in front of them on the riverbank fifty feet below. With a perfect natural barrier protecting the onlookers and the bear from each other, and with the hill I was parked on providing an already good view, I stayed behind at the bus.

The bear nosed around, foraging for edible roots or shoots, or if luck was with it, an elk calf. It was only a couple hundred pounds in weight, so it was probably a subadult, the ursine equivalent of a teenager. A coyote was nearby, searching for its breakfast too—an unsuspecting rodent, most likely. From downriver came the prehistoric cries of a pair of sandhill cranes, possibly telling the coyote to stay away: they knew it was there and were prepared to defend their colt (chick). A herd of bison grazed on the hillside above the bear, the orangey young calves closely following their mothers. Morning freshets brought the pungent scents of damp sage and grass, the smells of the American West, while the strengthening sunshine dissipated any vapors still lingering above the river. All in all, it was the quintessential Yellowstone bear sighting, probably the most memorable part of the vacation for some of the crowd.

It was soon to become *the* most memorable wildlife encounter for everyone present—and the most amusing one I witnessed in over two decades living and working in this Wonderland. Not finding what it wanted, the bear paused, looked our way, and strolled on over to the river's edge where it hesitated for a moment. Then it waded in and began swimming across the river, its strokes much like those of a dog in water. Slowly it came our way, the river's languid current there barely pushing it downstream. Even from my remove, I could sense the electric excitement in the crowd of onlookers: seeing any bear was a rare treat, let alone witnessing one swim across a river.

From my elevation, I could see something else: the griz was rapidly eroding the natural safety barrier, swimming directly toward the small group of people on the riverbank. Engrossed in nature's show, no one was moving aside to make way for the swimmer, which was approaching the halfway mark. No ranger was present to wake them from their reverie; I was the only uniformed park employee present. Because my blue polyester pants, white dress shirt, and tacky clip-on tie were more suitable for the driver of an ice-cream truck than for a well-trained Yellowstone guide, I hoped a voice of authority coming from the driver of a large yellow bus that screamed "Yellowstone Park" in bold lettering on its side would be taken seriously (Figure I.1). So, when the bear reached the middle of the river and still no one had moved, I assumed that voice and hollered down to them, "Folks, that's a BEAR swimming toward you!" Whether it was the voice or the bus—or even the misfit tie—I'll never know, but light bulbs actually went on, and those near the river retreated to the relative safety of the larger crowd.

The bear reached the shallows, climbed out of the water,

Figure I.1: Yellowstone bus and the author and former driver / guide, 1999. Despite the lack of the ice-cream-truck-driver tie, which was no longer required from 1999 on, the presumed authority of this bus's driver is evident, at least when park rangers are not present (I gave park tours in such buses for four years in the late 1990s, which was between my two periods of being a park ranger). AUTHOR COLLECTION.

and shook itself off like a dog. For a minute or two, it poked around the riverbank, looking for food. Then, without warning, it bolted, taking off at a dead run—right for the middle of the line of people. That's when the Red Sea parted, the line of people breaking into two waves, washing in opposite directions as fast as they could away from the bear. Never have I seen my fellow sluggish Americans move so quickly, the white of their eyeballs visible even from my perch. Moses the griz darted between the two waves of humanity, crossed the road, and disappeared into the forest on the other side. The waves of people crested, then spilled back over themselves in breathless disarray, closing the break in the sea. The onlookers swirled and frothed about, restoring their oxygen balance and chattering with excitement. Gradually, they climbed into their cars and motored away, while my passengers came back to the bus and found their seats.

But not before one more notable animal made a cameo appearance. As if four charismatic animals plus the biblical reenactment weren't enough for one Yellowstone wildlife showing, a bald eagle was perched in a nearby tree. Maybe it watched the parting, or maybe it was trying to find the ice-cream truck. Failing that, maybe it was trying to figure out what was up with the stupid tie. Whatever the case, it was the encore to the show we'd just finished; it was Yellowstone at its Best.

As this reenactment so aptly illustrates, Yellowstone is a living, moving landscape that creates powerful experiences, memories, and connections. For generations, people have been coming to this Rocky Mountain Wonderland, regaling in its geysers, waterfalls, and wildlife. Some of them stay in the park's comfortable hotels and rustic lodges; more of them camp out; all of them make memories, bonding with each other and with this land of steam and animals. No one forgets a visit to Yellowstone; some return again and again. One in four Americans has been to Yellowstone, confirming that the park does indeed have a powerful hold on the American imagination.

I am one such American, happily afflicted with a Yellowstone obsession at an early age. Visiting when I was just a tot, an event at the Grand Canyon of the Yellowstone formed my earliest childhood memory. My Daddy wore sunglasses on that vacation—a major violation of this two-year-old's knowledge of male dress code (until then, only Mommy had ever worn them). But Mother Nature soon restored the order when a sudden gust of wind blew them off his face and into the canyon. They were not retrievable, and Daddy conformed to my dress code for the rest of the trip (some of the wrinkles on his face are probably from squinting against the bright western sun for the rest of that trip; Figure I.2). Returning in my impressionable teens, I not only reencountered the park's wonders, but I had my first

Figure I.2: Daddy (Jim) Yochim and his twin two-and-a-half-year-old boys (the author at left) on a Yellowstone Lake beach, 1969. The sunglasses incident had occurred by this time, explaining why Jim is not sporting any. AUTHOR COLLECTION.

encounters with the unique people who worked there, the rangers of the National Park Service. One of them, an older ranger leading us on a nature walk, made us get down on our knees on a floating boardwalk to "look at all the life down there." We obliged and saw a few bugs moving around in the water, and then got our knees wet when the overloaded boardwalk no longer floated so buoyantly. On a different ranger-led hike, a younger ranger let a mosquito bite herself, showing us how its abdomen gradually filled with blood, at which point the pest labored into the air and flew off to lay her eggs. Claiming she was immune to their bites, the ranger used the show to teach us that only female mosquitoes bite, using our blood to dramatically boost the number of eggs she lays. Whatever the intended lessons might have been, it was clear to me that this place had a lot of secrets to divulge—and that the people protecting it were an eclectic, dedicated, and memorable group.

Enjoying the same experiences on that trip, my twin brother commented that the rangers were cool and that he wanted to become one someday. To this day I don't know why, but my immediate reaction was the thought, "You won't, but I will." Left unspoken, that thought became reality a few years later when I arrived in Yellowstone for my first college-year summer job (my brother remained in St. Louis for his college years and summer jobs). I sold rubber tomahawks in the Canyon Lodge gift shop, a meaningless job made meaningful by its location in the middle of the world's first national park. Five days a week, I did my time marketing kitsch to park visitors, but the evenings and weekends found me exploring the best backyard imaginable. One of the first hikes I took was an off-trail scramble to the summit of Top Notch Peak. Because it was early in June, the winter's snow hadn't fully melted, still lying several feet deep in shady areas. It was dense enough to support one's weight, except where an exposed log, warmed in the summer sun, had melted the snow it touched. Step too close to a log, we quickly discovered, and you'd break through, plunging down till you reached firm snow below the log. Sometimes we would fall in to our waists and flail helplessly until another member of the group came to the rescue. We didn't care; the exuberance of youth pulled us up, out, and onward.

Top Notch does indeed have a notch near the summit; take the wrong route up the mountain and you'll arrive at the lower of its two summits with no easy way to get to the true summit. Despite being a group of teens and twenty-somethings, our leader Stephanie had done her homework and led us up the correct route. We went part way around the mountain, crossing a lovely little valley with a gurgling brook, marsh marigolds and glacier lilies welcoming us where the snow had melted out. Climbing the far ridge, we soon reached the true summit, where we all sat down to lunch with a view of Yellowstone. Before us, the land dropped away to Yellowstone Lake, the forests and meadows of the Yellowstone plateau picking up where the waters ended and sprawling away to the Gallatin and Madison mountain ranges forming the distant horizon. Behind us and to our right and left spread the Absaroka Mountains, a hundred-mile crazy quilt of mountaintop, cliff, forest, and snow. We were high on wilderness and drunk on wildness—and shortly overcome with laughter as we slipped and slid our way down the snow back to our cars. It was to be, for me, the first of hundreds of encounters with the wonders of Yellowstone.

The West has a lot of places equal in magnificence to Yellowstone: the Colorado Rockies, the rugged coasts of California and Oregon, the granite peaks of the Sierra Nevada, the canyons of the Colorado Plateau, the Cascade volcanoes, the layered mountains of Glacier National Park. Yellowstone, though, is perhaps unique in its strong sense of place, one with many dimensions of meaning. Many authors have tried to articulate these, some by examining the voluminous literature on the park and its natural and cultural history. Writer Paul Schullery, for example, traces the park's history, finding a constant evolution in the meanings we ascribe to the park, while geographer Judy Meyer finds both continuity and evolution in those meanings. Historian Lee Whittlesey details the park's meanings around the turn of the twentieth century, while his colleagues Mark Daniel Barringer and Chris Magoc explore its significance as a marketplace. Environmental historian James Pritchard chronicles Yellowstone's role as a laboratory and crucible of science, while his colleague Richard Sellers did the same thing with all national parks more broadly. Finally, a number of authors have turned to their experiences in Yellowstone to write memoirs, many of which explore the meanings they have personally found there. Writers such as Marjane Ambler, Jerry Mernin, and Paul Schullery (again) have each published books drawing upon their time as park rangers to relate stories of Yellowstone's wonders and the many ways we have experienced them. Together with the historians and geographer—and many other writers—they paint a picture of an endlessly fascinating place that has amused people for generations, a place of beauty and significance that has few equals in America and in the hearts of Americans.

As diverse as the meanings of this hallowed place are, there is ample room for more investigations and explorations of that complexity. This book is my humble contribution to that dialogue, one that is informed as much by my experiences in the "real" Yellowstone—its two-million-acre backcountry—as by the research and study I have undertaken in the park's archives. As I have learned through these experiences, the Yellowstone wilderness is a world of powerful natural forces that can have powerfully transformative effects on the people who experience it. Away from the park's roads, boardwalks, and tourist villages, the natural forces creating Yellowstone are everywhere on display, in the thermal features peppering the land, the forests and meadows clothing it, and the animals inhabiting it. This native power can give rise to enduring connections between and among the people who explore the land, the landscape, and the animals that populate the landscape. More importantly, experiences in the Yellowstone wilderness provide insight into many of Yellowstone's core meanings, from its value as a preserve for some of the continent's most fearsome animals to its value as a contemplative retreat, from a place to unlock nature's secrets through careful research to a place to connect with family and friends, and from a place to experience the overwhelming power of nature to a place to experience nature as spiritual teacher and comforter.

This book is about that power and the enduring connections we can form with it and to each other, as seen through the lens of my experiences here. Hooked on Yellowstone from an early age, I ended up spending half my life living, working, hiking, camping, and cross-country skiing in that place, much of it as a ranger with the National Park Service. These experiences have given me a rich collection of encounters with the Yellowstone landscape and its inhabitants, both biped and quadruped. Some of these stories fill the pages of this book: tales about this land, the power that it has, some of the ways my companions and I have interacted with it, and some of the lessons we have learned. The stories include adventures and misadventures, love and fear, surprise and wonder, humor and seriousness, expeditions and quiet reflection, and teachable moments and the ursine biblical reenactment. Almost all the stories take place in the park's vast, exquisite backcountry, on some of the hundreds of hikes I took there, but a few are from the wilderness areas surrounding the park or its "front country," Yellowstone's small tourist villages and roadsides. This is a Yellowstone storybook and wilderness sampler, then, with some yarns that are amusing, others more poignant, but all illustrating the vital force that is Yellowstone and the insights and understanding I have been fortunate to receive.

I have grouped the stories into four chapters—wildlife encounters, natural forces, winter adventures, and journeys of immersion—because they are the defining elements of my experiences in Yellowstone. The stories begin with several of my more memorable wildlife encounters, experiences illustrating that the Yellowstone landscape is not just scenic, but very much alive. Roadside wildlife encounters are what most visitors enjoy and remember, but encounters in the backcountry, away from our vehicles, cabins, and lodges and the security they provide, seem more authentic, more enduring. They reverse the typical relationship of humans to the natural world, from manager and manipulator to subject and visitor. The next group of stories, Chapter Two, focuses on the ecological, geological, and atmospheric forces that create the Yellowstone landscape, seen through some of my own experiences. From fires and predation to volcanic eruptions and summertime snowfalls, Yellowstone is constantly being shaped and transformed by forces infinitely more far-reaching than human engineering. Chapter Three hones in on winter, by far the longest—and most influential—of Yellowstone's four seasons. Four stories (the norm for all chapters) illustrate the extremes of the Yellowstone winter and their importance to the flora and fauna of the Yellowstone landscape. The stories also discuss our efforts to experience winter and safeguard the frosty park. The final group of stories, Chapter Four, takes us on some hikes through the park's wilder regions, and into a pastoral backcountry valley in all four seasons. This group of stories brings together some of my deepest immersions in the Yellowstone wilderness, journeys that perhaps provide the most profound insights. Each chapter closes with some reflections, and the chapters overlap somewhat, illustrating that their subjects intertwine to create the singular Yellowstone landscape.

An epilogue rounds out the book by looking to the future, one in which humans will play as decisive a role as nature and its forces did in creating Wonderland. Taken together, this collection of stories brings to life the essential Yellowstone, a world that showcases nature's forces, teaches humility and restraint, and offers peace, joy, and endless fascination.

CHAPTER 1

Wildlife Encounters

My tracks in the snow
criss-crossed by hares and squirrels—
My cousins, all!
—David Kirtley

CAMPED AT THE BASE of Mount Holmes one night in 2007, my partner Ellen and I awoke to a most unusual nighttime visitor. It was not a bear—every camper's first and worst fear—but what it was, we hadn't a clue. We had both worked and hiked in Yellowstone for many years, but neither of us had ever heard anything like this before. It sounded a bit like R2D2 from the *Star Wars* movies, the Droid whose vocalizations were mechanical squeaks and squeals, not the noise of any creature from this planet. Whatever this was, it didn't sound like anything to fear, even though it was approaching our tent and was soon just a few feet away. We shouted at it and waited a couple of minutes for it to disappear, but it apparently didn't speak the language of earthlings and continued making its extraterrestrial noises. Failing to think of any other way to scare it away, and with it showing no sign of leaving, I decided to get out of the tent and frighten it away as best I could. Shivering as I stood up in the cold June night with my headlamp on, I looked the beast in the eyes. It was actually an earthling, of the quadruped variety, and though only eighteen inches tall, it was well endowed with defensive armor. I wondered for a moment if I had misjudged its non-threatening nature. Many visitors make that mistake in Yellowstone, and I did not want to join the ranks of the ill-prepared.

If I had been injured by the intruder, I would not have been the first to be ignominiously quilled, for I was looking at a porcupine and two of its young. The strange sounds we'd been hearing were evidently the mother communicating with her young, known as porcupettes. Relieved to see I was facing an adversary only as tall as my kneecaps, I still had a problem on my hands: exactly how does one frighten away an animal that has no fear of humans? Nudging it with my foot was a risky proposition even if I'd had boots on, but mine were in the tent. I looked around for some sticks to drive them away, but none were handy. There were some rocks, though, so I gathered a few and began pelting the adult with them, hard enough to make her feel unwelcome but not enough to hurt her. Porcupines aren't the fastest critters in the woods, but with repeated rocks hitting her, she strolled off with her porcupettes following. They made a repeat visit the next night, but I'd gathered a long stout stick for that situation, half expecting them to come calling again. As they did on the previous night, their departure was anything but rushed, more like a forced march in slow motion. Our departure the next day was similar, with sleep deprivation from those two nights slowing us down. Nonetheless, it was a great trip, with a beautiful climb of Mount Holmes providing a scenic counterpoint to the nighttime entertainment.

The porcupine incident is one of my stranger Yellowstone wildlife encounters, not only because of its extraterrestrial nature, but also because it did not involve one of the park's charismatic megafauna, the large animals that most visitors want to see. More and more, people *really* want to encounter those animals during their time in Yellowstone, so much so that when asked to list their reasons for traveling to the park, visitors rank the geysers and hot springs second. Seeing wildlife takes the prize for first, though geysers are not far behind (and, lest you fear we Americans are straying too far from our consumer habits, shopping is on that list—and not that far down from geysers). Indeed, it's hard to avoid animals in this land of wonders; whether you stay on the roads or venture out for a hike, animals constantly flavor life there.

Here are some of my more memorable encounters with Yellowstone's wildlife, three of which focus on the larger creatures that so many visitors want to see, and that strongly influence the wilderness experience. Merely by virtue of their larger size, grizzly bears, moose, and bison hold sway over us when we venture into their homes. The fourth story brings us into contact with some smaller creatures, encounters that remind us that not all of Yellowstone's animals are charismatic megafauna.

Be Prepared in the Land of Grizzly Bears

HAYDEN VALLEY IS ONE of Yellowstone's many surprises for park visitors. The park's main loop road traverses its eastern reaches, providing tranquil views of America the Beautiful, complete with amber waves of grasses, purple Washburn Mountain majesties, endless azure skyways, and the Yellowstone River substituting for the shining seas. During my Yellowstone tenure, it was hard to drive that road without encountering bison; the noble animals were almost always near or on the road itself.

Millions of people have thrilled to the sight and sound of buffalo crossing the road, grazing the lush vegetation, and going through the annual rut, with 2000-pound bulls tussling each other and jockeying for mating privileges with the females. As Moses the bear demonstrated, the valley is also good grizzly bear habitat, with its abundance of edible shoots, tubers, carrion, and elk calves. The valley is also much larger than meets the automobile passenger's eye, extending some eight or nine miles west of the road. Wanting to explore it further in 1986, my first summer working in the park, I came across a description of an 18-mile route up one side of the valley and back down the other, and found a fellow hotel employee willing to do the hike with me. He was Daniel Barbir, a Romanian fellow who, by the end of the day, was as lucky as he was happy.

Neither of us owned a car, so we got a ride to the trailhead at the north end of the valley and set off. A few paces in, I stopped for a drink of water. Pulling out my trusty Boy Scout canteen from my Boy Scout knapsack, I noticed that Daniel was not carrying a backpack of any kind (Figure 1.1). Despite my gear, I was not much of a scout (I had dropped out before even earning the lowest rank, "Tenderfoot"), but I could understand and employ the scout motto written on both canteen and knapsack: "Be Prepared." So, I asked him where his pack was, to which he replied that he didn't bring one. He had no food or water, and we were going to be out all day! If scouting had a parallel in Romania, it was clear he hadn't learned its motto. Our choices were either to abandon the hike and hitchhike back to Canyon Village, or continue on and share my supplies, which consisted of two quarts of water and a sack lunch. On a hike of this length, that was barely enough for one person, so we made a decision reflecting the exuberance and confidence of youth: we resumed hiking. The resilience of young bodies would see us through the day.

Figure 1.1: Hayden Valley and an unprepared hiker, 1986. Daniel Barbir pauses before embarking upon a full-day, eighteen-mile hike, sans food, water, rain jacket, or any other emergency or wilderness hiking gear AUTHOR COLLECTION.

Hiking westward, we became immersed in the wilds of this high elevation prairie. Here, we strode through a valley within the valley, the trail charting a course between the forested plateau bounding Hayden Valley on the north and a large island of trees in this sea of grass (to our left, or south of us). Growing vigorously in the warm July sunshine, the grasses colored the valley in various shades of summer green, a pleasing contrast to the dark green forest rimming our view. Gentle breezes swept through the knee-high graminoid seed heads, producing waves only our eyes could surf. Occasional fringed gentian and yarrow added speckles of midnight blue and cream to the visual feast, with sagebrush adding a scattering of gray. Emerging into the open sea beyond the island of forest, we came to Violet Creek, one of Yellowstone's hot streams. Diverting from our route, we followed the creek up a short way to its source, a collection of small springs clustered around a five-foot waterfall. In any state east of the Rockies, this would be a state park; here in Wonder-land, it was only another group of hot springs, seen by just a few dozen people per year.

Continuing on, the day grew warm but not unpleasant. The trail became a latticework of intertwined human and bison trails with occasional branches forking off to select grazing spots. We gave up trying to stay on the maintained trail, using my trail guide and map to pilot ourselves in the general direction of the valley's west end. The hiking wasn't difficult, as open as it was and with bison trails frequently appearing where the valley's rolling topography funneled the animals around some hill or other obstacle. Hayden Valley was once part of Yellow-stone Lake, enlarged and raised by an ice dam in the glacial era that ended around ten thousand years ago. Fine sediments accumulated in that lake bottom, producing the clay soils com-mon in the valley today. Those clays prevent lodgepole pines from establishing here (the park's most common tree, they need well-drained, sandier soils) and also made us choose our steps carefully in a few places, the going made tricky by standing wa-ter and squishy mud. We still made it to the valley's western edge by about noon, found our return trail (the stagecoach road that once went from the Lower Geyser Basin to the Yellowstone River near Mud Volcano), and looked around for a place to sit and eat our sumptuous lunch for one. We had not seen humans nor beasts all morning—but that was about to change.

Before we could sit down for lunch, we heard something bark. Barking? There were no dogs here (nor wolves, which would not be reintroduced for another nine years), and this sound was too deep for coyotes, whose bark is best described as a yip. Turning toward the sound, we saw what every Yellowstone hiker fears: a grizzly bear sow with three cubs. Sows are very protective of their cubs and likely to attack if they perceive a threat to them. Flight is their more common response, away from the threat—

and that was what they were doing when our eyes found them, about a hundred yards away. Barking is an alarm call of sorts for the cubs, who were following their mother at a dead run. Relieved to see them running in the correct direction—away—I knew our situation was still perilous. One wrong move on our part and the sow might do an about-face and charge us; she might do it even without a provocation. Looking quickly at my inexperienced partner, I saw that he was turning to run, which even I, a scout of no rank, knew was almost guaranteed to turn the sow around for a charge and attack. Grabbing ahold of him and stopping his flight with a death grip, we stood our ground and watched the griz family. They continued running away, never looking back and disappearing in the forest from which the stagecoach road emerged. The threat had passed, so I relaxed my hold on Daniel, who may still have the marks of my hand in his arm. We decided that our lunch spot had lost its appeal and we had lost our appetites anyway, so we moved on, down the stagecoach road, keeping a nervous eye over our shoulders lest the grizzly family turn around and catch up to us.

Half an hour later, my appetite returned, so we found a place to sit for lunch. Daniel ate my apple but refused more, so I happily devoured the rest of what I'd brought. We ate in silence, having already discussed the event and the proper response to a bear should we see another. Preventing an encounter by making noise to alert bears to our presence was the best thing to do; they don't like tangling with us any more than we do them, so upon hearing hikers coming, they usually take off. Should we surprise one, we should stand our ground or slowly back away. If the bear were to charge, we should climb a tree or drop to the ground, curl into the fetal position, and play dead. Either action would remove the threat in the bear's mind, although it might take a while before it realizes that you are not coming down from the tree and that, therefore, it can stop trying to pull you down. For that reason, and because I would find it difficult to scale a tree fifteen feet in the best of circumstances—let alone with an angry mother bear racing toward me—I knew I would take my chances playing possum. I would rather be sniffed and inspected by the bruin (their typical reaction to a person playing dead, sometimes with a bite or two thrown in to make sure you really are dead) than look into the eyes of an angry griz, perhaps for several hours or even overnight, all the while wondering if it will catch hold of me or climb up after me (all have happened to people treed by a bear). With these thoughts on our minds, small wonder our lunch was quiet.

The food now a memory, we resumed hiking. The stagecoach road, now grown over with grasses, was easy to follow, its once-graded and flattened road prism at odds with the landscape anywhere there was some relief. Soon it entered a peninsula of open forest jutting into the grassland sea through which we'd been journeying. We were enjoying the change of scenery when we were suddenly jolted to a stop by the sound of—unbelievably—more barking. Now knowing what to expect, we looked across the ravine on our right and saw another grizzly bear sow, this one with two cubs. Again luck was with us, for they were running away, probably having heard our talking. Daniel, either putting into practice what he'd learned from me or fearing another death grip (or both), stood still this time. With the ravine providing a partial safety barrier for us, we watched them run out of sight, the pinnacle of wild beauty in the feast we had been immersed in all day.

We saw no other bears that day; two sows with cubs was more than enough. In fact, never again would I see two sows or that many individual grizzly bears—seven—on a hike, despite eventually hiking all 1,200 miles of trails in Yellowstone, most of the trails in the national forest wildernesses surrounding the park, and almost all of the trails in neighboring Grand Teton

National Park. Hayden Valley was *the* place in the 1980s to see grizzlies, but sightings were nonetheless uncommon, both because few visitors ventured far from their cars and also because bear numbers were low, owing to changes in the way the National Park Service (NPS) had managed them. A decade earlier, park managers had closed the last open garbage dumps at which the bruins fed in an effort to return them to more natural diets. Some did, but others really didn't want to give up our high-fat foods and sought them instead in nearby campgrounds, where some bruins became nuisances, hurting people and damaging vehicles. Park managers tried moving such bears to remote areas far from human food, only to see them show up again where they'd been trapped, often within a few days. Managers had little choice but to remove such bears: over a hundred in all, a hit to the grizzly population that resulted in Endangered Species Act protection in 1975 and from which the bruin was just beginning to recover when we took our hike. We had indeed been lucky that day, in more ways than one.

How much of this were we aware of at the time? Very little. I knew that Hayden Valley had grizzlies, but I had driven through it several times and done several hikes in other parts of the park that summer, and had yet to see one. Daniel, obviously, preferred experiential education, gaining most of what he knew about grizzlies that day. Perhaps the best indication of our youthful state of knowledge came later in the afternoon, when we had to detour widely around some large herds of bison grazing on and near the stagecoach road. The charismatic animals were scattered so widely that we abandoned the road, proceeding eastward as best we could. In so doing, we came across another former road; this one was wider, with chunks of asphalt still present, and led directly east. It was the old Trout Creek Road, leading to the dump that had been most utilized by grizzly bears (Figure 1.2). Two or three dozen sometimes had been

Figure 1.2: Grizzly bears feed on human garbage at the Trout Creek Dump, 1970. Scenes like this prompted some to question how wild Yellowstone's grizzly bears really were—and a decade of controversy over closing the dump and the associated effects on the bear. NPS PHOTO, PHOTOGRAPHER UNKNOWN; COURTESY OF NPS, YELLOWSTONE NATIONAL PARK (WWW.NPS.GOV/FEATURES/YELL/SLIDEFILE/INDEX.HTM, ACCESSED MAY 30, 2017).

counted there at one time, and up to half of the park's grizzlies had fed there at some point in the year. More than any other, this dump's closure produced the grizzly bear population crash that was still affecting the bear. About all this, we knew nothing; all that mattered to us was that this road went in the direction we needed to go, and that no bison were near it—or bears.

We reached the modern road an hour later, hungry and thirsty, but otherwise none the worse for wear. Thumbing a ride back to Canyon, we arrived just before the employee dining room closed and ate a hearty meal. Daniel and I didn't hike together again, but I took several other hikes in the remaining few weeks of that season, all with groups of three or more people, and generally in areas with a lower bear density. Those hikes were without bear incidents, perhaps affirming that my learning curve was beginning to level out—a good thing in grizzly bear terrain. In a place as rich in wildlife and ecological complexities as Yellowstone, though, the learning curve should never become flat, especially for those who travel deeply into the backcountry. I learned that lesson many times over in Yellowstone, for grizzlies and the other large animals are never completely predictable, affirming the "wild" in wildlife. Indeed, Yellowstone and its wonders make for a lifetime of learning, as time, change, understanding, and personal growth occur.

Perhaps the best illustration of this dynamic ecological complexity is the story of grizzly bears after Daniel and I took that exceptional hike. Yellowstone's grizzly bears continued their slow comeback, doubling their numbers by 1990 and again by 2004. Key to this growth were the other management changes the NPS put in place at the time of the dump closures, such as installing bear-proof garbage cans throughout the park and ticketing people who fed bears, all of which had the effect of divorcing bears from human food. Park managers also closed parts of the backcountry during seasons when bears converged in those areas to eat seasonally available foods, so the bears could forage without disruption. These actions, combined with the termination of grizzly bear hunting in Wyoming and Montana, led to the bear's removal from the threatened and endangered species list in 2007 (pursuant to the outcome of lawsuits contesting that decision, the grizzly was relisted as a threatened species in 2009, but the US Fish and Wildlife Service took the bear back off the list in 2017 for many of the same reasons). Estimates of their population in and around Yellowstone today center at seven hundred but run as high as a thousand, which is an order of magnitude larger than it was in the late 1970s. Such significant population growth sent ecological ripples throughout the region, particularly in the elk population. Grizzly bears can outrun and take down elk calves in their first month of life, so more bears have translated into fewer elk surviving to adulthood. Since 1995, Yellowstone's elk population has declined by 50 to 75 percent, but that reduction is commonly attributed to wolves, which were reintroduced to Yellowstone that same year. Wolves have certainly preyed heavily on elk, but it is ecological naiveté to blame wolves exclusively for the drop in elk numbers when grizzly bears clearly have an additive effect. Even attributing the elk decline to both species simplifies reality, for an abundance of dry years since 1995 has produced poor forage for elk, resulting in fewer calves. Still other factors such as elk hunting outside Yellowstone and resurging mountain lion numbers likely contribute to this story or may come into play in the future. The complexity and dynamism of Yellowstone's ecology is clear, as is the success of grizzly bear conservation.

As Daniel and I experienced that day in 1986, grizzlies are not only successful, they are also fearsome, a powerful symbol of nature's wildness. Although I never again saw so many in one day, I had many more run-ins with them, including one in spring, when bears emerge from hibernation. Two decades after the hike of the grizzlies, I trekked again to the head of Hayden Valley, this time on cross country skis. It was April, and snow still lay heavy on the land. A string of warm days and cold nights had successively melted and refrozen the snowpack, transforming it from soft powder into solid firmness upon which skiers could veritably fly. Such conditions don't occur every year, so my buddy Mike Tercek and I made plans to ski to Glen Africa Basin, a thermal area at the west end of Hayden Valley that I'd missed on the hike with Daniel. Knowing the sun would gradually soften the snow and slow us down, Mike and I—the Doctors Mike, for we both have doctorates—hit the snow-covered trail early, zooming across the frozen sea of grass to Violet Creek. There we dismounted our boards of speed to hop the stream, whose waters were still warm enough here, a few hundred yards from the hot springs, to melt the snow back a foot or two on either side. Donning our skis again after the easy jump, we made steady progress on the firm snow, arriving at the thermal basin just as the snow was starting to soften. The nine-mile journey took us two and a half hours, two-thirds of the hiking time.

My first impression of Glen Africa Basin, other than the steam that guided us in the last half mile, was the field of grass fronting it, grass that had no snow cover but that did have a liberal scattering of bison droppings (Figure 1.3). Warmed enough to melt snow but cool enough for grass to grow, the field sustained bison when the rest of Hayden Valley's grass was buried by snow and harder or impossible to reach. None of the furry beasts were there that day, having migrated west to the lower-lying Firehole River Valley when even this patch of grass had become insufficient. We poked around the thermal area, finding a few fumaroles (gas vents) and small hot springs, one or two of which were spouters, continuously erupting water three or four feet high (Figure 1.4). Satisfied that we'd seen the basin's major features, we found a dry patch of grass and sat down for lunch. Dessert consisted of cookies with a chaser of Jim Beam bourbon (one must always Be Prepared!). In the warm Rocky Mountain sunshine, with full bellies and Mr. Beam helping us forget any worries we may have had, we both nodded off, enjoying an hour of bliss in an already exceptional day.

The return trip was slower, the snow having softened enough that our skis sank in an inch or two. Our tracks from the morning were gone, melted in the sunshine that had me in shorts and a T-shirt. An hour after we'd begun skiing out, though, I went reaching for warmer clothing because we came across something that sent a chill down my spine: grizzly bear tracks. They were fresh, and they were big (Figure 1.5). Not only were they new

Figure 1.3: Bison pasture at Glen Africa Basin, 2005. This thermally warmed patch of grass is a field of dreams for some Yellowstone bison, sustaining some when the rest of Hayden Valley gets buried by snow. As the skull attests, some of the dreams become nightmares, perhaps because the pasture is too small to support a bison all winter. Mike Tercek is in the background. AUTHOR COLLECTION.

Figure 1.4: Alum Creek, Glen Africa Basin, 2005. Bison aren't the only animals sustained by the thermal warmth and associated life at this small thermal area, as the elk rack suggests. AUTHOR COLLECTION.

since the morning, the afternoon sun had barely begun to melt them, indicating the bear had passed this way in the last fifteen or twenty minutes. Including the claws, the bear's hind feet were almost a foot long, and its front claws—the bear's business set—were at least three inches long. These were the tracks of a sizable boar (a male), and it was walking east, the same as us— and he was probably hungry, anxious to end his five-month fast. We could see that he had come down from the hill to our left, which prompted Mike to mention that he'd heard the sounds of a large animal breaking branches coming from that vicinity as we skied by this morning. Stopping momentarily, he had failed to see movement, so he caught back up to me. We snapped some photos of the tracks and resumed skiing, following them and keeping a wary eye for their owner. In the brilliantly white landscape we were a part of that day, the bruin would have been easily seen. We never saw him, though, and his tracks eventually diverged from those we were leaving.

The five-month fast that our track artist had just finished is quite different from the hibernation some smaller animals undergo. Marmots and some ground squirrels, for example, will see a radical drop in body temperature, to just above freezing, but they will occasionally warm up and rouse themselves to eat, drink, and eliminate wastes. Not so for the grizzly, whose body temperature falls only ten or fifteen degrees. More remarkable, though, is that grizzly bear bodies become a closed metabolic system for the duration of hibernation. For four to six months (depending on such variables as winter severity and food availability), they will not eat, drink, urinate, or defecate. Instead, they subsist on body fat, reprocessing wastes into proteins and other substances they need. Pregnant females, moreover, will give birth to two to four cubs while hibernating, and then nourish them to grow from a pound or two at birth to about twelve pounds when spring arrives. The huge metabolic demands of hibernation for bears of either sex mean they lose a third of their body weight by springtime, which is why putting on fat is the bear's sole focus in the weeks leading up to hibernation. Fattening up in the fall is so important that the bear has evolved to delay implantation of fertilized eggs in the uterus until November, the start of hibernation. Mating, short as it is for bears, would take too much time away from eating in the fall, so they have also evolved to mate in June, when food is plentiful. But with gestation taking just two months, the female's body suspends pregnancy until she is hibernating. The blind and helpless cubs are born in January, and they spend the following two years with their mother before she mates again and drives them off. So begins anew the extraordinary ursine cycle of life and hibernation. As that cycle demonstrates, grizzly bears hold endless fascination for the wilderness traveler and armchair naturalist, much like the landscape they inhabit.

As one would surmise from this discussion, bears have one, and only one, thing on their mind once the winter fast is over: food, so we were right to be cautious that April day. While grizzly bears seldom prey on humans, they are possessive of animal carcasses (their main food in spring), so we maintained our vigilance the rest of the day. We finished the day without further incident, and although I saw many more grizzly tracks in my time in Yellowstone, none were as perfect and purposeful as those in the springtime snow. The tracks were clear evidence that Hayden Valley was still the grizzly bear haunt it had been in the 1980s. Blessed with an abundance of naturally occurring foods and nearby cover, the valley still held the same allure for the bear—and for us. It was not only a reminder of how the continent looked before settlement, but also of how it acted. Many western landscapes do the former, but few are able to do the latter, for almost none have the griz. In the contiguous United States, only the Greater Yellowstone Ecosystem and the Crown

Figure 1.5: Grizzly bear tracks, Hayden Valley, 2005. Boars (males) emerge from hibernation before females with cubs. At the time they emerge (March and April), scavenging on winter-killed carcasses is the main way the bear breaks its five-month fast. AUTHOR COLLECTION.

of the Continent Ecosystem, which includes Glacier National Park and the Bob Marshall Wilderness Complex in Montana, have a healthy population of grizzlies, the two redoubts for the bear and the wildness that sustains them.

Grizzly bears change the way elk and other prey animals act and move in the landscape, they change the distribution of favored plant foods (by roto-tilling the soil digging for edible roots and tubers), and they change us. They sharpen our focus on our surroundings, forcing us to be aware of tracks and other signs they have been this way. In a way that no other animal in the contiguous states can do, they growl, bark, and roar that we are not the ultimate power here. Just as I learned my first time through Hayden Valley, we must always be aware and humble in their haunt and home, this landscape of power.

A Weekend with Family and Yellowstone Wildlife, Large and Small

A HOUSE IS NOT A HOME without food to eat and water to drink, and Yellowstone has plenty of both for its resident grizzly bears. The Hayden Valley adventures emphasized the importance of red meat in the form of carrion and elk calves, but two other hikes I took in the Yellowstone area illustrated the importance of three other key foods. The first of the outings was in 2004, when my youngest brother Brian and his wife Jill paid me a visit. Knowing they wanted a combination of adventure and relaxation while they were with me, I got permission to stay in the Clear Creek Cabin on Yellowstone Lake. We would canoe the three miles down the shoreline to it, spend the night, and then climb nearby Avalanche Peak the next day. This sounded good to them, so we packed our overnight bags, loaded the canoe on my truck, and drove the sixty miles to the put-in early the next morning. We were embarking upon a journey that would give us what we were seeking and more; indeed, Yellowstone rarely disappoints its visitors, and it would outdo itself this time, with both megafauna and microfauna starring in the show.

With the canoe on the beach and our gear in it, we launched and began paddling. This part of the lakeshore has a fifteen-mile fetch aligned with the prevailing wind direction (from the southwest), so waves the size of ocean swells are not unusual. Adding to the challenge for canoeists, whose craft can be swamped by mere whitecaps, are the rocky shores here, the easily eroded sand and gravel long since carried away by the waves. For the unfortunate paddler caught in rough water, there is no place to land on these stretches (some more than a mile long), putting one at risk of capsizing and drowning or dying of hypothermia in the lake's frigid water. More people have died in such boating accidents in Yellowstone's history than in any other manner (excluding traffic accidents and medical reasons). For this reason, we got an early start, paddling to the cabin in the morning calm. Jill, who was not afflicted with the gene that made Yochims wake up with the roosters, called this "Yochim time," an expression that reflected both her sympathy and pity for the afflicted. Nonetheless, she could see that it was occasionally useful, as we sat down for a relaxed lunch on the cabin beach.

After lunch, the wind stayed light and the waves small, so we canoed an additional three miles to Park Point, where the shoreline bends slightly to the east, affording a spectacular view south to the lake's remotest reaches. The point is named for the meadow that spills down to the lake from a sloping hill. Putting to shore, we climbed that hill to take in one of my favorite views in Yellowstone (Figure 1.6). Beyond the golden meadow, the lakeshore gracefully curves to a forested point, conifers replacing the meadow a hundred yards from us but then shrinking in size as they approach the distant point. To the right of that point, across the opening to the lake's Southeast Arm, rises the Promontory, its triangular form clothed in dark forest. The Arm recedes a dozen or so miles into the distance, finally ending at the foot of a gray, flat-topped ridge, the northern end of the Two Ocean Plateau. The Continental Divide runs down the middle of that long plateau, splitting its snowmelt between the two oceans cradling the contiguous states. About a dozen more miles south (and out of view), the plateau looks down upon the most remote point in the contiguous states, a place some nineteen or twenty miles from the nearest road (as the raven flies, there being no crows here). That is a land of broad valleys and high mountains, alpine plateaus and rushing streams, dense forests and flower-filled meadows, elk and moose, wolves and grizzly bears. Only trails penetrate that vast wilderness, many of which I have been fortunate to hike. Some of the stories later in

Figure 1.6: Yellowstone Lake from Park Point, 2006. This is a view into Yellowstone's Thorofare region, which is part of a sprawling wilderness area about 2700 square miles in size—larger than the state of Delaware. Author collection.

this book are from those hikes; for now, we satisfied ourselves with a long, relaxed peek into a country of remoteness and wildness.

We arrived back at the cabin in time for some wine and cheese on the lakeshore. The light breeze we'd been enjoying began to calm, and some mosquitoes began to emerge, so we finished the hors d'oeuvres and moved inside to make supper. Like most of Yellowstone's backcountry cabins, this one was rustic, with a wood-burning stove for heat, a basic table and folding chairs for dining, Coleman lanterns for lighting, a filter and bucket for drinking water (UHaul it from the nearby creek), and bunks and mattresses for sleeping. A Holiday Inn they are not, but this one was a step above the other cabins I'd used, with a separate bedroom for the bunks—two of which, for some reason, were under what looked like a tent suspended from the ceiling. The cabins provide a bed and shelter from the elements for rangers patrolling and maintaining the park's 1200-mile trail system. Off-duty rangers like me could use the cabins if the local rangers approved and if the users agreed to leave it in better shape than they found it. I had long taken advantage of this employee perk, expanding my hiking range (because I didn't need to carry the gear that the cabins provided, my pack was lighter, so I could hike faster and farther) and knowledge of the park (which benefits the agency). I also brought guests who didn't ordinarily backpack to a cabin for a unique park experience, the cabins providing the shelter they couldn't carry.

The Clear Creek Cabin is different from most Yellowstone patrol cabins in that it was specifically built to shelter employees counting cutthroat trout swimming up the nearby creek to spawn in June, something the NPS does every year to monitor their population health. Park managers have monitored this number for over half a century; it peaked around 70,000 in the late 1970s. So many cutthroats swimming up the creek in one month would have been a feast in fins for a well-positioned grizzly bear; trout are high in protein and are a key food in early summer. In fact, the hungriest and most skillful bears could consume over fifty trout in one day! With the same opportunity available on 35 other Yellowstone Lake tributaries, cutthroats were one of the four most important foods for grizzlies—until lake trout began decimating cutthroat numbers in the late 1990s. Lake trout are invaders to Yellowstone Lake, brought there in the 1980s by a misinformed or ill-intentioned person or group of people. Lake trout feed on cutthroats (over forty cutthroats annually per lake trout) and they don't spawn in tributary streams, so they were not good news for those concerned with grizzly bear recovery. Park managers, alarmed at the prospect of ecological collapse from that voracious predator (besides grizzlies, twenty other birds and mammals feed on cutthroats), immediately began a gill-netting program targeting the invaders. These efforts have been doubled and redoubled in the years since, and may finally be paying off, for the number of lake trout per unit effort has declined in the last few years, and cutthroat numbers at Clear Creek have risen modestly. Still, the numbers at Clear Creek tell the story best, for spawning cutthroat numbers bottomed out at only 538 in the late 2000s—a 99% decline—before rising to 743 in 2015 and 801 in 2016.[1] For now, the cutthroat is still effectively eliminated from the grizzly bear's diet, a situation that NPS netting efforts may yet change. Fortunately, the grizzly seems to have taken the situation in stride, finding replacement foods elsewhere in and around Yellowstone, but the bear would undoubtedly welcome the cutthroat back into its diet.

Back at Clear Creek, we wondered if the resident mosquito population was facing the same food deprivation, because an occasional one made its presence known—inside the cabin—while

---

1 Technical difficulties precluded an accurate count in 2017 and 2018.

we cooked and ate supper that evening. I had seen this before in some cabins; a few of the pests would get in as we went out to get water or use the outhouse. With the fish counting crew here for a month or more at the height of the mosquito hatch, repeatedly going in and out throughout the day, such indoor mosquitoes were probably a recurring problem, explaining the tents over two of the beds: they were mosquito netting. Knowing that even one mosquito would manage to find the ear of the person in the open bed (probably me, since I would offer the netting-covered beds to my two guests), I did my best to put the whiners out of my misery, and Brian and Jill did likewise. A few well-timed whacks and the cabin should be free of the sleep-destroying bloodsuckers. But something was wrong, for the mosquitoes didn't disappear. I reasoned then that with the fish counting season ending just days before we arrived, there might be more of the pests still hanging on in the cabin, and so a few more smacks should do it. So we continued waging war as we cleaned up from dinner, each of us looking for the expected reprieve. It was not to be, however; rather, as we ate dessert and then tried to relax, the whining and whacking intensified. Soon it sounded like a Three Stooges episode, complete with the same expressions ("Why you!" "Take that!" and even a "Nyuck, nyuck" or two) and, of course, plenty of slaps, some of them hard enough to spatter blood (ours, but from the abdomens of the mosquitoes that were already filling up on us). Now we really knew what the netting over the beds was for: to help us survive the night! Somehow mosquitoes were getting in (perhaps through cracks in the chinking between the logs), and there was no sign of a let up. It was time to concede defeat and seek shelter. Forgetting chivalry, I dove to safety in one of the netting-covered beds, leaving the other for them to share (the beds were twins, but they didn't care about being crowded). We had lost the battle but not the war, thanks to the netting.

The netting was our shelter in the mosquito storm, giving us more rest than the alternative. Actually, as the cabin cooled, the mosquitoes gradually went back to wherever they'd come from, so Brian took his life in his hands and crept out after the whining ceased to one of the uncovered beds. He survived without any whining in his ears, sleeping as well as Jill and I did (which is to say, mediocre). Once the sun rose, we did too, anxious to be long gone before warming temperatures reawakened the swarms (Jill was beginning to wish she had our gene). We broke our fast and cleaned the cabin in good time, hopping in the canoe before the sun's rays had found the cabin. An hour later, the first half of our adventure came to an end when we loaded the canoe back onto my truck. We had seen thirty-six of Yellowstone's thirty-five mosquito species, an experience with Yellowstone's microfauna that was, to be positive, unforgettable.

We then made the short drive to the Avalanche Peak trailhead and began the mountain ascent. The trail is one of the steepest in the park, climbing 2,200 feet in just over two miles. After passing through a lush spruce-fir forest, the trail enters a small, flowery meadow. Hopping the little creek bisecting it, we climbed to the top of the meadow and sat down for second breakfast. It was a lovely spot, with Top Notch Peak across the valley rising above the rainbows of color surrounding us. Part way through our snack, though, a member of Yellowstone's megafauna appeared at the bottom of the meadow: a grizzly bear. It was not that big, but it was coming our way. We hollered to get its attention and scare it away, but it either didn't hear us or didn't care, for it kept coming. We continued shouting and it continued walking toward us, approaching the halfway point. Grizzlies have poor eyesight, so it may not have registered our existence visually, but their hearing is good, so it had to hear us by now—unless it was deaf or, again, didn't care (the creek was too small to mask our calls). Either way, I had not seen this behavior before (bears had always fled as soon as they heard or saw me and my hiking partners), so I realized we needed to move. But our food was scattered around us, and some of the containers were open! We couldn't let the bear get any human food, so Scene Two of the Three Stooges show began as we madly scrambled to get the food in our backpacks. Ziploc bags were flying between us as we shoved them in, sealed shut or not, all the while shouting at the bear and watching it get closer. Adding to the entertainment was that one of us—me—was shoeless, having taken my boots off to let my socks dry. I pulled them on and improvised a knot on both, managing to avoid tying the two together but not to avoid dropping a couple pieces of the gorp I'd been eating in one of my boots. The bear now just a few yards away, we grabbed our packs and walked, hobbled, and limped the only direction we could go: up the trail. The party's fearless leader—again, me—brought up the rear, ostensibly because I had the only container of bear pepper spray, but perhaps also because my feet didn't enjoy the gorp as much as my stomach had. Still, the unwitting Stooges were making their escape.

As we soon would discover, however, Scene Two wasn't quite finished. After five minutes of our slow motion escape, we paused, gasping for breath (all of us) and gimping with gorp-inflicted pain (one of us). The trail was still steep, and the high elevation air thin, so even a steady walk—the fastest one should move away from a griz at any time—was difficult to maintain. I had just emptied my boot and was tying its laces when I saw movement down the trail. It was the bear again, back for more laughs. That's what it got as we repeated the panic, again realizing that our only option was to continue up the trail, the mountain slope here being too steep to safely step to the side and let the bruin pass. We walked farther this time, stopping well after we'd rounded a switchback that we hoped would sideline the bear. Moments later, though, we saw its familiar face approaching, yet again. And so Scene Two played out: walk, stop, gasp for breath, see bear, move on. Up through the switchbacks we went in this oxygen-deprived, slow motion, modern-day Three Stooges episode. Walk, stop, gasp for breath, see bear, move on. After four or five rounds of this ursine entertainment, the slope finally leveled out, allowing us to step aside and let the bruin mountaineer pass. It passed on by, walked a short distance farther, then left the trail itself, slowly disappearing from view in the forest across from us.

That forest is what it may have been seeking, for the stand of trees was dominated by whitebark pine, one of the highest-growing trees in Yellowstone. Whitebarks produce a nut so rich in fat, carbohydrates, and protein that it is as nutritious for the bear as animal foods like elk calves and cutthroat trout. What's more, the cones are borne in autumn, right when grizzly bears are eating everything they can find in preparation for their marathon fast. The nuts are so wholesome that pregnant females have larger litters of cubs in winters following good pine nut production (whitebarks only bear cones an average of every other year). Years that the trees don't produce a sizable crop will see grizzlies heading for the lowlands in search of food in fall. Since those areas are where people live, conflicts sometimes arise, such as when bears find food in unsecured garbage cans. When the whitebarks do produce cones, bears face a minor dilemma in getting them, for the trees don't drop them and they are only found on the uppermost branches, out of ursine reach. Red squirrels are the solution, for they stockpile the cones at the base of a favorite tree, to eat over winter. The task for the bear, then, is only to find one of these food caches, known as middens. Once in awhile, the whitebarks will outdo themselves, producing so many cones that some of them are still on the trees the following spring. Our bear may have been searching for a midden containing these or other leftovers; either way, he had exited the scene.

My two fellow Stooges looked at me after the bear left us, the expression on their faces posing the question of what to do now: abort the hike or resume the climb? Notwithstanding its behavior that morning, the bear seemed to be truly done with its game of cat and mouse, and I knew the trail was about to leave the forest for the final pitch to the summit, so we decided to finish the ascent. A half hour later, we sat down to a 360 degree view much like the one I had enjoyed from Top Notch Peak eighteen years earlier (Figure 1.7). This mountain's summit is a pile of rock just a few feet higher than the broad crescent-shaped ridge that defines the peak, so we could easily see anything coming our way. Thankfully, our only visitors were the booted bipedal

Figure 1.7: Brian and Jill Yochim and the author (at right) on Avalanche Peak, 2006. Yellowstone Lake can be seen in the background. Between the lake and us is a mountain ridge with some snow on it; the ridge continues rising to Top Notch Peak, out of view to the left. COURTESY BRIAN AND JILL YOCHIM.

variety, whom we regaled with our story of how to amuse a bear. Scene Two of the Three Stooges episode had clearly ended, allowing us to relax and enjoy the view and our tossed-about lunch. It was everything the climb had not been: tranquil and serene, with any worries momentarily forgotten.

The descent was thankfully unremarkable, but the showers we took at home that evening quite the opposite, as each of us washed off the accumulated sweat, trail dust, mosquito guts, and dried blood of two eventful days. Back among the civilized, we treated ourselves to dinner out and laughed about our experiences. Brian and Jill left for home the next day. As they said goodbye, they thanked me for adventures that would be difficult to forget or, for that matter, to repeat. Maybe that's why they chose winter for their next visit, a time when mosquitoes are nonexistent, bears are in hibernation, and unwitting stooges are in scarce supply.

That's not the only time I saw a bear climbing a mountain in the Yellowstone area. Not long after the Avalanche Peak incident, the Doctors Mike took another outing, this time with Mike's now-wife Ashea Mills. We set out to climb Emigrant Peak, an imposing mountain rising 6,000 feet above the Yellowstone River, some twenty miles north of the park. Once we gained the ridge leading to the summit, I pulled ahead of the other two. The ridge presented no climbing or route finding problems, but it does get steep and rocky near the summit. Concentrating on finding safe footing, I had my head down as I approached the top. As I crested it, I saw a flash of knee-high brown fur that disappeared as quickly as I saw it (had I blinked at the wrong time, I would have missed it). At this elevation (almost 11,000 feet), I realized it had to be a grizzly bear because the other animals that frequent such elevations were either a different color (mountain goats, white, and bighorn sheep, light gray) or too small (marmots). So it was a griz, but where was it? I frantically looked down all sides of the peak, but didn't see it. Emigrant's summit is small with steep sides all around, so it must have been hidden behind some rock outcrop below me. But where, and what was it doing? Was it running away, or was it coming back to reclaim its lofty perch? I waited uneasily for my climbing partners, repeatedly looking down for the bear.

Mike arrived a few minutes later, with Ashea close behind. I was relieved to learn they hadn't seen the bear, but I soon found that they thought my tale was a little tall. Just at that moment, I spotted the bruin a thousand feet below us and moving fast. Shouting "there it is!" I pointed to it, and then we all watched it disappear in the forest clothing the mountainside. In a mere ten minutes the bear had descended a thousand feet of steep mountainside covered in loose volcanic cobbles, a pace the best alpinist would struggle to match. This griz was very real and very agile—and very selective in its choice of mountaintops to scale and take in the view. Space yawned in three dimensions, from Paradise Valley a vertical mile below us, to the seemingly never-ending collage of mountains and mountain ranges stretching dozens of miles in all directions. To the north were the Crazy, Bangtail, and Bridger Mountains; to the west, the Gallatin, Madison, and Gravelly Ranges, one behind another; to the south, the Washburn and Red Mountains in Yellowstone and beyond them, more than a hundred miles distant, the Tetons; and to the east, beyond the Absaroka and Beartooth Ranges, their lingering snow glinting in the bright sunshine. Almost all of those mountain ranges are protected, which is why the grizzly bear is thriving—and there at all, given the dozens, sometimes hundreds of square miles each bear needs.

If the view was not the reason the bear I glimpsed was there, army cutworm moths might have been. These small nocturnal moths, the bane of low-land wheat farmers, migrate to the high country to escape the summer heat and feed on alpine flower nectar there. During the day, they escape the warmth by crawl-ing under the rocks in talus piles (fields of loose rocks). Grizzlies will overturn the rocks, slurping up the moths—by the thou-sands, up to forty thousand in a day! At about a half calorie each and made mostly of fat, they rival the whitebark nuts as a hiber-nation prep. Most of the known moth sites are south and east of Yellowstone, but Emigrant Peak has an abundance of talus on its sides, so the bear I glimpsed may well have been enjoying a private feast, sleeping it off, or taking in the space.

As these two encounters reveal, grizzly bears find a variety of high quality foods in Yellowstone and the surrounding area. Most important among those are elk calves, cutthroat trout, whitebark pine nuts, and army cutworm moths, but there are many others. With three of these important foods being animals and with an abundance of other animals to opportunistically eat (such as wolf kills), it's perhaps not a surprise to learn that, relative to other grizzly populations, Yellowstone's grizzly bears have a taste for meat. The grizzlies in Glacier National Park, for example, rely more heavily on that park's lush vegetation (especially huckleberries), to the extent that their diet is only 20 percent meat, compared to 50 percent for Yellowstone's bruins. The disparity in their diets also indicates that grizzlies are flex-ible, able to mold their diets to the foods available in different habitats. This adaptability is what enabled them to recover from the dump closures and other management changes in the 1970s, what led them to the dumps in the first place, what enabled them to thrive when lake trout took away cutthroats—and what has enabled them to continue flourishing when the whitebark pine crashed in the 2000s. Since I climbed Avalanche Peak with Brian and Jill, the whitebarks on that mountainside have all suc-cumbed to white pine blister rust (a fungus that attacks certain pines) or mountain pine beetle (which tunnel into and destroy the cambium, the tree's growing layer). Some three-fourths of the whitebark pines in and around Yellowstone have gone the same way. Despite the loss, grizzlies appear to be doing well, perhaps because some whitebarks have survived, because the moths persist, because the bears are substituting a different food, or a combination of these possibilities. With this omnivorous plasticity, the long-term outlook for the bear is good, as long as it is protected. This adaptability is partly why the US Fish and Wildlife Service took the bear back off the list of threatened and endangered species in 2017. Given protection, the grizzly is a remarkable survivor indeed.

The grizzly bear is also, for many of us, the ultimate symbol of wilderness, wildness, and nature's power. Both of these bear-on-mountain encounters were with subadult bears, basically bear teenagers. Much like their human counterparts, subadult bears are still learning how the world works, occasionally producing unusual and unpredictable behavior. As bears age, their behavior may become more routine and predictable, but it always retains elements of wildness, never becoming sedate and fully controlled. Wilderness travelers never know when they will see the bruins, or any of nature's creatures, or what they will do when we encounter them. Their presence in the landscape and their variability in responding to our interruptions and encounters demand recognition and awareness when we travel through their homeland. Animals and their unpredictability enliven both the landscape and us, helping make Yellowstone so vibrant and compelling, ever-changing and alive.

Traveling Through Time on the Mirror Plateau

THE MIRROR PLATEAU rises 9,000 feet into the sky in Yellowstone's northeast corner. As high as it is, the plateau is equally remote, with a point on it being over thirteen miles from the nearest road in any direction. That makes it the sixth most remote place in the country outside of Alaska, putting it among the ranks of the Big Wild—places with names like the Bob Marshall, Frank Church, and Selway-Bitterroot Wildernesses, not to mention Yellowstone's own Thorofare. While any wilderness aficionado will recognize those names, they might draw a blank with the Mirror (or, as it's sometimes known, the Upper Lamar/ North Absaroka wilderness complex). This could be because no trails cross the plateau; only a few approach it, turning back before reaching its loftiest heights, as if deterred by some power unwilling to give up its secrets. As well, the Mirror is made the more inaccessible by the rugged depths of the Lamar and Yellowstone River canyons, flanking its northern half like a pair of linear sentinels. These attributes make the Mirror even more remote than its distance from a road would indicate; to really explore it, you must be willing to hike off trail, navigate by map and compass, and climb over or around the obstacles in the way, all while dealing with Yellowstone's micro- and megafauna. Few people are willing to confront such challenges, so the Mirror remains little known—which is just fine with the animals that call it home, along with its occasional explorers.

In 2002, I was fortunate to become one of those explorers. I had just moved back to Yellowstone from Wisconsin to take a more permanent park ranger position with the NPS (my previous appointments had been seasonal) and to do my dissertation research. The year before, I had suffered through Independence Day in Gardiner, a late night, lawless pandemonium featuring every kind of pyrotechnic noisemaker known to red-blooded Americans. Near and far, louder and loudest, and continuing well after midnight, pyrotechnics fans competed with each other to see who could be the loudest and latest celebrant. I wasn't anxious to subject myself to that chaotic cacophony again, so I decided to get as far as I could into the backcountry and away from the noisemakers this time around. When I heard that some fellow employees were planning a four-day hike across the Mirror Plateau over the July 4th weekend, I asked if I could join them. They welcomed me along, so on July 4th we escaped, in the nick of time.

Our hike began at the Pelican Valley trailhead on the north shore of Yellowstone Lake. For this hike, I was with Ivan Kowski, who worked in the park's backcountry office, his wife and park interpreter Beth Taylor, bear biologist Kerry Gunther, and fisheries biologist Pat Bigelow. Pelican Valley has one of the highest bear densities in Yellowstone; it is so important for the bear that the NPS closes it to human entry every spring so the bruins can utilize its rich food resources without being disturbed. May and June bring a variety of edible roots and tender shoots out of dormancy, but the real prizes for bears at that time are newborn elk calves and cutthroat trout swimming up the creek to spawn (cutthroats, of course, are no longer an important food source for them). As well, the valley's lush grasses and nearby forest cover are perfect habitat for elk and bison, making the valley a miniature Serengeti.

Into this wildlife bonanza we happily strode on Independence Day, the day the valley opens to hiking every spring. After a mile of forest, the trail emerged into the valley's open grasslands. As I imagine most hikers do there, we paused, the view practically demanding a moment of admiration. Before us sprawled the verdant carpet of grass, bounded by forest two or three miles across from us and by the ramparts of the Absaroka Mountains seven or eight miles away to our right. Separated from, and to the left of, the mountain range was a lone peak, rising more directly above the valley: Pelican Cone, with a little knob on the summit. The bump was a fire lookout, our destination for the night. Meandering its lazy way through this real-life Thomas

Moran canvas was the valley's namesake creek. Absent from view were any other people or animals, save a solitary bull bison or two, grazing peacefully in the distance. At our feet, though, were scattered and dried pies of bison dung, along with the pellets that elk leave behind—evidence of their presence, and that they apparently were also inclined to survey their surroundings from this knoll. Accentuating the tranquility here was the bright sunshine and gentle breeze bringing us the aromas of dew, grass, and wildflower. It was a picture of loveliness, sensual and serene.

Turning right with the trail, we began hiking up the broad valley. After a couple of miles, we arrived at a rickety bridge across the creek. This was our cue to turn left and cross the valley, where a few more miles of hiking brought us to a second crossing of the creek and, shortly after that, the trail up Pelican Cone. Two hours later, with a quick stop to fill our water bottles at the last spring (the only water at the lookout would be from snow that we would have to melt), we were at the lookout, perched almost two thousand feet above the valley. We hadn't seen any bears, probably because we were chatting with each other and making enough noise to alert and send them to the nearest cover. Once in the lookout, we settled in for the evening, sharing stories and food as we watched the shadows lengthen. The mountain afforded a good view not only of the terrain we had sojourned through that day, but also of that which we would hike through the next three days. The Mirror Plateau spread out to the north, a rumpled quilt of forest and meadow, with a number of thermal areas belying their presence with wisps of steam. Cradling our lair were four shallow, linear valleys, a pair on each side. The setting sun highlighted the forested ridges between them, at the same time progressively hiding the valleys behind a deepening curtain of darkness (Figure 1.8). Soon, the fingers of forest also eased into shadow, leaving only the cone and the Absarokas in sunlight. For a few minutes, the mountains turned dusky shades of orange and crimson, but gradually they too became one with the world of softening shadows and purples and midnight blues. This light show had covered the entire landscape, with nature's tranquility providing an auditory accompaniment that no pyrotechnic explosion could equal.

Looking down from on high, it was easy to see why Yellowstone bison found their last, and ultimately successful, refuge in this land of grassland and hideaway. They found year-round forage, from the plateau's high meadows in summer to the less snow-bound Pelican Valley grassland in winter. Perhaps giving them just enough of an edge to get through winter's bitterly cold nights were the thermal areas, which provided warm ground to bed down on as well as a modest amount of more easily accessible grass. Equally important was the security of the area: this place was hard to get to, then and now. Once

Figure 1.8: View northeast at sunset from atop Pelican Cone, 2002. Lengthening shadows highlight parallel valleys (center, on either side of the linear shadow) and Absaroka peaks (background). The Mirror Plateau is out of view to the left. AUTHOR COLLECTION.

bison were eliminated from the Great Plains and everywhere else in America in the 1880s, poachers began taking the remaining bison in Yellowstone for trophies and hides. By the turn of the century, there were only twenty-three bison left in the park—all in the remote headwaters of Pelican Creek—despite the sometimes valiant protective efforts of the US Army scouts (Congress didn't create the National Park Service until 1916). Assuming the last twenty-three would also go the way of their forbears, the Army bought another couple dozen bison from conservation herds and had them shipped to Yellowstone, where they were put in protective custody first at Mammoth Hot Springs (Figure 1.9) and then, five years later, at the Buffalo Ranch in Lamar Valley. There the buffalo prospered, numbering over a thousand by the 1920s. The last 23, though, did not succumb to the poacher's bullet; rather, they hung on in their wild fastness. Eventually the NPS allowed the Buffalo Ranch herd to roam freely and the two herds comingled and interbred. The bison we see throughout the park today, then, are all descended at least in part from those 23, the only herd in America that has continuously roamed freely in the wild. The legacy of Pelican Valley and the Mirror Plateau looms large indeed; it is one that all Americans can enjoy, whether they partake of the long Yellowstone tradition of watching bison cross the road slowly, as if they own the place (in many ways, they do) or simply take delight in knowing that it still roams the wilds much as it did before the continent was transformed into cities and farms.

For the next three days, we became time travelers of sorts, exploring the secret haunts of the twenty-three survivors: a world that looked, sounded, and acted like the land did when bison were the dominant herbivore on the continent. The only trails we would encounter would be those created by their hoofs (known as game trails) and even those would be rare. For navi-

Figure 1.9: Bison in show corral at Mammoth Hot Springs, no date. Bison were so rare in the early twentieth century that the Army felt it necessary to locate this corral near park headquarters, where the animals could be more securely guarded against poachers. NPS PHOTO, PHOTOGRAPHER UNKNOWN; COURTESY OF NPS, YELLOWSTONE NATIONAL PARK (HTTP://WWW.NPS. GOV/FEATURES/YELL/SLIDEFILE/INDEX.HTM, ACCESSED MAY 30, 2017).

gation we had US Geological Survey maps and a compass or two, and for our route of travel, we would connect the many meadows along the backbone of the plateau. We began our exploration the next day by descending to Raven Creek, a tributary to Pelican Creek and one of the linear valleys on the east side of Pelican Cone; it was to be our ramp up to the plateau. The open valley was easy walking, one or two hundred yards wide, and sloped up so gently that the creek, whose direction of travel opposed ours, sometimes meandered through marshes. It wasn't long before we saw a small herd of bison, contentedly grazing the lush green grasses. The herd was about two dozen in size; it could easily have been the twenty-three historic survivors, in their very same home. We passed others as we continued up the small valley, all grazing, all playing the same ecological role bison have played for millennia.

All around us was evidence of another such force: fire, in the form of dead, standing trees bordering the valley. It's hard to go anywhere in Yellowstone without seeing such evidence, for the last thirty years have seen an abundance of forest fires in the park, especially in 1988 (and a topic I'll explore more thoroughly in the next chapter). In fact, if you are a Yellowstone regular, you get to the point where you hardly notice burned forests, there having been so many fires. But we do still take note of smoke plumes, like the one we soon saw rising above Raven Creek that day. It was the Broad Fire, which park managers were allowing to burn because it was surrounded by things that don't burn well, like previously burned forests and the Grand Canyon of the Yellowstone. The fire would probably remain within those boundaries (which were well outside our route), playing its natural role and further enhancing the illusion that we were hiking through time.

We continued hiking, leaving the creek and its lovely valley behind and ascending the final rise to the plateau. After threading our way through some forest and past Mirror Lake (an appropriate name, the lake surface looking like an inverted forest), we emerged into another large meadow. Not surprisingly, more bison were present, so we detoured around them and walked to the northern edge of the meadow, where we made camp for the night. With a rivulet nearby for water and a view out over the meadow, the campsite was delightful enough; soon, a local resident decided to welcome us in a way that made the site as educational as it was enjoyable. After we had the tents set up and supper on the way, one of us noticed a bison coming our way. It was a bull—a big one—and he was walking along the edge of the meadow, which would have him coming right through our camp. And that is precisely what he did, much like a surly supervisor who brushes by his employees as though they don't exist. Bison are Yellowstone's most dangerous animals, at least in terms of numbers of people who are injured every year, and bulls account for most of the injuries. Most of those are not life-threatening and result from visitors invading the bison's personal space, though two bison gorings in Yellowstone's history were fatal, and many more send victims to the hospital. For these reasons, we gave the bull all due respect, stepping into the woods behind camp while he barreled right through, between our tents and the backpacking stoves, simmering away under unattended pots. He didn't stop or take notice of us in any way, although his actions certainly spoke loudly enough, effectively conveying his lesson: he was the boss here and he knew it, and we had better get out of the way.

Because we did as instructed, we lived to see another day, one in which the plateau divulged some of its sweetest secrets. Strung along its northern heights are a series of large meadows, a necklace of vibrant emeralds in the Yellowstone sky. We linked the jewels the next day, connecting them with our footsteps through the skeins of forest or isthmuses of wetland separating them. Along the way, we passed directly east of one of the plateau's thermal areas, another secret for the wilderness traveler. I had visited the area a few years earlier and found an unforgettable hot spring, one that is mute testimony of power: a small green pool with a complete bison skull lying on the ground next to it (Figure 1.10). The animal had obviously found some shelter there, but in one of nature's paradoxes, life became death. Most likely, the bison was already weak when he took refuge on the snow-free ground by the pool, but he soon succumbed to winter's severity. At the same pool was an elk antler, evidence that the pool's warmth was succor for many. The elk may or may not have died there, for we didn't see a skeleton nearby, but combined with the skull it was enough for us to christen the spring "Death Pool." Perhaps a better name would be "Circle of Life Spring," a moniker that captures more of the relationship between it and the animal life around it. Regardless, the antler was clear indication that elk also roamed these high meadows.

Another animal whose signs we had been seeing was moose. Moose are big, almost the size a horse, and seemingly more so in fall, when the bulls have antlers (moose shed the antlers in January, the better to cope with deep snow). That size means they are another animal for the wilderness traveler to watch for, particularly in fall, their mating season—as I had personally experienced the previous fall. My friend Sean Miculka and I were hiking out from Union Falls in the park's southwest corner, and I had pulled ahead of him climbing a hill. My eyes were down, focusing on safe footing, when a small sound made me look up and to the right. About fifty feet away was a bull moose, look-

Figure 1.10: "Circle of Life Spring," 1997. A bison skull and elk antler by this small hot spring indicate the importance of thermal warmth for Yellowstone's wild animals trying to survive the park's long, cold winters—but not always succeeding in the endeavor. AUTHOR COLLECTION.

ing right at me, and a quick glance beyond the bull revealed a female lurking in some willows. Bulls don't appreciate interlopers—quadruped or otherwise—and are formidably equipped to defend their cows, with muscle, height, and weaponry (spreading, hardened antlers with a dozen or more lance-like tines) that made me feel outgunned. Quickly, my fears were realized when he began to come my way. There was no hope of outrunning him, even without a forty-pound backpack weighing me down; running with it would have been like one of those dreams in which you're trying to run but are going nowhere. Looking around, the forest here offered no obvious protection—except something to hide behind. Moving partly *toward* the moose, I put a tree between him and me, arriving to my side of the tree just as he did to his. The forest there was open, so some trees, including my momentary savior, had kept their lower branches, giving me something more than just a spindly tree trunk for concealment. As bushy as this tree was, though, the moose and I could see each other through the branches, so he knew I was still there, still a potential threat.

But how to get to me? The bull could see that crashing his way through the branches would not be possible, and he may have understood that going around the tree would probably be no more successful, for I would just follow him step-by-step, always staying just out of reach. At least for the moment, then, he remained where he was. On my side of the tree, my thoughts were similar. I prayed I could move fast enough to keep my savior between us; certainly, I would die trying, because the alternative promised much the same fate. Otherwise, unless and until he moved away, I had little choice but to wait for Sean and hope the extra human would send the moose back to his would-be mate. For these reasons, then, we both stood our ground, watching each other through the needles and twigs. It must have been a tragicomic sight to behold: one of the most intelligent animals on Earth squared off against one of the most powerful, brains versus brawn, fear versus power, but both temporary equals. There we stood, stalled, and stayed for several minutes, a quintessential Yellowstone standoff.

Into this quiet but volatile situation Sean strode, finally. Using a low voice and waving my hand, I got his attention, and he quickly realized my—now our—predicament and paused. The bull saw him at the same time and seemed to realize that the tables had turned. Nothing happened for a moment, an uncertain stillness in which time seemed to freeze. Then he slowly turned and walked over to the female, strolling without urgency, clearly telling us who was still the boss in these woods. Sean and I got the message and got out of there while we safely could, ending one of the most frightening and potentially dangerous animal encounters in all my Yellowstone career. Animals as gentle as deer have killed people; the moose could easily have done the same to me if that tree not been where it was, or to Sean if I had not been positioned where I could get his attention so easily. Just like the bison on the Mirror Plateau, the moose demonstrated that grizzly bears aren't the only ambulatory evidence of nature's power in Yellowstone.

After our last evening at another lovely campsite on the Mirror Plateau, we set off on our return to twenty-first century reality. We trekked through our last meadow and then crossed a short but narrow ridge yawning above two steep ravines, the drawbridge off the Mirror Plateau and its treasures, as it were. Climbing the hill on the other side, we walked onto the broad open summit of Amethyst Mountain, the highest point of Specimen Ridge. There, we came across the skull of a bull elk, complete with a pair of six-point antlers, the complement to the bison skull of yesteryear and a prelude to what was to come (Figure 1.11). Specimen Ridge towers above Lamar Valley, which really is the Serengeti of America, a wide, open grassland where one can find, if you look hard enough and have patience, every species of large animal native to Yellowstone: elk, bison, moose, bighorn sheep, pronghorn, mule deer, and white-tailed deer—all of Yellowstone's native ungulates. Complementing (and eating) the ungulates is a similar diversity of predators, with wolves, coyotes, grizzlies, and black bears being the most frequently sighted. In addition to diversity, there is abundance: as many as five thousand or more bison and elk call Yellowstone home, along with two or three thousand mule deer, a hundred wolves, a few dozen white-tailed deer and mountain lions, and a few hundred each of the remaining ungulates and predators. Lamar Valley is especially good habitat for bison and elk: I've seen upward of 2,000 elk and several hundred bison there in the depth of winter, at one time. So many elk were present in the

Figure 1.11: Elk skull and antlers, Amethyst Mountain, 2002. Some bull elk overwinter on high mountain ridges and plateaus, where their larger size (relative to females and calves) enables them to stride through the deep snow linking patches of windswept grass. Some make it through, but others don't. AUTHOR COLLECTION.

1990s that the first wolf reintroduction sites were all in Lamar Valley. Wolves have dropped elk numbers considerably, but not so much that signs of them are hard to find, like the mountaintop skull. In fall, bull elk run themselves ragged in the rut, growing weaker as they guard their harems. When the rut ends, many bulls remain on or scale this ridge, where winter winds keep some patches of grass free of snow. For the weakest bulls, though, that's not enough, so they perish, while those that make it through will drop their antlers in spring. It's a cycle that has gone on here for decades, centuries, and probably millennia; when I first climbed this peak fifteen years earlier, my hiking partners and I found a similar bull elk rack on the summit.

Reminders of elk abundance were with us the rest of the day, with antlers and an occasional skull scattered along much of the route down and out. On Amethyst Mountain, we had met up with a trail that traverses the length of Specimen Ridge, which is open and windswept all the way. Today, the trail had us traveling forward in time as it descended, this time from spring into summer, and from the late 1800s to the twenty-first century. The grasses became more and more golden as we travelled, while sticky geranium and aster took the place of phlox and forget-me-not. Endless, ever-changing panoramas greeted us in every direction. To the right, cloud shadows and sunshine played tug-of-war with each other, the sun standing its ground over Lamar Valley while the clouds held firm over the Absaroka Mountains, occasionally kissing them with a fleeting shower. Meanwhile, on the left brooded the northern end of the Grand Canyon of the Yellowstone, the river hidden within the dense forest rimming its banks and dark volcanic rock rising a thousand feet above. After a full afternoon of these unbelievable views, we arrived at a trail junction marking the impending end of the journey. A mile later the four days of wonder were complete, and we were back in 2002.

We arrived in Gardiner an hour later to find our houses intact but the smell of gunpowder still lingering, slowly dissipating in the breezes that regularly blow up the Yellowstone River, which bisects the town. Other than this one holiday, most of us feel fortunate to live in this funky western town, in part because the wildlife abundance we had witnessed the past few days is even visible in town. Anyone who wants a garden there needs to put up an eight-foot fence to keep deer and elk out, and every winter bison find the grass on the high school football field too good to pass up (which gives the school principal the opportunity to exact a unique punishment on any rule-breakers: picking up the hundreds of bison droppings littering the field in spring, when bison have moved back into Yellowstone). These animals come into town in winter because it is low-lying, and the free lunch available there has less snow covering it than just about anything in the park. Extending down valley are thousands more acres of similar winter range, which sustains a sizeable portion of the ungulates that summer in the park. Without the low elevation winter range, we wouldn't have such an abundance of wildlife, just as we wouldn't have it without Yellowstone's summer range. The two work together to support the country's most complete and abundant wildlife assemblage outside of Alaska, a visceral reminder of how the continent looked, felt, and acted before it was so drastically and irrevocably altered.

No matter where we live, Yellowstone gives us all the opportunity to experience that primeval abundance and diversity today, either by becoming time travelers ourselves or by enjoying armchair travel. Those who are fortunate to journey into Yellowstone's wild country, though, get to feel firsthand the fear that comes with surprising a grizzly bear, the uncertainty associated with threatening a bull moose's intended mate, and the concern about whether the bison will leave you alone. These are some of the emotions and feelings missing from wilderness areas that don't have animals known to harm humans. Equally intense are the opposing sensations: the joy of seeing the grizzly move on, the relief from being freed from an angry and hormonal moose, and the thrill of seeing a bison claim its rightful territory. Movies and stories can provide a taste of the real, but only the authentic can move the blood, can provide the adrenaline boost, can touch the soul. This is the Yellowstone we sampled that holiday weekend, a place everyone can experience themselves.

Wildlife Surprise

I THINK YOU REMEMBER the wilderness trips you did solo best, at least in some ways. Without a person to converse with, and with grizzly bears present, your thoughts turn inward and outward. Introspection and vigilance take the place of conviviality and relaxation. No longer can you trust that someone in your group of hikers will discover a bear or other large creature that has not been frightened away by your conversation. More than on hikes with others, you become acutely aware that your safety depends on you alone. Awareness of the land you travel through becomes an absolute necessity, demanding you to look ahead for blind spots where the trail goes over a hill or around a bend, places where a moose could be browsing willows, places where a griz might be searching out pine nuts. Watching for sign is also wise: scat piles, tracks, overturned soil where bears have been digging for edible tubers like spring beauty and yampa. These are some of the costs; rewards include seeing the landscape come alive by noticing, for example, where sage disappears because a fire recently passed through, hearing the cries of Clark's nutcrackers as they go about stashing whitebark pine cones for winter, and smelling the sweetness of willows as you approach a creek crossing. The landscape seems more vivid, both in the present and in memory.

Perhaps this is why I remember better the second of my two trips to Fawn Pass in 1991, because I was alone on it. The pass is in the Gallatin Mountains, which dominate Yellowstone's northwest corner. The Gallatins are an area of Northern Rockies beauty, with mountains reaching above treeline, crystalline lakes, rushing streams, and abundant wildlife. Three trails cross the mountain range, and a few others approach it, but roads and automobiles stay more than eight miles from the mountaintops. To experience this isolated range, then, you must put your boots on and hike, which I happily did several times that year, my first time in Yellowstone after I had earned my bachelor's degree. The first time I went to Fawn Pass was in July, with two buddies from Mammoth Hot Springs, where I was stationed. After they had left the park (because their seasonal jobs had ended earlier than mine), I set out on a solo three-day hike that featured two mountain passes, two mountaintops, and two NPS patrol cabins. Despite being more than a quarter century ago, I still remember the solo trip well, but an experience on the first visit would come to color both of them. It was a non-threatening wildlife encounter, which probably constitute the majority of our experiences with our furry, feathery, scaly, and slippery friends (which you wouldn't guess that from Yellowstone's representation in the popular press, including this book thus far!). This story, plus two postscripts, will demonstrate, then, that as much as trepidation and fright color our interactions with Yellowstone's charismatic wildlife, so too do charm, amusement, and fascination.

The Fawn Pass trail begins on Swan Lake Flats, a large mid-elevation prairie a few miles south of Mammoth. The view to the west there is one I have always loved, with the Gallatin Mountains parading to the south in clusters separated by the major drainages spilling out from the range: Indian, Panther, and Fawn Creeks, and the Gardiner River. I shouldered my pack that October morning and began walking generally northwest across the flats and then generally southwest up the Fawn Creek Valley, which is partly open. Autumn's look and feel were in the air, from the golden grasses to the crisp air. Indian summer was upon the land though, so the sun was rapidly warming the air and melting the overnight frost. Once I turned into the Fawn Creek drainage, forest closed in, broken up by a liberal sprinkling of meadows. The patches of forest held on to cooler air (until afternoon breezes began to stir), while the meadows told me that they had traded their abundant flowers for dried flower arrangements, rattling when pushed by breezes of warmth or by solitary hiker's legs. Above me rose the two quadrants: Quadrant Mountain on my left and Little Quadrant Mountain on my right, both given their names because their summits are relatively square, almost flat islands of alpine tundra, two miles square on the greater one (with a bite taken out of it, descriptively—and enticingly—called "The Pocket"), and considerably smaller on the lesser (a half mile square). Above all of this was the cobalt Indian summer sky, the deep blue a perfect complement to the auburns I was hiking through.

By mid-afternoon, I was at the Fawn Pass Cabin, situated on a knoll across a small stream from the trail. I let myself in, dropped my pack, and set the place up for the night. Because few of the backcountry patrol cabins are mouse-proof, the bedding is hung over a bar hanging from the ceiling, and the simple dinner table is turned on its side. Canned and dry goods are stored in metal lockers, while dishes are in close-fitting drawers and pots hang from nails in the cabin's log walls. To make the cabins bear-proof, heavy shutters cover the windows, which are locked from inside. Some cabins even have bars or heavy-duty barbed wire covering the windows—in addition to the shutters!

As confirmation of the need for these measures, most cabins, including the Fawn Pass Cabin, have gouges and scratches on the sides from bears trying to get in (the cabins also have plenty of mouse traps for the smaller food thieves).

Once I had the cabin opened up and ready to use, I took a folding chair to the front porch and parked it and myself there to enjoy the remaining daylight. The sun sets early in October, especially on places that face northeast, as the cabin did. The temperature was already dropping in the lengthening shadows there, but I wanted to look for the tree I thought I had seen three months earlier. It was a sapling about five or six feet tall, about a hundred feet from the porch I was sitting on, with unusually dense foliage. That's what I remembered, anyway, from the July visit with my buddy Alan Brown and a friend of his (whose identity I have long forgotten). They had packed in a beer for each of us, which I certainly enjoyed, but I had to let it out after we went to bed. For a simple errand like that, I didn't grab my glasses; I could find my way outside and open the relief valve just fine with blurred vision. Standing there in the moonlight, though, I noticed the odd tree and decided to check it out come daylight and corrected vision. When I finished marking my territory, I returned to my lair and then dreamed of grizzly bears standing up to get a good look at a urinating man who they soon had for dinner. But the next morning, there was no such tree to be found, just as there wasn't that October evening. What I had seen remains a mystery to me. It's unlikely, even with blurred vision, that I could mistake a grizzly bear for a tree, just as it's unlikely a bear would stand still that long. But there was no tree resembling what I had seen there, not even close.

The next day was as glorious as the first, the more so because of the route I traveled. In July, I had paged through the cabin logbook, a journal all cabins have in which rangers using them record their activities and observations. By recording their visits, other rangers also know their colleagues had made it to the particular cabin, along with their intended route upon departure, something cabin users also record in the logbook. In this way, should something befall a ranger after she leaves the cabin, search parties will know more where to focus their efforts. In this cabin's logbook, I had read an entry by a ranger who described traveling the crest of the Gallatin Mountains north from Fawn Pass to Sportsman Divide, where another trail crossed the range. From there, a ranger could hike west to Sportsman Lake, where the NPS had another cabin, or east and back to the trailhead where I began the hike. I would do both, staying at the Sportsman Lake Cabin and returning to my car the third day.

There are few things finer, more liberating, and more beautiful than walking a mountain ridge on an autumn day glittering with sunshine. I walked the crest that day, summitting Joseph and Gray Peaks and two others without names, all of them over ten thousand feet high (or close to it). I looked up to that cobalt sky again, the only thing higher than the ridge I was on besides Electric Peak. That imposing presence is the tallest mountain in the Gallatin Range and the only one to flirt with 11,000 feet, coming up just eight feet short—and looking me in the face (Figure 1.12). I looked down on alpine basins awaiting the first snowfall, tanned by autumn frosts and peppered with stands of whitebark pine. One basin had two small ponds, as blue as the sky they reflected. Others had ribbon forests, linear strips of trees separated by the snowdrifts that build up behind them and that discourage seedling establishment, the drifts taking half of an already fleeting summer to fully melt. I inhaled the warmth of a day so fine it must have been a gift straight from the weather gods. I felt the silence of a place whose loudest sound is thunder, whose most common sound is wind, whose quietest times see decibel levels in the single digits of the decibel scale, or below. I heard the breeze blow air as pure as snow into my lungs, air so

Figure 1.12: Electric Peak (right) and the Gallatin crest, 1991. In the foreground are many ribbon forests, which form at treeline where winter winds blow snow into drifts behind a row of trees. The drifts take too much of the brief Northern Rockies summer to melt away for trees to occupy that ground, so the next strip of forest takes root on the other side of the drift. Another drift forms behind that ribbon, and so on, eventually resulting in many ribbon forests, as seen here. AUTHOR COLLECTION.

clean it hurt to exhale. And all of this was mine alone to fathom, to swallow, to delight in.

From Sportsman Divide, I dropped down to the lake of the same name and let myself into the cabin. The original building there had burned down three years previously, so the NPS rebuilt it the following year, on the same site. It is quite a bit larger than the Fawn Pass Cabin, giving me, when combined with its newness, the feeling I was temporarily wilderness royalty. Royalty or peasant, the setting was fit for a king, with Electric Peak rising over three thousand feet from the lake. That evening, I strolled over to the lake and watched the sun setting, the show doubled in the reflection on the lake surface (Figure 1.13). Sitting there quietly, I became aware of movement in the water just a few feet away. It was a muskrat, swimming around in the lake shallows right in front of me. It didn't seem aware of me, so I continued silently watching the dual light show and muskrat wanderings. I couldn't hold my silence, though, when I saw the little creature pawing at his nose and, shortly thereafter, sneeze! I gave a short laugh, which it heard, sending it diving for cover. It was a delightful and intimate encounter with a friend who did the most earthly of things, an experience I probably would not have had with another person around.

I climbed back up to Sportsman Divide the next day, and from there, out to my car. I had many more memorable encounters with Yellowstone's wildlife in the 1990s, with another notable one happening in 1995. My platonic friend and

Figure 1.13: Electric Peak and Sportsman Lake at sunset, 1991. Many rewards like this scene and memorable wildlife encounters await the wilderness traveler. AUTHOR COLLECTION.

avid hiking partner Carla Polk[2] and I were starting a long hike through the Thorofare, the first half of which was hiking Yellowstone's South Boundary Trail from the South Entrance to the Thorofare Ranger Station. The second day was all uphill—a vertical half-mile—with the last thousand feet coming in the last mile and a half. It was steep, our packs weighed over fifty pounds each, it was hot, and the forest provided no shade, having burned recently. We made camp just before the trail leveled out on Big Game Ridge, on a knoll amid a blackened forest. I remember the campsite for the charcoal that seemed to be everywhere, which made it difficult to keep from getting blackened ourselves. The site had a small creek nearby, though, and the view to the west through the fire-killed snags was good, promising a nice sunset. The hike that day had covered only six or seven miles, but with the conditions being what they were, we were happy to stop.

We had another reason to camp there: to climb Mount Hancock, just two more miles away. The mountain was the highest point of Big Game Ridge, and it has few neighboring peaks, so it provides a unique perspective of the park. It's also visible from many other high points in Yellowstone, so we knew it would have a commanding view. With camp set up and most of the afternoon before us, we climbed the last two hundred feet to the ridge and began sauntering north along the ridgeline (when you've carried a heavy backpack for several hours and then walk without it, you feel as though you are floating). The ridge is broad-backed and gently rising in that area and is mostly open, so it made for easy, enjoyable walking, a welcome contrast to the morning. Just an hour after we left camp, we reached the top and surprised an animal I have rarely ever seen in Yellowstone, and one I surely did not expect to see on a mountaintop: a red

---

2 Pseudonym.

fox. The smallest canine found in the park, foxes can't cope with the deep snow found in most of Yellowstone. Their typical prey, small rodents, tunnel under the snow, and though foxes can successfully pounce on them by triangulating their location with their keen hearing, snow more than two feet deep is too much for them. Additionally, fox numbers were suppressed before wolves were reintroduced in 1995-96; the absence of wolves led to more coyotes, which prey on foxes. The elapsed time between our hike and the first wolf release four months earlier was not enough time to restore foxes, so our fox was the more surprising and perplexing. What was it doing there on Mount Hancock, one of the snowier locations in Yellowstone? Where did it spend the winter? Did it have a den nearby? We wished it could talk and tell us its story.

We puzzled over these questions for a while after the fox trotted off, which was not long after we interrupted its mountaintop snooze. It didn't run away, as the grizzly I startled on Emigrant Peak did. Rather, it just loped away, perhaps with a pause to look back at two hominids that *it* found equally surprising (I don't remember what it did, other than cede the summit to us). We lingered on the summit about an hour and then returned to our camp. The next day we moved on, leaving Big Game Ridge to the big game (none of which we saw) and the intriguing red canine. We crossed the ridge, descended to Fox Creek (the name certainly suggesting the canine's presence in the landscape), and then made camp at Mariposa Lake for two nights. On the layover day, we climbed to the high point of Two Ocean Plateau, the long ridge bisected by the Continental Divide. There, we met with some of the big game that we'd missed two days earlier, a gang (herd) of 100-150 elk. Even though we were a half mile away, they took flight as soon as they saw us. Elk migrate from all directions, sometimes from fifty or sixty miles away and over rugged mountain terrain, to spend the summer amid the breezy meadows and subalpine ponds on that plateau. We pondered the same questions about the elk as we had of the red fox: where did the elk winter? Why migrate so far to the Two Ocean Plateau and Big Game Ridge when there is plenty of good summer range elsewhere in Yellowstone? What is so special about the plateau and ridge? It became a second experience of wonder, another benign but rewarding wildlife encounter on that lengthy hike. We left the elk to their delightful home the next day, descending to the Yellowstone River Valley and then following the river to its source, a wilderness odyssey enriched by the two wildlife encounters ("Absaroka Journey" in Chapter 4 describes a different hike that essentially picks up where I leave off here).

That would not be my last encounter with animals on mountaintops, though, for nine years later, I had another memorable experience with a different native quadruped. It was winter, and my grad school buddy Eric Compas and I had driven out to Lamar Valley for a day of cross country skiing. We strapped on our climbing skins (strips of knapped fabric that adhere to the bottom of skis and enable one to climb uphill), and began ascending Specimen Ridge. The snow was crusty from rain five days earlier, but an inch of new snow on top softened the surface. As we climbed, the song of coyotes howling interrupted our breathing and conversation; their song seemed like a welcome to their home. In another hour, we reached the ridgetop, blown almost bare of snow by the wind. Taking off our skis, we walked to a nearby rock outcrop for shelter and to eat lunch. Low-hanging clouds and falling snow obscured the view, but we still knew we were in a vast winter wilderness.

We had only been there a few minutes when I looked up to see a small herd of bighorn sheep approaching. One of Yellowstone's rarer ungulates, sheep are not commonly seen, and sightings of more than six or eight are uncommon. About twenty sheep in size, the herd of mature rams, ewes, and lambs of the year followed a ewe to a point barely fifty feet away, exchanging looks with us. Stopping there, the herd milled about, seemingly trying to decide what to do with us—accept or fear us? Graze or run away? Thrilled and entranced by their proximity and seeming acceptance of us, we stood calmly, waiting to see what they would do. Shortly, they decided to stay and began grazing, chewing their cuds, and even napping, all within fifty feet. Growing hungry myself, I sat down and began to eat. Eric did likewise, and sheep and humans all enjoyed lunch with fellow residents of Planet Earth, both consuming the Earth's goodness, both aware of the other species, neither feeling threatened (Figure 1.14). The sheep remained in place, only giving us a look when we made a sudden move or when we reluctantly stood to leave. It was a moment of magic, too brief a time of faunal conviviality. Shivering, we went on our way, skiing back to the car, pausing to listen to more coyote howling and to savor an unforgettable experience. We—sheep, humans, coyotes—were all creatures of nature in love with this homeland.

As the wildlife encounters in this story reveal, not all encounters with Yellowstone's wildlife bring forth fear and related emotions; indeed, most of them are run-of-the-mill, a regular part of life for those of us lucky to live in this fascinating region. But a few of the not-so-harrowing ones stand out for other reasons. They make us smile, shake our heads in amazement, and stir our hearts and minds with wonder. They show us some of nature's many other faces, aspects of the natural world that range from mystery to amusement, intimacy to awe, fascination to camaraderie. They are also rewards for those who approach nature's creatures with humility and restraint, who are quiet and non-dominating when in the presence of the animals we share the planet. Ultimately, they hint at the complexity of the natural world, a tapestry so detailed and interwoven that we can-

Figure 1.14: Bighorn sheep and the author on Specimen Ridge, 2004. Bighorns can be surprisingly docile, like these sheep, which approached the author and his friend Eric and then stayed nearby while both species had lunch. AUTHOR COLLECTION.

not hope to fully comprehend it. We are left with wonder and amazement at Yellowstone's landscape of power.

Reflections

SOMETHING WITHIN US YEARNS for places like Yellowstone, for many reasons, some of which are contradictory. For some, it's a desire to assuage our conscience, to know that there are still some places largely untouched by human hands, unsullied by the rapacious forces of capitalism. Others see a frontier, a place where they can relive the experiences of Lewis and Clark, or John Colter, or perhaps their own ancestor. Some see a howling wilderness, a place that vindicates the ongoing triumph of capitalism and civilization over nature and its entropic forces. Still others find solace, healing, and renewal, a retreat from the everyday existence that wears them down. Others celebrate a Garden of Eden, a tangible look at what many would call paradise. Whatever the reason, wildlife are a fundamental part of the story; they transform the landscape from a still life to a moving picture, from a diorama to a reincarnation, from a house to a home, from scenery to the American Serengeti.

While most American landscapes have some wildlife—even the largest urban areas—few have the diversity of large herbivores present in Yellowstone; most have only deer, and bison are, sadly, almost unknown in other landscapes. Few as well have any predators larger than coyotes and black bears; Yellowstone not only has these, but also grizzlies, wolves, and mountain lions. Small wonder, then, that wildlife watching is more popular than geyser gazing, for many of us are attempting to satisfy that desire to experience something meaningful. That wildlife watching even eclipses shopping—the most important expression of identity for many Americans—confirms that Yellowstone truly is a landscape of power, one with few equals in the 48 contiguous states.

That power is readily apparent to anyone who journeys through Yellowstone, but especially to those who travel away from the road and into the home of Yellowstone's native residents. Just as we do when we enter someone else's home, we must adhere to the rules of Yellowstone's wildlife when we hike into their home. Wildlife are random and unpredictable, two traits that give them the edge in an encounter (Figure 1.15). They demand preparation and forethought, vigilance and alertness, observation and awareness: all signs of deference. They have important lessons to give about life and coexisting with the land, suggesting a wisdom we would do well to absorb and emulate. The presence of grizzly bears, in particular, demands hu-

Figure 1.15: Hotpotting with the bison in Alum Creek, 2005. En route to Glen Africa Basin, the Doctors Mike found this small hotpot for a quick soak. While we were in, a group of bison silently approached us from behind. Neither of us noticed them until they were quite close, so we had little choice but to stay where we were and hope they kept going, without disturbing our packs. That is indeed what they did. PHOTO BY MIKE TERCEK, AUTHOR COLLECTION.

mility and restraint, key things one accords any more powerful being or authority. In short, wildlife empower the Yellowstone landscape, demanding an entirely different approach to relating with the natural world, one that our society has too rarely adopted. Instead of domination and destruction, they require reverence and community in their world, and hint that these would be fundamental elements of a more rewarding approach to nature more generally. This approach holds rich possibilities, not least that we may come to understand, appreciate, and further the innumerable bonds that exist within and between them and us. Indeed, by embracing such an approach, we may even come to share in the power of Yellowstone.

CHAPTER 2

Natural Forces

While mudpots boil,
a grizzly dines on an elk —
the calls of ravens.
—David Kirtley

SITTING ON THE DIVIDE between Open and Granite Canyons in the Tetons one summer day in the 1990s, I was enjoying a solitary lunch with a glorious view, one of in-your-face mountain geology. At my feet were the two parallel canyons, both carved by glaciers in the recent geologic past into broad, U-shaped troughs that descend eastward below the rugged spires for which the mountain range is famous. Where the creeks that have replaced the glaciers spill out onto the flats of Jackson Hole, they cross one of two faults whose movements created the mountain range. That one, the eastern one at the base of the mountain range, separates the upwardly rising Tetons from the downwardly sinking valley floor, while another on the west side of the range acts as a hinge, allowing the range to rise a mile and a half into the sky in the last ten million years. Sometimes hard to grasp (most of us will be lucky to live .000001%

as long as these mountains are old—and the Tetons are *young* mountains), the geology here was hard to ignore, the forces almost as tangible as they get. I enjoyed that tangibility for an hour or so and was preparing to hike back when a loud crash made me look across Open Canyon to the side of Prospectors Mountain. A slab of rock the size and approximate shape of a fifteen-passenger van had broken loose and was tumbling down the mountainside, taking out everything in its path and shaking other rocks and boulders loose. The van-sized boulder dominated the show, making the canyon boom as solid rock collided repeatedly with solid rock. The boulder's angularity prevented gravity from accelerating its fall, so the slow-motion descent continued, the boulder's booming echoing off the canyon walls in a sort of geologic thunderstorm. Geologic forces—this time, freeze-thaw action and erosion—were now overwhelmingly real and present.

The boulder and its associated detritus landed on the canyon floor a few moments later, but the show had several encores as other boulders (none quite as large as the first) broke off from the same fractured rock face and careened downslope. The show finally ended when the rocks peeling off exposed a face that freeze-thaw action had not yet weakened. No one else saw the show (so far as I know), and no one was killed or injured, there being no trails below the shattered rock face. To this day, that rockslide (especially the first, massive boulder) ranks among the most obvious displays of nature's erosive force I have witnessed in the Yellowstone area. It was almost deafening evidence of the geologic forces creating and shaping this place. Such forces are not the only ones leaving their mark on the Yellowstone area; a suite of atmospheric and ecological forces do as well. This chapter will shed some light on all of these forces through another set of stories. Because no amount of storytelling can hope to elucidate the innumerable forces, large and small, that together create Wonderland, the stories that follow cover the three broad groups: ecologic, geologic, and atmospheric. While they are just a sample, they still illustrate the immense powers that shape this remarkable landscape.

Cache Creek and Fire

CACHE CREEK IS A LARGE drainage in the Absaroka Mountains, a wide valley of (once) luxurious forest, cold rushing streams, and rugged mountain peaks in Yellowstone's northeast corner. During my time in Yellowstone, I had the pleasure of visiting this wilderness hideaway several times, giving me the opportunity to observe ecological change—sometimes drastic—over time. The first such visit was in 1988, shortly after I had begun my first job as a park ranger with the NPS. This job was slightly more meaningful than the gift shop one, as I was wearing the NPS uniform and flat hat, the "Smoky Bear" ranger hat that symbolizes the agency to many Americans. In a big way, few jobs could have been better than the one I had, welcoming visitors to the world's first national park. Better yet, I was stationed at the Northeast Entrance near Cooke City, Montana, the least-used entrance, giving me the time to actually talk with the excited travelers and help plan their visits. I was living well, enjoying the highest hourly wage I'd ever earned, a job in which I could use my brain, and living in my own place (another first). Topping it all off was that, as a park ranger, I could use the NPS patrol cabins scattered around the park's backcountry. Learning about this perk a few weeks after starting work, I quickly made plans to hike to the Cache Creek Cabin with my buddy Garrett Seal. On our weekend adventure, we would climb a mountain on the way in and another on the way out, staying at the cabin for the night in between. Along the way, we would get our first taste of

an ecological force so powerful it defeated the mightiest government in the world.

The hike began with a ford of Soda Butte Creek, a foot-
numbing welcome to the wilderness. That done, we made the
two-hour climb to the ridge separating Soda Butte Creek from
Cache Creek, a glorious spot with an inglorious name: Chaw
Pass. Not Lightning Pass or Thunderbolt Pass or, better yet,
Zeus Pass, all more befitting names taking their cue from the
nearby mountain we were about to climb, The Thunderer. But
then Garrett, who enjoyed an occasional plug of chewing tobacco, pointed out that this would be a helluva spot to kick back
and enjoy a moment of existential pleasure. Even I could agree
that it was such, although the pleasure seemed more redneck to
me (not to mention carcinogenic and revolting). Whatever the
pleasure, that was the place for us to turn right, leave the trail,
and climb the last thousand feet to Zeus's home. The ascent
involved some hand-over-foot climbing, the slope steepening to
the point where we needed to hold on with our hands for stabil-
ity and then becoming vertical for ten or fifteen feet at a time.
Hand- and toeholds were plentiful and conditions were otherwise safe for climbing, so we made our way through the cliff
bands and soon walked up the final rocky slope. Emerging onto
the summit, we were surprised to find a broad, flat, grassy patch
of alpine tundra about a hundred yards across. Dotted here and
there with pincushions of blue forget-me-nots and white phlox,
it was the sky miniaturized in a field of living energy, Zeus's
parlor. Zeus himself was nowhere to be found, so we sat down
to have our lunch, taking care not to crush the drops of sky.

Looking around the landscape below us, Cache Creek was
clothed with dark green forest broken only by small meadows
and stretching east almost to Republic Pass, which we would
cross on our way out of the valley the next day. Looking to the
west, we saw a thin plume of smoke rising from a forest fire on

the Mirror Plateau. It was the Clover Fire, which had started a few days previously. Since 1972, the NPS has allowed some lightning-caused fires to burn, resuming the natural role they have played in Yellowstone for millennia. The signature of fire was ubiquitous in the park, especially in the lodgepole pine forests that blanket much of it. Those pines produce two different cones, one that opens normally and another that needs temperatures of 120 degrees to open (Figure 2.1). Fire in lodgepole pine forests typically kills the trees, but much like a life insurance policy bearing dividends when the owner dies, the serotinous cones open after the flames subside, releasing the seeds onto a freshly cleared and fertilized seedbed. The next generation forest gradually supplants the former one, growing slowly in the cold Northern Rockies climate and finally becoming susceptible to another stand-replacing fire in one to three hundred years.

Figure 2.1: Serotinous lodgepole pine cone, no date. Sealed closed with resinous bonds that melt when burned, these cones open and release the seeds inside after a fire moves through, ensuring the species' survival. NPS PHOTO, PHOTOGRAPHER UNKNOWN; COURTESY OF NPS, YELLOWSTONE NATIONAL PARK.

As the forest ages, Engelmann spruce and subalpine fir also invade, further increasing the forest flammability because, unlike lodgepole pine, the two don't shed their lower branches as they grow, giving fire a ladder to get into the canopy and become a fast-moving—and more powerful—crown fire, if conditions are right. This recurring fire pattern has produced a patchwork forest throughout Yellowstone, each patch the result of an individual fire. The same pattern also meant that Yellowstone's forests were ready to burn in 1988, because many of the patches were 150 years old or older. Perhaps ominously, years like the one we were seeing unfold before us were the right kind for such radical environmental change, for it was only early July and that fire had already begun—and the Clover Fire had several companions also smoldering away elsewhere in the park.

With lunch done, we decided it was time to explore Cache Creek. For the next twenty-four hours, we immersed ourselves in its wonders, beginning with the cabin (Figure 2.2). Each of the forty parkwide patrol cabins (four of which are fire lookouts like the one on Pelican Cone) has a unique personality, depending on its setting, design, and amenities. The Cache Creek Cabin was strongly flavored by the Thunderer towering 2,800 above, the God of Thunder's citadel. Inside, the place had the rustic ambience that characterized most of the cabins, a blend of wood smoke, native material construction, and subdued lighting. This one also had something to enhance the culinary part of the cabin experience: silverware that lived up to the name (probably silver plated, the set was almost certainly donated to the NPS). With this touch of class in its glorious setting, the cabin was a worthy welcome to Cache Creek.

The next day, we awoke to find the day already warm, unusually so—and by day's end, it was one of the warmest in my Yellowstone experience. Nonetheless, the three-hour climb to Republic Pass was a delightful journey through old-growth for-

Figure 2.2: Cache Creek Patrol Cabin, July, 1988. The dead trees around the cabin indicate that the forest in Cache Creek was senescent, with sub-alpine fir and Engelmann spruce replacing the lodgepole pines that had sprouted after the last stand-replacing fire. The diverse forest is lush and pretty, but quite flammable in dry years. Spruce and fir hold onto their lower branches, giving fire a ladder to climb into the canopy, as can be seen in the large spruce just left of the cabin. AUTHOR COLLECTION.

est, an interesting mix of pine, spruce, and fir. Interspersed with the trees were small meadows laced with the flowers of moistness: deep blue Columbia monkshood, hot pink Lewis monkey flower, magenta sticky geranium, its white cousin Richardson's geranium, and a host of others I have long forgotten. I have not lost my dominant impression from that morning's hike, however: the Cache Creek Valley was lush, full of life, and colorful, with a generous scattering of springs, seeps, and freshets.

Republic Pass sits at ten thousand feet, above treeline. It's a spot not unlike Chaw Pass, one of those places that demand pause and reflection, but without the suggestion of tobacco spit and drool. The view is even more expansive atop Republic Peak, which rises an additional four hundred feet above the pass. Twenty minutes after we arrived at the pass, we were on its summit, sitting down for another unbeatable lunch. The Clover Fire was still sending a delicate smoke plume into the nearly cloudless sky, a second reminder that day that 1988 could become a year of change, possibly significant change. Sitting on that mountaintop, though, it was hard to be too concerned, for a seemingly limitless panorama of wilderness spread out before us. To the south and west we looked over all of Yellowstone, the largest national park in the forty-eight contiguous states (at that time; Death Valley took that status from Yellowstone in 1994 when Congress enlarged and upgraded it to a national park). To the east and north we looked upon the Absaroka and Beartooth Mountains, two ranges every bit as wild as the park (or more so) and both largely protected as designated wilderness. We were momentary lords of one of the largest blocks of protected land in the country, a cohesive whole known to many as the Greater Yellowstone Ecosystem. Some eighteen million acres in extent, this vast chunk of Montana, Wyoming, and Idaho is mostly undeveloped federal land with a thin scattering of small towns and a sparse road network. The area functions as one ecological whole—an ecosystem—with many interlocking and interrelated parts, one of the largest and relatively intact ecosystems in Earth's temperate regions. In such ecosystems, natural forces dominate over human ones, as we would soon—very soon—see happening in the world at our feet.

That afternoon, we finished the hike, walking four miles down Republic Creek, through Republic Creek Meadows, and past another mountain bearing the same name, Republic Mountain (not to be confused with the *Peak* we'd just descended from)—all things Republic, in other words. In the meadows, we turned to look back at the pass and saw something I'll never forget: a massive smoke plume, blowing laterally in the wind just above the graceful curve that defined the pass (Figure 2.3). It was a portent, perhaps, of things to come, and a sign that Zeus might be preparing for action. The warmth I had been noticing had dried the vegetation enough that afternoon breezes blew up the Clover Fire; I later learned it exploded from 350 to 5,000 acres that day. We watched the plume blow in the wind for a few minutes and then walked out to Cooke City. With that, we headed home to reality, a very different one from the one we had left the morning before. If the smoke plume were not enough to make that clear, the note on my door telling me to call my boss right away certainly was. I obliged, and found that he wanted to be sure we had made it out okay—and to tell me that the NPS had

Figure 2.3: Smoke plume over Republic Pass, 1988. Plumes like this indicate significant fire activity, such as a crown fire (one that has climbed into the treetops and is jumping from tree to tree), which resembles a moving wall of flame. AUTHOR COLLECTION.

closed Cache Creek to human entry, because the fire could burn into the drainage.

In the weeks that followed, the weather got progressively warmer and windier, the fires bigger and more erratic. Zeus started more blazes, their very names suggesting his involvement: the Storm Creek Fire, the Hellroaring Fire. Some, such as the Clover and Mist Fires, burned into one another, joining forces to become a mega fire with a mega name, the Clover-Mist Fire. Air quality grew increasingly degraded, the smoke settling in the valleys overnight but dispersing in the afternoon breeze, the same wind fanning the flames. Defying the weather gods, though, firefighters managed to keep the Clover-Mist Fire out of Cache Creek until August 20, a day that would become known as Black Saturday. That day began like many others before it that August, with a thick pall of smoke obscuring the mountains rising above the entrance station, where I was on duty. The smoke cleared out by midday, but around five o'clock an ugly gray line of clouds overtook the station from the southwest. About the same time, the Cooke City phone began ringing nonstop with town residents concerned about the same cloud and what it might portend for them. They knew, better than I, that the cloud meant a storm was coming—a firestorm, not a thunderstorm, for the cloud was too gray to be only water vapor. The storm was in Cache Creek, which fell that afternoon, the Clover-Mist Fire devouring it in about six hours. Stoked by the wind from a dry cold front, the fire roared up the valley faster than a person can walk, the flames reaching two or three hundred feet toward the heavens. Not till it reached Republic Pass did the inferno stop, there being no more trees to feed its voracious appetite. Hardly a drop of chlorophyll remained in Cache Creek, though the cabin and a few adjacent trees survived, protected by a sprinkler system firefighters had set up. Parkwide, 160,000 acres burned that day—20% of the year's total—much of that in Cache Creek. The fires continued burning well into October, eventually affecting 793,880 acres, or 36% of the park. The North Fork Fire achieved the most notoriety, running some fifty miles across the park and right through the Old Faithful area, despite being fought from its inception. The federal government staged one of its largest firefighting efforts in history that summer in Yellowstone, with about 10,000 men and women on the ground at one point. In the park villages and gateway communities, they were remarkably successful in saving all homes and buildings of note (like the Old Faithful Inn), but in the backcountry they were just as remarkably unsuccessful at stopping, or even making a dent in, the fires and their spread. Zeus was firmly in control there; the fires were a force every bit as powerful as tornadoes and hurricanes.

Six years later, I returned to Cache Creek, staying again at the cabin. My friend Carla and I entered the drainage at Republic Pass, again taking the time to climb nearby Republic Peak. We were temporary lords of the wilderness again, one that looked different but acted much the same. The forest was still one of fire, except that now it was in a different phase; instead of old growth, it was a seedling forest under a canopy of gray ghosts. At least that's what I expected to find when we hiked down into the valley, based on what I'd seen in other burned areas I had hiked through. But after a few miles of hiking, it was clear that something was different in Cache Creek. Gone were the seeps and springs, along with the flowers that needed them; in their place were dusty soil and dryland flowers that had already gone to seed in the ubiquitous sunshine. Lodgepole seedlings were scarce, although the ones we found seemed as vigorous as those we'd encountered elsewhere. Where before we heard the trickle of water, now we heard the rattle and whistle of wind through barren trees. The difference probably had to do with the forest that was there in 1988 and how it burned. As I saw when I had hiked through with Garrett, the forest there was dominated by spruce and fir, neither of which is well adapted for fire. Like lodgepole pine, they succumb easily to flame, but unlike the pine, they don't have serotinous cones. Compounding the lack of seedlings was the nature of the fire, which burned hot enough to incinerate some of the serotinous lodgepole cones that were present in 1988. With so few seed sources, it would probably take much longer than expected for this forest to regenerate. It was saddening to walk through, knowing what had been here before. Life was present, to be sure, but the contrast to what had been here before could hardly have been more stark. Indeed, the same word could be used to describe the entire drainage.

We relaxed at the cabin, enjoying the fine silverware and the first shelter from the sun we'd had all day. The next day, we climbed the Needle, a mountain with a large natural arch at the summit (and visible from Chaw Pass). Having lunch and photographing ourselves in the Eye of the Needle, we descended back to Cache Creek and hiked out, a long but powerful tour of that firescape. It was one to which I would not return for more than a decade, my impression of sadness and destruction working against a third visit—and when I did come back, it was winter, when I assumed the starkness would be covered by a blanket of white. With my buddy Jared White and his girlfriend Jill McMurray, we made the climb up to Chaw Pass, this time on cross-country skis with climbing skins attached. At the pass we stopped to peel the skins off, chow down some lunch, and inhale the view (Figure 2.4). The cabin was easy to see with the live trees around it standing out from the surrounding whiteness. Also easy to pick out were some other isolated pockets of trees, appearing black against the snow, that had somehow survived the 1988 inferno, all shielded from the flames by the stream or wrinkles of topography. Otherwise, Cache Creek was a world of white, a valley of brilliance enveloped by mountains that practically glowed in the midday sunshine. Thousands upon thousands of gray, weathered trees still stood in the valley, adding texture and bridging the grayscale between dazzling white and the brooding black survivors. Snow has a way of transforming the mundane into the wonderful, of whitewashing the unappealing into the lovely. For that reason, Cache Creek was now winter beauty, a wilderness in ermine.

Our hunger for sustenance and beauty temporarily sated, we dropped off the ridge into Cache Creek, doing telemark turns in the powder but finding an occasional crust on southwest exposures. Alternately graceful in the powder and awkward in the crust, we made the descent to the cabin in less than an hour. Letting ourselves in, we fired up the woodstove and soon had a

Figure 2.4: The Needle, 2007. This mountain forms the southern boundary of Cache Creek, with the Eye of the Needle just visible left of center on the rocky horizon. The 1988 fire effects were plain to see, almost two decades afterwards. AUTHOR COLLECTION.

cozy home in the wilderness for the next two nights. The afternoon was waning, and we were all pretty tired from the morning
climb, so we relaxed in the warmth and watched the shadows
lengthen outside. The low-angle January sun set on us by four
o'clock, instantly dropping the temperature ten degrees outside.
An hour later, the mountains surrounding us were also in shadow, leaving only the sky in color, soft shades of pink, purple,
and blue. Quickly then, night overtook the valley, replacing
brilliance with blackness, glitter with ink, resplendence with
dim of night. We stayed in our refuge, passing the long evening
with dinner, card games, and reading. Stepping outside to brush
my teeth at bedtime, I saw that the glitter had returned, migrating to the night sky, now sprinkled with a million stars. Twelve
hours later, radiance gradually returned, the sun slowly burning
through a thin veil of fog that had crept in from down valley.
The Thunderer slowly returned to view, a mirage transformed
into reality. Night or day, sunset or sunrise, Cache Creek was
indeed a winter world of beauty.

After breakfast, Jared and Jill took off to find some powder
while I remained at the cabin to relax. Work had been hectic
recently, so I relished the opportunity for some down time. The
two of them returned for lunch, after which we all set off to do
some turns. Climbing to some meadows on the slopes of the
Thunderer, we stopped at the top to remove our skins and to
savor the view again. It was much the same as yesterday's, but
this time I noticed something across and up the valley: a hint
of green under the gray ghosts of fires past. It was a seedling
forest, tall enough to rise above the snow and dense enough
to be visible from three or four miles away (Figure 2.5). With
the snow providing a contrast and the passage of time enabling
seedlings to grow, the new generation forest was finally taking
shape. Looking around at other slopes, I saw the same green
shading on some, but not on others (seedlings don't appear as

dark as mature trees). The hint of green was more prevalent in moister areas such as the valley bottom and north-facing slopes that receive less direct sun, but there were some seedlings even in the drier areas. It was refreshing and enlivening to see this valley, where I had once found such a lovely forest with flowers in abundance, showing signs that it could become that way again. This inspired us to shove off into the powder, carving our way down the meadow. After we had climbed back up for a second run, we called it a day—a refreshing one—and returned to the cabin, noticing more young trees below the meadow. They weren't everywhere, but there were enough to see that my impression of sadness and destruction could now give way to one of happiness and life.

Figure 2.5: Jared and Jill above Cache Creek, 2007. Between the left-most live foreground tree and the white mountain on the horizon can be seen some dark gray slopes angling up to the right. This is the forest of seedlings established after the 1988 wildfires. AUTHOR COLLECTION.

The next day, we climbed the hill to Chaw Pass and took a final look at the valley fire had so radically changed almost two decades earlier. It was to be my last look into that valley, as life's unexpected turns soon took me away from Yellowstone. Nonetheless, the three visits I'd had to Cache Creek gave me a peek into natural processes that few of us are fortunate to have. If Zeus is the most powerful god in Greek mythology, then fire is perhaps the best parallel among the many ecological forces at play in Yellowstone. More powerful than the U.S. government, fire not only radically changed the forests of Cache Creek, but also the valley's hydrology, drying up many seeps and springs that were present in 1988. That wasn't the only thing I learned from my visits to the valley, though; for another, it's clear that natural cycles can take much longer than human time frames. I was not wrong to feel the emotions that I did upon my initial return, but Cache Creek teaches nature's observers to be patient. As well, the valley teaches us that natural cycles may not be circular; the future forests one finds there may never be the same as what they were. These revelations are part of the mystery and majesty of nature: innumerable forces and interrelationships constantly interacting to produce a dynamism that challenges our attempts to predict, understand, and categorize.

Predators and Predation

NOT LONG AFTER my 1988 visit to Cache Creek, I went to the Tetons with my friend Dave Moser and his sister Cathy, in search of smoke-free air and a mountain to climb. We found both there, climbing Mount St. John and enjoying world-class views of Jackson Hole, the other Tetons, and the lower mountains across the valley. Memorable enough, but the truly unforgettable events of that weekend happened on the drive home. By this time, the fires had crossed the South Entrance Road linking Yellowstone and the Tetons, restricting travel to nighttime and mornings, times when the fires were not as active. Driving north after dark, we knew we'd entered the active fire zone when we saw dozens of seeming campfires appear across the valley. Glowing bright in the blackness, they gave the appearance of an army encampment, when they were really an indication that this fire was going strong. That vitality suddenly exploded before us, as we rounded the bend to Lewis Falls, where an entire tree was going up in flames, right next to the road. We screeched to a halt and jumped out of the car to watch nature's fireworks, so brightly contrasted against the dark of night. Barely had we stood up when the flames subsided, all the readily flammable material already consumed. Still, we lingered, watching other bushes and spot fires burning near the falls and turning the cascading water a subtle shade of orange. As if reassuring us not to be alarmed at the power on the loose around us, the sound of falling water dampened the crackles and pops of the fires still simmering—and masked the other sound of that eerie night.

With no other trees going up in flames, we turned around and walked back to the car, which is when we heard it: a woman in distress, screaming at the top of her lungs, across the valley. Long screams, as though she were being approached by an assailant and were unable to flee. The sound was unsettling, seemingly demanding immediate efforts to find and rescue her. But there were no trails or roads over there, and the river and surrounding marshes would discourage most anyone from going across the valley. Plus, if it were a woman, she would most likely be calling for help, between the screams. For these reasons (which were intuitive and therefore unspoken), we knew it was probably an animal, but what? And why was it screaming? We shivered in spite of the warm night, hopped in the car, and escaped the screams, but the spooky night stayed with me. I eventually learned that the calls were probably those of a mountain lion (also known as a cougar, catamount, panther, or puma). Although fires don't maim or kill wildlife anywhere near as much as *Bambi* would have us believe, it does happen, so the screams may have been from a lion in distress. Ordinarily, however, lion screaming is associated with their mating, such as a female advertising that she is in heat, a male defending his female, or two of them mating, so the screams we heard could have been from a big cat experiencing a more typical part of life. I will never know what prompted that cat or cats to scream that eerie night, but the combination of auditory and visual effects created a scene of deep and penetrating power.

Mountain lions were eliminated from Yellowstone early in the twentieth century (Figure 2.6), but as their numbers recovered throughout the West in the last few decades, they drifted back into the park, today numbering two or three dozen park-wide. Preying mostly on deer, elk, bighorn sheep, and smaller animals like marmots and porcupines (lions flip the latter on their back, exposing their unguarded bellies), they are found where those prey live, mostly in the park's lower, northern elevations. That was where I actually saw one five years later, on an early spring hike along the Yellowstone River. On its way to Gardiner, Montana, the river flows through the Black Canyon, a thousand-foot-deep gorge of dark volcanic rock, rushing river, and tall Douglas-fir trees. It's also one of the lowest elevations in the park, so the trail was mostly free of snow as my friend Tom Richards and I hiked upriver. The day was warm and sunny, one of those special spring days that hold the promise of still warmer weather, emerging wildflowers, and newborn animals. The day before I'd seen a flock of trumpeter swans flying north on their spring migration, a down payment of sorts on the wildlife we would see that day. Signs of wildlife were plentiful, the canyon's relative warmth and snow-free south-facing slopes sustaining elk, deer, and bighorn sheep through the long Northern Rockies winter. Tracks and piles of scat were abundant, along with an occasional carcass with tufts of fur scattered about, reminding us that the land and its residents were just emerging from the season of want.

Lost in our thoughts and the world of wildlife through which we walked, we were brought to a sudden halt when we rounded a bend in the trail and saw the mountain lion, lapping water from the river. A hundred feet away, it didn't see us initially, so we gave each other congratulatory looks and quietly watched the cat to see what it would do. Shortly thereafter, it raised its head and looked our way, staring at us for a moment as if it was trying to figure out what we were. We expected it would run away once

Figure 2.6: Mountain lion carcass, 1927. Park managers targeted mainly wolves and mountain lions in their predator elimination program in the early twentieth century. Wolves were gone by the time this photo was taken; lions were soon to follow. NPS PHOTO, PHOTOGRAPHER UNKNOWN; COURTESY OF NPS, YELLOWSTONE NATIONAL PARK (HTTP://WWW.NPS.GOV/FEA-TURES/YELL/SLIDEFILE/INDEX.HTM, ACCESSED MAY 30, 2017).

it realized we were its main enemy, but instead it did something that would remind any parent of a hide-and-seek game with a toddler. Like the two-year-old who thinks she's hiding when she closes her eyes, the lion "hid" from us by lowering its head—but not the rest of its body—behind an adjacent boulder. We could plainly see its haunches and long tail, which is how the situation remained for the next minute or two. We soon decided to move along, leaving the feline to think it had been successful in hiding from us. It continued to "hide" as we exited the scene, and was long gone when we hiked back through that afternoon. Seeing the wild predator up close in its native habitat was thrilling, a personal view of a top predator—and an amusingly memorable encounter, for it's not every day that you can play games with a large predator and escape unscathed.

Black Canyon is typical habitat for mountain lions, which prefer the rugged, rocky canyon walls for stalking their prey. With hind legs slightly longer than their front legs, they are powerfully adapted for jumping and short bursts of speed (up to 40 or 50 mph). In contrast to wolves and other predators that chase down their quarry, lions are ambush predators, lying in wait or sneaking up on an unsuspecting deer or elk (their two most common prey in Yellowstone). The cats are generalists, able to take a wide variety of prey in habitats from deserts and tropical jungle to grassland and boreal forest. This flexibility means mountain lions can be found in every country in the Americas, from the southern Andes to Canada's Yukon Territory; in fact, mountain lions have the largest range of any land animal in the western hemisphere, crossing 110 degrees of latitude. Lions are often apex predators, at the top of the food chain—but not in Yellowstone, where both wolves and grizzly bears are usually dominant. Grizzlies and black bears visit a fourth of lion kills, completely usurping a tenth of them. Similarly, wolf packs will displace lions from kills, but if the wolf is alone, the lion usually holds its own. Surging wolf and grizzly numbers in the last twenty years has resulted in competition for elk calves, with the lion on the losing end. Still, the lion population has grown in that same time period, illustrating the cat's adaptability. The competition can also be deadly; lions have been known to kill single wolves, but wolf packs can reverse that mortal relationship. In Yellowstone, then, lions are part of a complex and robust community of life, one that we are fortunate to visit and observe.

When you mention predators and Yellowstone in the same sentence, most people don't think of felines. They think instead of ursines and canines, and understandably so, given the prominence of grizzly bears in the park's history and wolf reintroduction in the 1990s. Sightings of both wolves and grizzly bears are now almost common, easily obtained if you know where to go and which direction to look. But it wasn't always that way; just as grizzlies were scarce (along with their sightings) in the 1980s, wolves were completely absent from the Yellowstone ecosystem for most of the twentieth century. Eradicated from the park by the NPS in the 1920s, wolves were returned to the ecosystem in 1995 by the same agency (in cooperation with the US Fish and Wildlife Service), a policy reversal mirroring the nation's shifting environmental ethic (Figure 2.7). Once reviled as wanton killers of livestock and threats to Little Red Riding Hood, wolves have been more recently seen as essential components of an ecosystem, apex predators that have tremendous influence on their prey. Since reintroduction, wolf numbers and range have grown to about five hundred throughout most of the ecosystem, with about one hundred of those in Yellowstone. The canids have become the centerpiece of a thriving wildlife viewing industry, with dozens of individuals and businesses offering guided tours of their territory. They have indeed become a mainstay of the ecosystem and of many park visitors' experiences.

Figure 2.7: Gray wolf in acclimation pen, 1995. After a seventy-year absence, wolves were brought back to the Greater Yellowstone Ecosystem by
the US Fish and Wildlife Service and National Park Service, beginning in
1995. To discourage the canids from returning to their Canadian home,
the wolves were held in several one-acre pens for two months prior to
being released into the wild. NPS PHOTO BY JIM PEACO, COURTESY OF NPS,
YELLOWSTONE NATIONAL PARK (HTTP://WWW.NPS.GOV/FEATURES/YELL/SLIDEFILE/
INDEX.HTM, ACCESSED MAY 30, 2017).

Wolves have also become the focus of an impressive and
growing body of research. Upon reintroduction, the wolf population grew rapidly as the canids overtook a landscape with one
of the highest prey densities in the world. Wolves prospered,
with some packs seeing multiple pregnancies as the alpha male
bred with more than one female. One pack grew to 37 animals,
perhaps the largest ever recorded. Like mountain lions, wolf
densities have been highest in the park's northern, low elevation
grasslands, where their prey are most abundant (lions have effectively been restricted to steeper terrain like the Black Canyon
by wolves colonizing those low elevations). Yellowstone's wolves

have a clear preference for elk, with the animal comprising 85 to 97 percent of their diet, depending on time of year and elk availability. Wolves have also caused elk to shift to more marginal habitats, to become more stressed, and to have fewer calves. With elk numbers dropping significantly under the combined and increased predation of wolves, grizzly bears, and mountain lions (and the stresses of Yellowstone's variable climate), wolves have been taking more bison in recent years, though the bovines still constitute less than five percent of wolf diets. Wolves have also affected Yellowstone's coyotes, which had partially filled the wolf's ecological niche. Wolves will kill their smaller cousins when opportunity strikes, which has caused coyote numbers to decline by up to half in areas wolves occupy. Some coyotes have also moved out of flatter valley bottoms, where wolves can easily outrun them, to hillsides where they can outmaneuver the more ponderous canine. Fewer coyotes, in turn, means more pronghorn (whose fawns coyotes will prey on but wolves will not bother with) and foxes (which coyotes will kill). These shifting carnivore and herbivore numbers translate to changes in the vegetation, and still further ecological ripples. With fewer elk browsing them, willows and aspen in Lamar Valley are now growing rapidly, sending up new shoots and/or getting appreciably taller for the first time in decades. While a warming climate may be contributing to this growth, it's clear that wolves are responsible for some of it. Moreover, if the growth continues, it may lead to more indirect effects, such as an increase in the number of beaver, since willows and aspen are two of their favorite foods (more beaver are already present, but it's too soon to tell if that is associated with wolf recovery). And, if elk numbers continue falling, the ecological roles of bison and elk might flip, with buffalo outnumbering elk for the first time in Yellowstone's recorded history (currently both number about five thousand). Ecologists call such a chain of effects a trophic cascade, one that scientists have only rarely seen to the extent present in Yellowstone. It will probably continue to unfold for years, even decades to come, promising continued research opportunities and fascination for students of Yellowstone.

As intriguing as these changes are to study and learn about, experiencing the predators on their own turf is an opportunity Yellowstone provides, something that brings them and their ecological role alive in a personal and sometimes visceral way. One of my first encounters with wolves in the wild was in 1996, on my thirtieth birthday. Driving over from Missoula, where I was working on my master's degree, I met up with Carla for a late fall outing. We headed to Lamar Valley to climb Bison Peak, a 9,600-foot mountain whose south-facing slopes were open, promising solar warmth for us and the local four-legged residents alike. The first snow had whitened the landscape a few days earlier, but the sun was thinning the coverage in the open areas. So, we connected the dots between bare patches and thin spots, gaining elevation steadily. We weren't on a trail, but the topography made for easy route finding: we were ascending a spur ridge, one that joined another spur to produce a single, more defining ridge that would lead us the rest of the way to the summit. Ninety minutes into the climb, we reached a point from which we could see the other spur. That's when we saw them, a whole pack of wolves, loosely following some elk. None of them were running, so the wolves were probably just testing the herd to see if there were any elk weak enough to chase down. The elk knew that was the object of the game, so they were not spending any more energy than necessary to keep the predators at bay. We watched them pass out of sight, crossing the ridge that we'd be walking in an hour. When we passed that spot, we saw their tracks, the wolf tracks twice the size of the elk's. We saw no more sign of wolves that day, but the encounter with them made our day, the epitome of wildness doing its thing in the wild.

As uplifting as that experience was, another run-in with wolves was raw, even brutal. In the mid-2000s, I took a seminar on wolf ecology from the Yellowstone Institute, based at the organization's Buffalo Ranch field campus in Lamar Valley. Wolves are most active at dawn and, to a lesser extent, dusk, so after striking out trying to find some to watch the first evening, we agreed to meet at 4:30 the next morning (wolf observation is not for late risers). We drove east and soon found other wolf watchers gathered at a pullout overlooking Soda Butte Creek. Tumbling out of the vehicle, we didn't need to ask anyone where to look, for a pack of wolves and a bull elk were in plain view, about two hundred yards away. They were so close that spotting scopes were unnecessary; in fact, we had a pretty good view with the naked eye, though binoculars were handy. Settling in to see what would happen, we realized we had arrived after the show had begun, for the bull already had a gaping wound on one of his flanks. He was also in the middle of the stream, which our instructor told us was a defensive move, for the current was too strong for the wolves. Indeed, the pack was on the bank, stationary and watching the bull. Occasionally, one would wade into the water and try to swim toward the bull, but the stream, still swollen with snowmelt, was too powerful and the wolf would have to turn around. It was clear that, as long as the bull remained where he was, he was safe, although the wound on his leg looked bad enough that if he did survive the attack, infection might kill him anyway.

Watching this fight for survival, it was tempting to feel for the bull, to root for him, as it were. It is human nature to map our feelings and emotions onto the situation, to view it in black and white, wolves as bad, the bull as the good guy. We do this all the time, but the world of nature is amoral; nature just...is. Soon, the bull, for whatever reason, made a move that set into motion the events leading to his demise—and that brought forth more conflicting emotions. He waded out of the water, to the bank opposite the wolves. Perhaps he thought they would not cross the stream, but they simply found a place where the water spread out, enabling them to cross in those shallows. Quickly, they ran his way, but he retreated to the deeper water he'd just left. However, he didn't stay there long; for whatever reason, he got back out on the same side as the pack. They promptly gave chase, and he began to run away. A healthy bull can easily outrun a wolf, but not this one. Before he could even hit his stride, wolves began nipping, biting, and eventually locking onto his haunches. That slowed him down enough for another wolf to run around to his front, lock onto his throat, and drag him down. The bull struggled for a moment, trying to shake the predator off, but then stopped moving. The wolf clung to his throat a while longer, but its mission was complete. The bull, sleek and very much alive a minute earlier, was now dead. At that point, the wolves began to feed, the relationship between predator and prey once more acted out.

As we watched the wolves feed, I thought about the feelings that experience had triggered in me: revulsion and excitement, disgust and thrill, sadness and fascination. As ecologically influential as wolves are, they are also emotionally powerful for us. Indeed, seeing any large predator in action can bring us face-to-face with discomforting emotions, as I saw with the other apex predator in the Yellowstone ecosystem a few years later. I had traveled to Jackson Lake Lodge to give a talk about some of my national park policy research, and took a short hike before the conference began. As I walked past Christian Pond across the road from the lodge, I saw something move on the other side of the pond. I didn't have binoculars with me, but it was clearly a grizzly bear. It looked to be feeding on a carcass, for it wasn't moving, except around the dead animal (Figure 2.8). The pond was more the size of a small lake, so with a safety barrier between me and the bear, I sat down to enjoy the private grizzly viewing. The bear, which looked to be quite large, continued what it was doing, moving around the carcass to get the best angle on the various strips of flesh that were exposed. I was excited and a bit nervous, for bears are possessive of high protein food sources like this one, so much so that park managers usually close a trail when they learn a carcass is nearby. It was unlikely that this bear would come after me at this distance, especially with the grizzly's poor eyesight, but a different bear could walk past me en route to the carcass. Consequently, I kept a wary eye on the trail, knowing that bears find our trails as convenient for travel as we do.

Figure 2.8: Grizzly bear on an elk carcass, 1964. Grizzlies are fast enough to pull down elk calves less than a month old, but are otherwise limited to smaller prey and opportunistic scavenging. NPS PHOTO BY BRYAN HARRY, COURTESY OF NPS, YELLOWSTONE NATIONAL PARK (HTTP://WWW.NPS.GOV/FEA-TURES/YELL/SLIDEFILE/INDEX.HTM, ACCESSED MAY 30, 2017).

Soon, a loud roar, and then a second one, brought my attention back to the carcass. Something had clearly changed, as the griz was making clear. I struggled to see what was making it roar—this really was a misnamed body of water—and thought I saw a second bear just behind the other one. I hadn't seen another bear arrive, though one could have approached the carcass from beyond it, appearing out of the nearby forest without my noticing. Another roar came barreling at me across the "pond," as clear an indication of displeasure as I've ever heard. Those roars bespoke power, enough to kill, even if grizzly roaring is not associated with preying on humans. Nonetheless, I thought of what a predatory nighttime attack by a grizzly intent on killing and consuming a person must be like. Such attacks are rare, but they do happen, as recently as 2015 in the Lake area. Mountain lions and wolves have been known to attack and kill people, but neither animal has done so in Yellowstone, and wolves killing humans is largely a thing of the past and of Europe. Therefore, at least in Yellowstone, grizzlies are the only animal that includes humans in their diet (if rarely), a disquieting realization when hearing an angry griz. Moreover, the thought of a grizzly bear hunting you for your flesh, pulling you out of your tent, and then violently tearing you apart, sent a grim chill down my back. It made me feel small and vulnerable—much like a prey animal, especially since I was not that much larger than the elk calf the bear was probably eating. I hadn't heard grizzly bears roar previously, so now I understood more why their scientific name is *Ursus arctos horribilis*.

I watched and listened a little while longer, and then went on my way. As I walked, I thought about the hold that large predators have on our emotions and our imagination, as well as the ecological hold they have on the Yellowstone ecosystem. They are a riveting exploration of our deepest instincts and distant beginnings. Their influence on the landscapes they inhabit is equally significant, if not more so. Wolves, grizzly bears, and mountain lions have a major direct influence on their prey and indirect influence on the foods they in turn eat, and throughout the ecological web of interrelationships. Much of the landscape in and around Yellowstone bears the influence of the predators that inhabit it, whether they are one of the large predators discussed here, or any of the many smaller predators that roam the ecosystem. Coyotes and foxes, lynx and bobcats, black bears and a variety of mustelids (members of the weasel family), hawks and eagles, pelicans and mergansers, and a host of other carnivores live and hunt throughout this marvelous region, generating myriad networks of influences and predator-prey relationships. Few other places in America have so many predators and prey species, interacting in innumerable ways and joining with the many other ecological, geologic, and atmospheric forces to create the greater Yellowstone ecosystem. We are incredibly fortunate to have it, to watch its processes unfold, and to safeguard the region for our children and their children.

A Geologic Tour of Yellowstone Lake

Yellowstone Lake is many things to Yellowstone and its people: the park's largest body of water, the (past and hopefully future) home of millions of cutthroat trout and the predators that they sustain, a scene of dramatic natural beauty, and many more treasures. Looking somewhat like a down-hanging, misshapen hand, the lake is 135 square miles in size, making it the largest lake in North America at its elevation, 7733 feet above sea level. It is big enough to contain evidence of all the major geologic forces creating Yellowstone, including volcanism, tectonic activity (earthquakes), and glaciation and erosion. The lake is also big enough for fantastic boat trips of a week or more in duration. Roads hug the lake's northern shores and motorboats have access to much of the lake, but its most distant hideaways are reserved for the canoeist and kayaker. In 2003, my buddy Eric and I—two aspiring geographers both working on our doctorates at the University of Wisconsin-Madison—paddled the entire 80-mile roadless shoreline over the course of a week. It was to be a tour of the geosciences—geology and geography—on Yellowstone Lake.

We began our tour at Grant Village, known to some in Yellowstone as the Mosquito Coast, a moniker that we soon came to personally understand—and feel. Due to the lake's afternoon winds, we put in shortly after dawn, a practice we continued for the duration of the trip. We also hugged the shore as we paddled, because gale force winds can arise within minutes, leaving too little time to get out of the water. For the first day, our route took us around the lake's thumb, which points west, giving it the name West Thumb. We had its south shore to ourselves that morning, but occasional flashes of light from sun glinting off the cars on the road opposite us were reminders of the world we had hoped to leave behind. So we kept paddling, keeping the canoe just clear of the trees that had fallen into the water. Many of them dangled over the edge of ten or twenty-foot tall banks, suspended in a state of perpetual anticipation. Climb those banks and you'd emerge into a trailless flatland of dense, partly burned, and mostly jack-strawed forest interspersed with marsh and occasional pond and lake. It's so flat that figuring out which way one of the lakes drained was a challenge to early cartographers; Riddle Lake and Solution Creek bear testament to their confusion and ultimate cartographic success. Similarly, Delusion Lake is so named because it looked to those early geographers that it was the index finger to Yellowstone Lake. It's in the right place and is the shape of a forefinger, but is detached, severed from the hand, an excellent geographic delusion.

Paddling on, we carved a wide arc around the thumb and then through the two-mile-long strait leading to the lake's palm. Once through the strait, we rounded Breeze Point and entered an area of sandy points and sheltered bays. Protected from the prevailing southwest wind by the upwind, forested shore, we stopped for lunch. We had made better time than anticipated, so when we resumed our travel, we had only a short way to go before arriving at our campsite for the night. We still had most of the afternoon to enjoy, so we took a swim and relaxed on the beach. Refreshed by the dip, I thought of how the topography of West Thumb was in large part a reflection of its geologic past. The thumb is round, like a dumbbell whose other half is subsumed in the larger body of Yellowstone Lake. That's because West Thumb is a collapsed volcano, or caldera, one that blew its top and then fell in upon itself 174,000 years ago. It was a large eruption, many times the size of the 1980 Mt. St. Helens event, though most of this one's ejecta are buried under more recent deposits. Water has since filled the crater in, making it part of a newly reconfigured Yellowstone Lake. It was the first, but not the last—or the most impressive—evidence of the volcanic forces that created Yellowstone we were to see on that trip.

In fact, the very next day we paddled past evidence that West Thumb is actually a fairly good-sized caldera within a much larger, massive caldera. We entered the Flat Mountain Arm, a body of water that is quite linear, narrow, and bounded on the south by the foot of the mountain lending its name to the arm. When we were about halfway down the arm, we beached the canoe, hung our food out of ursine reach, and climbed Flat Mountain. In so doing, we climbed out of the Yellowstone caldera, a 34-by-45-mile-wide collapsed volcano occupying much of Yellowstone. It's so big that its size can only really be appreciated from on high, a point from which the other side is visible. Flat Mountain's forested summit was not such a vantage point—the mountain merits the name—but its northern slope is. From there, we could see Mount Washburn, on the northern rim of the caldera (Figure 2.9). Everything between us and the mountain on the horizon, and extending westward out of sight and beyond Old Faithful, collapsed at the end of a gigantic eruption 640,000 years ago. It blew out enough ash and dust to form deposits as deep as 1200 feet locally, and covered places as distant as California, Texas, and Missouri with an inch or two. It was a climate-altering eruption the likes of which modern civilization has never seen, making the 1980 St. Helens eruption look like a miniscule belch. The eruption annihilated entire mountain ranges that were here before, leaving disconnected remnants now known as the Tetons and Red Mountains on the south side, and the Gallatin and Madison Ranges on the north. Much of the caldera was filled in by subsequent lava flows, but the palm of Yellowstone Lake occupies an area that was not. For the same reason, most of the caldera rim has been submerged beneath water or lava, but there are a few places where it can still be seen, including the Flat Mountain Arm. The northern slopes of the mountain we climbed are the caldera rim, which falls away into the arm's watery depths. The north shore is the edge of one of the later lava flows, covered in most places with even more recent sediments. To say that the Flat Mountain Arm landscape owes its existence to dynamic and extreme volcanism seems an understatement; it's hard to imagine a more violent origin.

Indeed, the energy driving that eruption is still present, so the lake may not have seen its last violent change. Yellowstone sits astride a hot spot, a stationary plume of magma upwelling from deep in the earth. The plume brings magma up slowly but continuously, pooling it into large reservoirs under Yellowstone's shallow crust. Eventually, enough magma will accumu-

Figure 2.9: The Yellowstone caldera, as seen from the side of Flat Mountain, 2003. The Flat Mountain Arm of Yellowstone Lake (in the foreground) marks the southern boundary, while the Washburn Mountains 34 miles away (and faintly visible on the horizon) do the same for the northern boundary. Everything between the arm and the mountain range is in the caldera. The main body of Yellowstone Lake (its palm) stretches across the photo in the background, while Delusion Lake can be seen in the forest just this side of Yellowstone Lake. AUTHOR COLLECTION.

late to produce an eruption, either as a mere lava flow or another massive eruption of ash and dust. The hot spot has powered several previous eruptions, and because North America is moving slowly southwest, one can follow the calderas left behind, a string of progressively older calderas arcing in that direction across southern Idaho. The last three eruptions averaged about 600,000 years apart, so you could say we are due for another, though there is no indication that it's imminent. Nonetheless, reminders of the power lying in wait under Yellowstone are ubiquitous, especially in the geysers and hot springs fueled by the hot spot's heat. Magma under Yellowstone is only two or three miles down, compared to about thirty in most other areas. That magma will erupt some day, adding another chapter of volcanism to an already fascinating book, one whose evidence we would continue to see as we paddled around the lake.

We paddled out of the Flat Mountain Arm and out of the caldera that afternoon, making camp at Plover Point, which guards the west side of the South Arm's mouth, a portal to the wilder side of Yellowstone Lake. Motorboats are allowed in the South and Southeast Arms, but only at 5 mph or less, a regulation that discourages most boaters from entering them. Silence and a semblance of wilderness experience would be ours to enjoy the next four days, as we explored both arms, which are considerably larger than the arm we'd just left. Buoyed with anticipation, we repeated the activities of the previous afternoon, the swim being especially invigorating, given the climb we had done and the warm day. Unfortunately, the repeat also included swatting a never ending supply of mosquitoes while we prepared supper; though we donned mosquito netting and long sleeves and pants after the swim, our hands were still exposed and a mosquito would occasionally find its way under the netting. However, Eric suggested a possible escape from them for the dinner itself: reasoning that the bugs might not follow us out over open water, we would load the meal and tableware into the canoe and paddle a short distance out from shore. The ploy worked, perhaps because desperation lent speed to our strokes (Figure 2.10). Once we were a hundred yards out, we glided to a stop. The evening was calm, as was the air, no longer stirred by the wings of a million flying pests. It was unconventional dining to be sure, but no restaurant could compare with the ambiance we had that evening. Adrift on a sea of glass, unaltered forest on the near shore and the knobs of the Promontory rising above a similar forest on the far one, we were seated at a table of wilderness beauty. That, and the reprieve from mosquito whine, made that meal one of the better backcountry dining experiences I have had. We remained adrift until the sun had set, whereupon we put the netting back on, paddled to camp, and resumed battling humanity's greatest pest while we finished the remaining camp chores and then jumped into the tents for shelter. Falling temperatures gradually quieted the high-pitched roar outside the tent walls, and we slept soundly, pleased that two geographers were able to outwit the hoard.

Paddling into the South Arm the next day, we kept to the western shore, which is fairly linear, running north-south. Looking at the map, I could see that the line continued on land further south, appearing as a line of valleys between long ridges and low mountains. The line continues to and beyond Yellowstone's south boundary, turning with the topography some but remaining generally linear. Including the west shore of the arm, the line is more than thirty miles long. When geologists see a line

Figure 2.10: A floating dinner for two in Yellowstone, 2003. Eric and the photographer / author enjoy mosquito-free dining in the canoe. AUTHOR COLLECTION.

like that, they suspect an earthquake fault. Not only do faults allow for movement of the earth's crust, but that movement also shatters and weakens the rock on either side, making it easier to erode. In this manner, valleys often follow faults, as with this one south of the lake. Examining the underlying rocks on both sides of the fault there, geologists see that those on the east side appear younger than those on the other side. That makes this a "normal" fault, one in which the movement is vertical, with one side subsiding relative to the other (the eastern Teton fault is also a normal fault). This subsidence explains, at least in part, the existence of the South Arm, for it is on the side of the fault that subsided. Several times in the last fifty years, small earthquakes have occurred on this fault, possibly deepening the arm an inch or two. Earthquakes occur regularly throughout Yellowstone, which is riddled with faults of all kinds (others allow for lateral movement of the two sides, subduction of one side under the other, and other movements). Most of the earthquakes are small and happen in swarms, and may be related to magma moving in or shifting around below. However, the quakes can occasionally be quite large, with one in 1959 registering 7.5 on the Richter scale and causing widespread damage throughout the Yellowstone area. That quake shook loose an entire mountainside near the park, causing a massive landslide that dammed the Madison River and buried two dozen people camped below. As that quake tragically illustrated and as we could see on the South Arm, earthquakes can be a powerful force in shaping a landscape, especially in the Yellowstone area.

We camped that night at the end of the arm, our buggiest night yet. We sought relief in the canoe again, without which it would have been a miserable dining experience and an early-to-bed evening. As it was, some mosquitoes followed us as we dove into our respective tents, prompting us both to embark on a round of pest eradication. In our sanctuaries, the roles of hunter and hunted reversed as we each squished them against the tent walls. It was man against nature, a contest of the primitive. Thankfully, modern tents don't leak insects like the Clear Creek Cabin did, enabling both of us to prevail. We slept soundly and woke up in the pre-dawn light, ready for another day of paddling and geologic inquiry.

Paddling along the arm's eastern shore that morning, we made a quick stop to thrash through the alders to Alder Lake (a fitting name). Continuing on, we reached our campsite for the night at the tip of the Promontory, the peninsula separating the South and Southeast Arms, in time for a second breakfast. With the hash browns eaten and camp set up, we took off to climb the Promontory. An hour later, we were enjoying a fabulous view of the Southeast Arm, its wind-ruffled water dark blue in the bright afternoon sun (Figure 2.11). Across the arm from us, the Yellowstone River joins the lake but seemed that day as if it preferred to flow through the lake more than mingle with it, for a pathway of calm wended its way through the darker, riffled lake water. It was as if the river, having flowed unshackled thus far, wanted to hold onto its freedom as it passed through the lake, not realizing that the lake was freedom of another kind, for no dam regulates its level. Above the aqueous confusion rose the Absaroka Mountains, lofty peaks on the north giving way to loftier alpine plateaus to the south, some still holding on to banks of snow. They are still another form of freedom, reaching for the sky with reckless abandon, visited by only those few willing to hike for miles on rudimentary trails and more miles off trail, and all protected from the many degradations we have wreaked on mountains elsewhere in the world. It was liberating and invigorating to gaze upon this panorama, and exciting to think that tomorrow we would be paddling into it.

The Absarokas extend far outside the park, some forty or fifty miles in every direction except west. They were once a mighty

Figure 2.11: View into the Thorofare from the Promontory, 2003. Across the Southeast Arm, the Yellowstone River flows into it, seemingly retaining its integrity as it flows through the wind-ruffled water closer to our vantage point. The Absaroka Mountains line the horizon, with the Trident's northern spear appearing as the ridge with a patch of snow on it. AUTHOR COLLECTION.

field of volcanoes that erupted off and on for ten million years, ending about 43 million years ago. The lava from those eruptions had accumulated to thousands of feet deep, but with no more lava being added, erosion and weathering gained the upper hand, carving and widening valleys, carrying sediment downstream, and making soil. Still, despite being highly erosive, much of the lava remains, the building blocks of the range lining the lake—indeed, the whole park—on the east, as well as the peninsula on which we stood. Mostly andesite, the lava is rich in calcium, potassium, phosphorus, and magnesium, and so are the soils derived from it. Those are all minerals plants need for growth, so a richer variety of them is present on andesitic soils than on the nutrient-poor soils derived from the rhyolite extruded from the Yellowstone caldera. This diversity was not so evident to us on the dry backbone of the Promontory, but its side slopes had deeper soil and a rich forest reminiscent of the one I first encountered in Cache Creek, including the flowers. It was another reminder of how much this landscape is a product of its sometimes distant geologic past—even, to some degree, the mixture of plants we saw that day.

That day was hot, so when we got back to camp we jumped in the lake, but instead of hopping out right away as had been our custom, we remained sitting in the shallows. It really was warm; in a decade and a half in Yellowstone, I had rarely swum in the lake, let alone sat in it at length. It was a reminder of that warm day in Cache Creek fifteen years earlier, but this time we got an unexpected reprieve in the form of a thunderstorm, one that would pass to our north but bring us a steady breeze. From our location at the tip of the Promontory, we had a commanding view of the lake, looking out over the entire palm of the down-hanging hand. The storm filled the sky across the lake from us, its slate blue reflected in the choppy water at our feet. The only thing falling from the sky was a shaft of sunlight breaking through the clouds and angling across the lake, a contrast of gold with the tempest behind it. Rain was elusive, falling beyond the lake, if at all. Mosquitoes were absent as well, blown off by the salvation breeze.

Paddling into the Southeast Arm the next morning was a delight, with the Absarokas standing guard across the way, seeming sentinels protecting the arm against those who would defile its wildness. Our pace was relaxed, the Promontory shielding us from the prevailing southwest breezes. We savored the quiet coves, the rich forest hugging the shore, the occasional osprey or bald eagle perched in a lakeshore tree. By midmorning we were in the bottom of the arm, the province of paddlers and pelicans. That was the nonmotorized zone, where motorboats are not allowed, and the home of the Molly Islands, two specks of land sustaining the only breeding colony of American white pelicans in Wyoming. The islands also harbored cormorants and California gulls, all drawn there (along with the birds of prey) by the abundance of fish in the lake (although lake trout had been in the lake for over a decade by then, their effects on cutthroat trout were just beginning to be felt). A variety of ducks plied the waters there as well, the mergansers being especially memorable with their flotillas of fuzzy chicks madly paddling to keep up with their parent. Some of the families had a dozen or fifteen chicks in tow, a clear testament to their fecundity, the fishy smorgasbord swimming around underneath us, perhaps both. We had been seeing some of these birds all along, particularly in the South Arm, but on the Southeast Arm the exuberance of life was especially obvious, probably because there was plenty of sheltered habitat and because the nesting ground for some of the birds was there.

As we rounded the arm's fingertip, we noticed some dead trees standing in a few inches of water (Figure 2.12). They had been lodgepole pines, but the species prefers sandy, well-drained soil, not frequently saturated substrates like these. When they germinated, the soil here was indeed amenable to them, but Yellowstone's restless geology changed that, eventually drowning the trees. Just north of the lake is one of two resurgent domes in Yellowstone, areas where the ground is slowly rising from magma moving in below from the hot spot. That one, known as the Sour Creek Dome, has risen about three feet in the last century, a rate of geologic change that is quite rapid. With the lake's outlet right there, the uplift has had the effect of tilting the lake to the south, slowly inundating and killing the shoreline trees. Rarely is geologic change so dynamic, with such visible ecological effects. If this trip was a tour of Yellowstone geology, the dead trees were a crash course in geologic dynamism.

Figure 2.12: Partially submerged lodgepole pine in Southeast Arm, 2003. This sentinel of rapid geologic change has many companions on the shores of the South and Southeast Arms of Yellowstone Lake. Uplift at the lake's outlet has shifted its waters south, drowning shoreline trees in some areas. AUTHOR COLLECTION.

Figure 2.13: Whitecaps and a thunderstorm on the Southeast Arm, 2003. Nature's power is always on display in Yellowstone, but especially so on Yellowstone Lake and in thunderstorms. In this view, Colter Peak (left) and Turret Mountain dominate the horizon. AUTHOR COLLECTION.

That evening, we had a repeat performance of the previous night's thunderstorm. This time, the merciful wind not only blew the mosquitoes away, but it also stirred the lake up enough to produce whitecaps (Figure 2.13). Had we still been out paddling, we would have been forced ashore, the waves tall enough to slop over the gunwales. The storm and light show featured two shafts of sunlight, one illuminating a line of bleached-white trees on the far shore, victims of the 1988 fires, and the other dancing around the Absaroka peaks above, flitting from one volcanic remnant to another. With the lake at our feet reflecting the sky's midnight blue, it was last night's show on steroids.

The next morning the thunderstorm was gone, replaced by brilliant sunshine, crystalline air, and aquatic tranquility. We paddled our way across the Yellowstone River delta, weaving in and out with the undulating, willow-studded shoreline (Figure

2.14). The river's mouth was surprisingly hard to discern, only given away by numerous logs stuck in the shallows, their roots too big a drag for even the snowmelt-swollen river to move further into the lake. Once past the delta, we turned north, following the shore out of the arm and out of the wild. It was quiet and peaceful, as marked a contrast to last night's power show as this landscape would have been fifteen thousand years ago, in the most recent ice age. Grinding and scraping its way down the Yellowstone River Valley, a glacier widened and deepened the long valley as it descended, scouring out the Southeast Arm as well. Joining forces with many other glaciers flowing into the park from the Absaroka Mountains, the rivers of ice coalesced into a giant icecap covering most of Yellowstone and reaching three or four thousand feet thick over the lake. The Absaroka

Figure 2.14: Yellowstone River delta on the Southeast Arm, 2014. The delta is a place where the river slows and drops the sediment it's carrying, producing an undulating shoreline and a place of exceptional diversity and wildlife habitat. Photo by Eric Compas, author collection.

peaks would have just poked out above the ice, rocky refuges in a world of white. The ice began to melt after another thousand years, disappearing entirely by thirteen thousand years before the present. At sometime in the melt, the ice dam formed in the Canyon area, leading to sediment deposition covering some of the lava extruded by the last eruption of the Yellowstone caldera, deposits we paddled past on the first two days of this voyage. With the ice gone, the Yellowstone River began filling in the U-shaped river valley left behind by the glacier that gouged out the Southeast Arm, gradually producing a flat valley floor and pushing the delta and arm downstream to their current locations. At times in the not-too-distant past, then, this was a radically different landscape, but still one of power—an icy, resculpting, reshaping one.

Eric and I soon got a personal taste of the landscape's continuing energy. When we paddled out of the Southeast Arm and into the lake's palm, we entered more dangerous waters, the area of the lake's longest fetch. Knowing our margin of error was small, we approached the longest rocky stretch with concern, for the gentle breeze we had been enjoying seemed to be strengthening, kicking the waves up a notch. We paddled on, anxious to get to our campsite for the night before wind and waves made the rocky stretch impassable. Then, when we were drawing near the last possible place to bail out, whitecaps appeared, so we hauled out, putting a deep gouge in the canoe as we pulled it, fully loaded, up over the rough rocks. Safe for the moment, we sat down and snacked, pondering our next move. The wind was in our face, so forward movement would be slow if we reentered the fray. Still, it was tempting to make a run for it, for the waves were not that tall, and we knew they would probably not get any smaller as the afternoon progressed. On the other hand, getting caught in impassable water off an unforgiving shore could be a fatal mistake. For that reason, we opted to stay put—better to arrive late than not at all.

Having time on our hands and wanting to put temptation out of reach, we took off for a hike on the nearby trail, which parallels the lakeshore. After twenty minutes, we emerged from the forest to a small bluff above the lake. Stopping to take in the view, we looked at each other—not to remark upon the sunlit beauty at our feet, but to confirm that the wind had let up some. Temptation was now irresistible; turning around, we hightailed it back to the canoe, gave it another gouge dragging it back to the water, and hopped in. Conditions had improved, but only a little, as we shortly realized. The waves were within an inch of splashing over; the wind, strong enough that our most powerful strokes advanced the boat a mere six inches. We were committed, though; turning the canoe around in these conditions would have been riskier than continuing on, so we kept paddling. We had to pass a point of land about a quarter mile ahead, after which the wind would be at our backs. Madly paddling, we inched our way forward, the wind neither abating nor increasing, the waves neither shrinking nor growing (but occasionally splashing a few drops inside the boat, to keep us committed). Finally, we drew up to the point and slowly rounded it, the waves a tussle of confusion with the changing wind directions. Rounding the corner, we saw our campsite a mile away, the grassy meadow of Park Point. With the wind now ushering us forward, we flew the rest of the way, but our arms and shoulders still welcomed the break from exertion as we landed. This effort had been the most arduous work of the trip.

That evening was our last, and as if to mark the occasion, nature threw us another thunderstorm, completing the trifecta of dramatic storms. This time the shaft of sunlight was on us, turning the meadow before us into a field of gold. That gave way to a lake of slate gray, across from which a black Promontory guarded the entrance to the Southeast Arm. In the distance rose a dark gray Two Ocean Plateau, brooding over the Thorofare.

The storm, the view, and the remaining six miles of paddling that we did the next morning brought the trip full circle, in several ways. Most immediately, we now had three evenings with a thunderstorm, balancing the first three evenings with swarming mosquitoes. This last storm actually provided only partial relief, clearing out before sunset, which allowed the nuisances to return for a final encore ("Park Point" seems too nice a name for a place where mosquitoes occur in such soul-searching abundance!). The view, though, made up for the place's deficiencies, encapsulating most of the trip, from West Thumb to Flat Mountain, from the three fingers to the palm, from wilderness solitude to motorized vehicles in the distance (this time, motorboats, whose noise we had also been noticing). And the last morning of canoeing completed the geological circle, for we reentered the Yellowstone caldera. Much like our trip, any tour of Yellowstone geology begins and ends with the caldera and the hot spot, which define the park in so many ways. But, as we had seen paddling, many other geologic forces also help create the unique landscape, including glaciations, more ancient volcanism, and tectonic activity. It was a whole panoply of geologic forces, signs of which are widely manifest in the Yellowstone landscape. Those signs indicate that the ground under our feet (and below the lake waters) is very much alive, still evolving and being created. Indeed, Yellowstone is a landscape of change, of geologic force, and of nature's power.

A Cold and Snowy Climate

There is a saying in Yellowstone that goes something like this: "I remember that summer; it was the day we had a picnic." Summer is indeed fleeting on the Yellowstone plateau; barely have residents remarked upon seeing their first bluebirds in spring before they find fireweed, the harbinger of autumn, blooming in late summer. Many a hike of mine has driven home the same point, but a few stand out, virtually shouting that summer is the shortest season. That was the case in 1998 when my cousin Tom from Missouri spent a week visiting me. He came in June, a busy time of year for my work group, so it took some coaxing of my boss to even get a day and a half off, but he made it happen. After a quick lunch on the half day, Tom and I made the drive to the Hellroaring trailhead as quickly as traffic permitted—and as quickly as human error allowed, for, halfway there, I realized I had forgotten my hiking boots, so we had to double back to retrieve them. By the time we finally set off, it was mid-afternoon. That's a later start than I usually get, but we had only nine miles to our campsite for the night. Barring unforeseen delays and enjoying the long days of June, we would be making camp well before dark, with plenty of time for supper.

Descending the switchbacks to the Yellowstone River, we paused at a suspension bridge, as I have done every time I have crossed it. Pinched between the hundred-foot walls of rock that made this a natural site for a bridge, the river was a watery turmoil, blasting its way through the narrow channel. Swollen with spring snowmelt, the river's ordinarily green water was a turbid brown, as if to highlight its amped-up power. After we had absorbed metaphorical energy from the river and caloric energy from a handful of trail mix, we shouldered our packs and resumed the hike. The trail soon left the forest, crossing an open plain dotted with sage and appearing refreshingly green. Sometimes hot, the plain was pleasant that afternoon, with a light breeze and meadowlarks singing the praises of the day. It was a place to look down, to hunt for the flashes of color among the sagebrush, the spring wildflowers that would be gone in a matter of a week or two. Each held its own reward, from the sweet scent of the white phlox clusters to the delicate heads of yellow bells to the ephemeral purple brilliance of the rare bitterroot. It was also a place to look skyward, to see what the heavens might have to offer. For us, the view was one of clouds and sheets of rain in the distance, complements to the cool, humid air we were feeling. For now, our spirits were not to be dampened, for we were underway and surrounded by beauty, so we continued across the plain and soon met up with Hellroaring Creek (Figure 2.15). Lined with bright green willows and dark green junipers or Douglas-firs, the creek was a miniaturized Yellowstone River and a complement of vibrancy to the land through which it flowed.

The creek was our cue to turn right and hike upstream on the trail that would lead us into the Absaroka-Beartooth Wilderness

Figure 2.15: Hellroaring Creek, spring 2008. The sights and sounds of spring in the Rockies are evident here: rushing streams, swollen with snowmelt; budding willows and emerging plants, turning the landscape green; and changing weather conditions, rain falling in the distance. AUTHOR COLLECTION.

bordering the park. Soon, the rain came to us, a gentle drizzle that hardly justified donning our rain gear. But after having seen the cloud cover, and with the drizzle intensifying, we made the move to rain jackets and pants. A wise move it was, for the rain kept falling, and we kept hiking. Two more miles passed, we crossed the creek on a footbridge, and the rain fell. Three miles passed, we entered a thicker forest, and the temperature began to fall along with the rain. Four miles passed, we entered the wilderness area, and the rain stayed with us. Five miles passed, the forest turned to spruce and pine, and the greater moisture that sustains those trees fell in increasing amounts from the sky. Six miles passed, Tom and I agreed that we would hike another mile and take shelter on the covered porch of the Forest Service cabin in the meadow we were to camp in, and the rain began to soak through our rain gear. Finally, in a steady rain and with the temperature hovering around forty degrees, we strode into the meadow, only to find smoke rising from the cabin stovepipe. The cabin was occupied, which meant we would not be able to use the porch—the only dry spot for miles around—so we began looking disconsolately for a place to pitch the tent in the sodden meadow. As soaked and cold as we were, hypothermia was a real danger, so we would probably forego cooking a hot supper and instead just inhale a few power bars and then dive into the tent and sleeping bags to warm up. Tom's first back-packing trip was looking more and more like a survival test, not an enjoyable outing.

Barely had we begun our search, though, when something drew my attention to the cabin. Someone was standing on the front porch, motioning for us to come over. Could it be that they would let us use the porch? We held our breath as we crossed the meadow and approached the coveted—and very dry—porch. The fellow standing there introduced himself as a US Forest Service employee, part of a group of four doing some work in the area and staying in the cabin. He invited us to drop our packs on the porch and to come inside and warm up. We stared at him in disbelief; did our hearing somehow get warped in the watery death march we had just finished? He repeated himself, so we figured it was not an illusion and dropped the two rain-soaked packs, which landed with a thud that announced our arrival to everyone inside and out. Though protected by their own rain covers, the packs had taken on water in the consuming wetness, much like the two guys bearing them. In weather like this, the only rain gear that truly keeps water out is rubberized plastic, but that ends up producing the same end result if the bearer so much as thinks about exerting himself, for the material doesn't breathe at all, leaving one soaked in his own sweat. Neither our angelic host nor his unexpected guests cared about the fine points of rain gear at that moment, though, so we practically tore the door off its hinges in our stampede to get inside. As we did, we each had something resembling an out-of-body experience, for the atmosphere inside made us think we had entered heaven. It was hard to imagine a more complete contrast with the world we'd been walking through for the past several hours; gone were the damp and chill, replaced by a heavenly glow of warmth and dryness. St. Peter introduced us to his fellow angels and then moved aside as we gravitated toward the god that made this paradise possible, the humble woodstove.

After we had finished worshipping the woodstove, our stomachs began to draw us back to Earth. By this time, we had chatted with our hosts enough for them to see that they had a lot in common with us and could trust us to be companionable dinner guests, so they suggested we prepare our meal in their kitchen. We happily did so, enjoying a hot meal that an hour earlier had seemed as out of reach as sleeping on the silky—and blissfully dry—sheets of a Hilton Hotel bed that night. Before sitting down to eat, a moose walked by the cabin, so close that it was frightened away when the automatic flash on someone's camera went off as they took its picture out the window. Not long thereafter, I noticed Tom looking intently out a different window. He had been a veritable bear magnet on his weeklong visit; it seemed that every time he turned around, there was another bear. I wanted to conscript him into service on my bus tours so my passengers would have a guarantee of seeing bears. Consequently, I recognized the look on his face and followed his gaze to see a small grizzly bear poking around across the meadow. Tom announced his sighting to the others in a calm, almost bored voice reflecting his recent experience, and then the cabin saw its second rapid movement of humanity to windows as the Forest Service crew rushed to see it. They had not yet seen a bear and were thrilled to break their ursine drought. Someone noted that it was in the very area in which we had been preparing to camp, a thought that made me hope for more divine intervention regarding the night's sleeping arrangements. I did not relish the thought of going back out to set the tent up in this weather, much less trying to sleep with a grizzly on the prowl, even though it soon left the meadow. As if reading my mind, when the excitement subsided one of our hosts showed us an unoccupied room with two beds that we could use for the night. I had been planning to ask them if we could sleep on the porch, but this was unexpected salvation. We put our sleeping bags on the beds and prepared for a night of pampered luxury. This was most certainly heaven, at least for the night!

Overnight, the rain ended, but precipitation continued: we woke up to an inch of new snow on the ground. In June, snow and the frost that often accompanies it are not uncommon in Yellowstone, though snow is still usually a surprise. Of the two, frost is generally the more damaging for plants because snow often acts like a blanket, insulating the plants it covers from the colder temperatures and potential frost. The frequency of summertime snow and frost means that anything that grows here needs to be able to withstand them. That's why ponderosa pine, one of the most widely distributed western trees, doesn't grow here; the tree cannot cope with summertime frost. Other trees cope with these adverse conditions by aborting reproduction after such a frost, knowing that (to be anthropomorphic) their life expectancy of two or three hundred years means they can afford to wait for years with more favorable weather. Whitebark pine is one such tree; other factors like drought can also make them fail to reproduce, but summer-time frost is one of the leading causes. The hardy species also tends to favor south-facing slopes, which gives it maximum solar expo-sure. Whitebarks, like most of the trees they share those haunts with, are slow-growing, limited as they are by a short—or some-times nonexistent—frost-free growing season. Six inches of new annual growth is typical; a foot, exceptional. Grasses and forbs take the opposite tack, growing quickly to flower and set seed be-fore the killing frosts of autumn arrive in September (sometimes even in August). They quite literally make hay while the summer sun shines. These are just some of the adaptations trees and other plants have to a short growing season, one that even includes the occasional snowfall and frost. There is a reason palm trees don't grow in Yellowstone.

Some statistics give a better idea of just how cold Yellowstone is. Rangers at the Lake Ranger Station have operated a weather station for decades, giving us an excellent picture of the climate on the Yellowstone plateau. The ranger station is at 7800 feet above sea level, while the plateau varies from 7500 to 9000 feet, so conditions at the higher elevations would be a little cooler and snowier. The average high in July, the warmest month, is 72° F. (all temperatures for this discussion will be in degrees Fahren-heit), and the average low in January, the coldest month, is 1°. The average overnight low temperature is only above freezing for three months, June through August, and never far from the freezing point (June, 35°, July, 40°, and August, 38°). Similarly, the average high temperature is below freezing for the equivalent winter months (December and January, 24°, and February, 27°) and near freezing in the two bookend months (November, 33° F., and March, 37° F.). Perhaps the most succinct measure of Yellowstone's cold climate is the annual average temperature, which is the average of all daily high and low temperatures: just 33.2°. Compare that to a typical American city like my home town of St. Louis, Missouri, whose annual average temperature is 56.1°, or a hot city like Phoenix, Arizona (72.6°), or even a town known for being cold, International Falls, Minnesota (36.8°), and the arctic quality of Yellowstone's climate becomes apparent. In fact, Yellowstone is so cold its annual average temperature is between those of Anchorage and Fairbanks, Alaska (35.9° and 26.9°, respectively). Statistics for the annual average snowfall are similar (and given in inches): Yellowstone (150-200 or more, generally corresponding with elevation); St. Louis (19.5); Phoenix (trace); International Falls (65.7); Anchorage (70.5); and Fairbanks (69.0). While there are snowier places in the West, Yellowstone's cold air means that much of the snow piles up, not melting until April and May—and that spring and summer snowfalls can always happen, as we saw out the cabin window that morning.

With one of the Forest Service crew joining us for the hike out, we set off on the climb out of the Hellroaring Creek Canyon. Our hike was to be a loop, returning via the Coyote Creek Trail, which crosses a plateau just east of and about a thousand feet higher than the canyon we had spent the night in. The higher elevation meant we would find more snow up there, but we correctly guessed it would not be deeper than our boot tops. The temperature remained around the freezing point, but we stayed warm through exertion, climbing through some switchbacks and then emerging onto the intermittently forested plateau. Under the trees, the trail was bare but wet, while out in the meadows it had two or three inches of snow on it. Laden with heavy wet snow, plants leaned over the trail, kissing us with cold moisture as we brushed our way through. Color had been whitewashed from the landscape, the sky a brooding grey, the trees appearing almost black under the mantle of white, and the dots of wildflower color gone for the moment. It was a taste of winter beauty and a reminder that the season of white is never far away in Yellowstone.

As we hiked on, repeatedly soaking our legs for an encore of yesterday's experience, I was reminded of a hike I'd taken five years earlier, to Hoodoo Basin, high on the park's east boundary. That was July of 1993, the coolest and wettest summer in my Yellowstone experience. Carla and I had done the steep hike in from Sunlight Basin outside the park, making camp among lingering snowdrifts. After checking out the eroded rock pinnacles for which the basin was named, we made the easy walk over to Parker Peak, climbed its short summit, and returned to camp for the evening meal. The evening was cool and overcast, so after supper we turned in early for a night of hard-earned slumber. The clouds gathered and dropped their moisture while we slept, but instead of hearing the pitter-pat of rain on the tent, we didn't hear anything, even when we roused to turn over. Had we listened more intently, we might have heard the soft whisper of snowflakes and noticed the tent begin to sag. A silent snowstorm moved through, blanketing the basin with three or four inches of snow by daybreak (Figure 2.16). The storm had moved out by the time we emerged from the tent, but the cold temperatures had not. Shivering as we broke camp, we gulped hot tea and contemplated the hike out. Hoodoo Basin is high, but the trail back to Sunlight Basin climbed higher, staying above treeline for about three miles before crossing the park boundary and descending to the trailhead. There was already a breeze, so we knew we could be in for some memorable hiking. Indeed it was, for the temperature and breeze remained wintry enough to produce blowing and drifting snow, something ordinarily seen only in winter, hardly in the warmest month of the year. The hiking was raw and windy, with an occasional flower poking above the snow as if to defy the weather gods—and the only evidence of what season this really was. It was by far the coldest day of summertime hiking I experienced in Yellowstone, perhaps the best example I've encountered of the climactic extremes present in the northern Rockies. Conditions are already so harsh above about ten thousand feet in the Yellowstone area that trees cannot grow. Hardy, diminutive grasses and flowers hang on in the tundra, adapting to the extreme conditions by hugging the ground and sometimes growing in a pincushion form or having hairy leaves, all to retain heat and moisture. Even on a good day in the alpine tundra the climate limitations

Figure 2.16: Snow in Hoodoo Basin, July, 1993. A wintry surprise at the height of summer illustrates the primacy of a cold climate in determining what plants and animals can exist in Yellowstone. AUTHOR COLLECTION.

are obvious, and days like the one we endured in Hoodoo Basin drive home the understanding that climate is one of the most powerful forces creating the Yellowstone ecosystem. To grow there, a plant absolutely must be adapted to cold, even in the heart of what is considered summer.

Summer was on our minds as we hiked with the forest ranger, crossed the plateau, and began the gradual descent back to the suspension bridge. Dropping down was a walk forward in time and a recapitulation of the life zones we had climbed through on the way in. We had only visited the alpine zone in my memory, that land above ten thousand feet that occasionally features winter in July. We were headed for the land of grass and sage below about six thousand feet, the proverbial banana belt where precipitation is not adequate for trees but where the temperatures are warm enough to make people happy. Between those two is a broad band of forest, the land we were hiking through. The blend of trees changes with elevation, from the spruce, fir, and whitebark pine up high, to the lodgepole pine zone we were about to drop out of, to the Douglas-fir zone down low. As we experienced dropping off the plateau, the temperature gradually rose, the snow disappeared, and the forest transitioned through the tree groupings and then to sagebrush and grassland. While the mountains were still shrouded in clouds and snow, it was warm and nearly dry on the open plain. By the time we reached the suspension bridge over the Yellowstone, the sun had begun to peek out from the clouds. Spring had returned, along with its colors, smells, and sounds, and summer was just around the corner.

We climbed the last hill to the trailhead and said goodbye to our Forest Service friend. It had been a unique experience for both Tom and me, an unexpectedly cold encounter with nature's moods and power, as well as a memorable experience with human generosity and community. We were able to personally experience the real presence and influence of climate in determining which plants could prosper here, and the variety of different climes in a relatively small cross section of Yellowstone. But for our generous and unexpected hosts, we would have had a miserable evening and perhaps a too personal glimpse into how natural selection operates. Climate, like the other forces manifest in Yellowstone, operates without preference or care, affecting anything and anyone.

Reflections

Natural forces like those on display in Yellowstone are the stuff and story of nature and our most powerful experiences with it. They stir the heart, the mind, and our imagination, on multiple levels, seen and unseen. They stir feelings that are visceral and primal, from awe to its cousin fear, from dread to its companion terror, from fascination to its neighbor inspiration. They spring into our consciousness when the right image, scent, or sound is encountered. They impel us to react, sometimes by smiling and reliving the encounter, other times by building walls, real or emotional, against another such experience. Either way, we return for more, sometimes voluntarily, sometimes unwittingly, subconsciously yearning for something that has been sanitized out of our everyday life. We may dabble in fear and terror at Halloween, but that is easily eclipsed by the gripping experience of seeing wolves take down an elk. We may be awed and impressed by New York's new Freedom Tower or Washington's Bonneville Dam, but those sensations don't have the intensity of watching a forest fire march its way up a river valley, heedless of our attempts to control it. In other words, the works of humanity, however grand and inspiring, are generally mere proxy to the real, the primordial, the original: nature, and its vast and seemingly limitless forces.

Moreover, places like Yellowstone are an art form, the canvas on which nature expresses its ideas, thoughts, and desires. Geologic forces provide the foundation, while atmospheric and ecological forces shape and mold the landscape into the Yellowstone we have today. The canvas is alive and evolving, changing across both time and space. Where once was a glacial icecap, today rivers flow, wildlife roam, and thunderstorms blow. Tomorrow, the land will be different, perhaps with the formation of a new geyser, a longer growing season, and/or a new distribution of prey that forces wolves to adjust their territories and hunting habits. All of these things have happened in the not-too-distant past, demonstrating again the restlessness and limitless possibilities of the Yellowstone landscape. Few things remain unchanged for long in this dynamic place, leading to the realization that the only constant in Yellowstone is change. It is an artist's canvas like few on the planet, the stage upon which nature evolves, experiments, and explores new possibilities. If wild animals are what turn the still life into a motion picture, nature's forces are what change the scene, the set, the program, and even the venue.

Whether we have a front row seat or watch from the balcony, the Yellowstone story is one of power, power beyond our wildest imagination. Wildfires, volcanic eruptions, and blizzards are all, to some degree, beyond our control. They are superhuman, instilling more than just emotions in us. When the rush of emotion subsides, restraint and humility remain—or should do so: restraint against turning the power that is simultaneously destructive and creative toward the negative, humility in the face of something far from being controllable. No matter who we are or where we live, we are not so far removed from nature's forces that we can afford to be without humility and restraint in living on planet Earth.

CHAPTER 3

Winter Experiences

Winter snow falling,
boughs bending slightly, slightly—
sunlight on mountains.
—David Kirtley

One frosty February morning in 1933 at the Riverside Ranger Station near West Yellowstone, Montana, rangers Al Bicknell and Frank Anderson faced a minor dilemma. The broad mountain valley in which the station sat was known for its cold temperatures, but that morning was exceptional, for the mercury had dropped below the lowest marking on the thermometer. Cold air is heavier than its opposite, so the valley was the final destination for the frigid air sinking down from the mountains all around. This attribute of physics was especially evident at the ranger station, which sat along the Madison River, one of the valley's lower locales. The coldest of the cold air would pool there, so the thermometer at the cabin was a special one, graduated down to -65° F. After reading the instrument, Bicknell probably hovered over the wood stove to warm up while he conferred with his colleague about the dilemma.

The two decided that Anderson should confirm the reading, which he did, giving Bicknell some company in the bitter cold. Reasoning that the actual temperature was at least one degree colder, the rangers reported -66° F for the low that morning. Lest anyone question their credibility, they marked the actual level of the mercury, which had not fully dropped into the bulb. They probably spent the rest of the day inside, wondering why Santa Claus bothered with the North Pole when Yellowstone was closer to the kiddies and just about as cold.

That temperature, which is hard for most of us to fathom, set a new record for the nation's all-time low outside of Alaska. It stood for more than two decades, until Rogers Pass, Montana, recorded -70° F in 1954, a record that still stands. The colder reading prompted the question of how cold it really had been at Riverside in 1933, so the NPS sent the thermometer to the Weather Bureau, who calibrated down from -65° F to the pivotal mark. The rangers that historic morning, it turned out, weren't far off in their supposition, for the bureau reported that the actual temperature there had been a degree colder, -67° F.[1] Either way, the frigid reading puts Yellowstone in the ranks of coldest places in North America, for Alaska's record low is -80°F, and Canada's all-time record low just a degree colder. Small comfort such distinctions would have been for the rangers shivering on that bitterly cold morning, or for the generations of rangers who have worked outside in Yellowstone's extreme cold. But those distinctions are hugely important and influential for the plants and animals that call Yellowstone home, to the point that winter could be considered the default season for them, since it is the

---

1   In doing the research for my first book, I came across a memorandum relating this part of the -67° F story. Unfortunately, I forgot to take note of the relevant source information for the memo, which is somewhere in the Yellowstone archives in Gardiner, Montana.

longest season and they all must have a way to survive it. Harsh as it is, winter in Yellowstone is also a time of exquisite beauty, as super-cooled air clashes with super-heated water to produce super-fantastic snowscapes and sculptures. Indeed, the season of snow and cold is never far away in Yellowstone, and one that no discussion of nature's power would be complete without. Following are some of my own encounters with Yellowstone in ermine, experiences in which I gradually came to understand that winter touches everything in the grand old park.

Snowbound at Old Faithful

Winter in Yellowstone is a time of contrasts and extremes. White light parries with crushing darkness, intense chill duels with scalding heat, screaming wind alternates with icy calm, all while subzero cold, whiteouts, and snow by the foot punish anything and anyone with the temerity to cling to life there, much less seek recreation. Snow and cold define the landscape, dominating from October to May in the high country, less if the gods are merciful. Snow falls anytime, anywhere, accumulating to depths of several feet—sometimes several yards—in the southern and eastern mountains while fleeting away from the sheltered northern valleys. It is the stuff of whiteout and whimsy, dousing all visibility one day and treating Alice to a frozen Wonderland the next. It drifts into immense pillows in leeward nooks, but wind scours it away into nothing in exposed areas. It hushes all sound one minute, then shouts it all away the next. It descends vertically from the heavens, turns into sideways snow in dimension-destroying whiteouts, and puffs into curly-cues in lighter moments. It is annihilated instantly by the thermal features but reborn as hoarfrost and rime caking nearby trees (hoarfrost is that which accumulates from nighttime air becoming saturated—like the frost on your windshield if you park outside on a frosty night—while rime is frost deposited from drifting fog). It suppresses all smells, putting them on hold for months. In a thousand ways, snow transforms, reshapes, creates, and sculpts the landscape.

Meanwhile, cold keeps company with snow, going everywhere it does and working its own wonders. It freezes any surface waters, transforming liquid into solid, lake into ice, gurgles into silence. Waterfalls become vertical caskets of ice that sometimes even entomb the sound. The sounds of life give way to those of cold: snow squeaks as you walk through it, trees pop as subzero cold pervades, lake ice groans as it expands. Moisture in the air freezes to create halos and sun dogs around the solar orb that gives light but little warmth; halos warn of impending storm, sun dogs of arctic air. Daytime highs above freezing decrease in frequency till they are the stuff of memory and daydream. Balm and comfort go south, replaced by brace and chill. Wind chills alternate with stillness to intensify the cold, the one by assaulting you with wind and gale, the other by releasing residual warmth to the heavens. Nighttime lows below zero become the norm, rising above only when a storm moves through, dropping more snow and, as soon as it moves on, a return to subzero nights. No heat source can compete for long with the coldest air, which freezes the moisture in your nose and even geyser water, clattering to the ground as ice pellets, Yellowstone's unique contribution to the winter soundscape. In myriad ways, then, whiteness and deep freeze are the essence of the Yellowstone plateau in winter.

Like many Yellowstone fans, I first came to the park in summertime, but began to hear about these winter wonders after a summer or two. Once I was out of college and in need of year-round employment, I worked for a nearby guest ranch in wintertime, pairing that with a summer job at Old Faithful.

Once a week, the ranch took guests into the snow-covered park, and it was on one of those tours that I got my first taste of the white world of Yellowstone, in December, 1992 (Figure 3.1). I was as excited as the paying guests—and I was being paid to have this fun! Entering the park at West Yellowstone, our first indication that geothermal heat created unusual winter conditions was the Madison River, which remains ice-free for much of its length. Drawn to its open water, a variety of waterfowl spend the winter on or near it, including trumpeter swans—an incongruous picture of grace in a season of such harshness—and ducks of several species. Ducks are an occasional meal for the bald eagles that we saw perched on nearby trees; their more

Figure 3.1: Snowcoaches in Yellowstone, 2008. The one in front is a Bombardier, used for winter transportation in Yellowstone for over sixty years, and in Canada to bring children to school and to enable doctors to make house calls, both before plowing was common. Innovations in oversnow travel have continued, often using fifteen passenger vans, as can be seen behind the Bomb. AUTHOR COLLECTION.

common meal is fish they snag from the open water. Traveling further along the Madison, we came to some large meadows in which we saw bison and elk grazing. The moderate snow depths at these middle elevations allows the herbivores access to the dried grass underneath; elk paw the snow aside with their front hooves while bison shovel it away with their muzzles and powerful neck muscles. Bulls of both species go their own way, perhaps with a few other studs, while females, their calves of the year, and yearlings group into herds of a few dozen to a few hundred. When bison and elk move to a new snowy dining room, they follow the leader, walking in the tracks that the matriarch up front makes. They generally stay in the Madison Valley or those of its two forks, the Firehole and Gibbon Rivers, connecting the dots between the meadows and thermal areas lining them. They might bed down for the night near a hot spring or fumarole, or on one of the extensive patches of warm ground that hide among the other meadows in summer but which stand out in winter, barren of snow. It was a wildlife surprise, an oasis of life made possible by Yellowstone's geothermal heat—and, as I would come to see in my own experience in Yellowstone, one of many wintry surprises the park had to share with those brave enough to enter it in the season of white and black.

Making these sights accessible for us was the Bombardier, a vehicle equipped to travel on unplowed, snow-covered roads. The NPS doesn't plow Yellowstone's higher elevation roads in winter, but people have long wanted to see the park's overwintering wildlife and thermal features, so when a vehicle made for oversnow travel came along in the mid-1950s, it didn't take long for an entrepreneur in West Yellowstone to purchase one and get permission to give park tours with it. It was the "snowmobile" made by the Bombardier Company in Quebec, Canada. Not to be confused with the smaller, sportier machines that arrived in the 1960s, this snowmobile had room for ten people in a heated, enclosed cab, with tracks for propulsion and skis for steering. It was a cozy experience, for the passengers sat on bench seats facing each other, and the machines topped out at about 40 mph. The Bombardiers schussed the snow-covered roads of Yellowstone for the next half century, introducing thousands of people to the park's winter wonders, including myself.

The "Bombs," as they came to be known, were actually not the first oversnow vehicle to be used in Yellowstone. That special status belongs to the snowplane, which was first used for tours in 1949, when a West Yellowstone resident took 35 trips to Old Faithful, each time with a passenger in the cab with him.

Figure 3.2: Snowplane along the Firehole River, no date. Yellowstone's winter wonders began to be made accessible to more people with these funky—and fun—machines in 1949 and the early 1950s. In the background are two steam clouds rising from Grand Prismatic Spring (far left) and Excelsior Geyser (center, and shadowed), in Midway Geyser Basin. The much brighter cloud behind the snowplane is powdery snow kicked up by propeller wash. NPS PHOTO, PHOTOGRAPHER UNKNOWN; COURTESY OF NPS, YELLOWSTONE NATIONAL PARK (HTTP://WWW.NPS.GOV/FEATURES/YELL/SLIDEFILE/INDEX.HTM, ACCESSED MAY 30, 2017).

Snowplanes were the progenitor of the modern-day snowmobile, a vehicle built to move a person or two over snow, *fast* (Figure 3.2). Take two skis, lay them side-by-side, put another pair in front of them, and then mount a small airplane engine on them with an enclosed cab in front of it, and you have a way to zoom down any snow-covered road or frozen lake surface, not to mention a fantastic grown-up toy. By the mid-1950s, a few hundred people went on snowplane tours every winter, with the mode of transportation providing as many memories as the park itself. The vehicles had no brakes, relying on the deep snow to slow the toys. If that wasn't enough fun, you could open up the throttle on Yellowstone Lake. One snowplane owner, for example, recalled screaming across it at 140 mph when his passenger noticed water filling his tracks behind him. Whether they were going so fast that their friction was melting the ice or there was a lens of water above more ice below was never determined, but they lived to tell more stories. Fast and fun, snowplanes were the stuff of thrill and memory.

Back at Old Faithful after my winter at the ranch, I learned that one of the NPS winter naturalist positions there would be opening, so I put in for it, and got it. There were precious few winter positions anywhere in the park system, and I was lucky enough to get one of the most coveted! I couldn't believe my good luck and told the ranch I would not be returning. I would be immersed in the park, living and working at Yellowstone's heart, and exploring it on my weekends. I'd like to say I would be living in a rustic log cabin in a lovely grove of snow-covered pine trees, wood smoke curling up from the chimney built of native stone, but the truth was otherwise. The pines I would have, but my abode was to be the rundown mobile home I was already inhabiting that summer. It could have been worse; unlike a lot of NPS housing, there were no mice in the place, for I had plugged all the cracks by which they had once gained entry.

(Until I did so, my morning routine had included emptying the mouse traps in the woods outside the door; not till I mouse-proofed the trailer did I learn where the carcasses went, for a raven appeared for the next couple days, sitting on the porch railing and peering in as if to say, "Hey! Where's my breakfast?"). I would also be snowbound, with only my cross-country skis for transportation. With the closest grocery store thirty miles away in West Yellowstone and no access to a snowmobile, I would have to lay in enough food to last me three months. That was no easy task for a seasonal employee struggling to get by, so I worked some volunteer hours at the local community food coop and still spent almost $500 with the 30% discount I had earned (with the other supplies I needed, it was a month's wages). I bought several cases of soy milk (sealed, and therefore non-perishable), fifty pounds of flour (for baking bread), several pounds of peanut butter, and loads of canned and dry goods. Friends gave me a bushel of apples from their tree, which I converted into sauce and pies, treats to pull from the freezer when fresh fruits ran out. With my larder full and the roads about to close for the season, I left the park in late October, full of anticipation about the season to come.

For the next month and a half, I traveled while nature piled up the white stuff in Yellowstone, transforming it into a winter delight and its roadways into oversnow vehicle routes (by then the modern snowmobile was also allowed in the park). On the appointed day in December, I met my boss at the park entrance, loaded my duffel bags and two coolers crammed with fresh fruits and vegetables onto his snowmobile cargo trailer, and then started putting on more clothing than I believed it was possible to wear. First, long underwear, then a turtleneck and other street clothes, a sweater, my winter parka, three layers of wool socks, oversized boots that barely accommodated my uber-sized feet, a super-insulated snowmobile suit that covered everything, a balaclava for the face, a wool stocking hat, insulated gloves, and, finally, a shiny black snowmobile helmet that made me look like Darth Vader. I sounded like him, too, struggling to breathe through all those layers. I felt more like a walrus, or that kid in *The Christmas Story* whose mother piles on so much clothing his arms stuck straight out. About to die of heat stroke, my boss and I waddled out to the snowmobile and lumbered on. Starting it up, we motored out of there and into the park, arriving at cruising speed (about 35 mph) within a few seconds, despite the load. Snowmobiles are built for speed, and I soon was enjoying a wind chill of about 200 degrees below zero. I now knew what all the clothing was for. I could also see why snowmobiling was so much fun, for I soon lost all feeling in my fingers and toes. Any aches and pains in them disappeared, leaving me in a state of pre-frostbite, painless bliss. The vehicle's ungodly noise amplified the otherworldly state, drowning out any distractions like my boss's instructions for hanging on to this speed demon. Its abundant fumes did the same thing, drugging my mind into a state that even Timothy Leary would envy. I was in my own world, zoned out and zooming through Wonderland. I glimpsed frosty bison, so impervious to cold that snow doesn't melt from their thick fur; screamed past trumpeter swans acting like royalty; and fumigated an elk in the river munching the grass exposed on the riverbank. It was an almost transcendental ride to a place almost out of this world, a weird, but in some ways fitting, introduction to Yellowstone in winter.

After an hour of this unforgettable, multi-dimensional tripping out, we arrived at my humble trailer, unloaded my stuff, and filled the fridge. When I came off the high, I remembered that I would use one of the coolers as a warmer for the case of oranges I'd brought in (they wouldn't fit in the fridge). I put the cooler-turned-warmer on the porch by day and inside at night, letting it even out the temperatures to preserve the fruit until I had eaten my way through its contents. That day didn't arrive until sometime in January, by which time I was settled in and happily snowbound. As expected, I was removed from the outside world, with only the radio stations I could receive on my stereo (and the long-distance antenna my grandpa had given me, strung between two trees out front) for news and entertainment. This far from civilization, even with the antenna, there was one, and only one, station that came in stereo: National Public Radio (NPR). If I could have chosen one station, it would have been NPR, so I was pleased. Better yet, this NPR station came with more than the typical NPR entertainment package, for it was broadcast from Ricks College, which is in southern Idaho, potato and sugar beet country. Along with *All Things Considered* came Phyllis Schlafly, and along with *Prairie Home Companion* came the Mormon Tabernacle Choir. It was Americana at its best, at least its western best, with something for everyone.

The radio was but a sidelight to the real show, Yellowstone in winter. I cross-country skied most everyday, to and from work, sometimes at work, before work when I went in late, and always on my weekends. As I did, the magic and wonder of Old Faithful and the Firehole Valley in winter set in. Lodgepole pine forests that had seemed monotonous in summer became Christmas trees by the thousands, each tree dusted by the snow of Santa's most whimsical elves (Figure 3.3). Rivers that had seemed ordinary (if a river can ever be commonplace) were transformed into ribbons of life, their hot-spring-warmed waters defying winter and sheltering aquatic plants, streamers of green in a whitened world. Geysers that had appeared little different than fountains morphed into billowing clouds of pure white steam, the vapors sometimes rising hundreds of feet into the frozen sky. Thermal areas that had seemed barren in July were oases of warmth and life in January, crucial habitat for animal and plant alike. Snow depths and cold that, elsewhere in the Rockies, would drive bison and elk to lower, more hospitable climes were made tolerable here by thermal warmth and easier walking. Bison came over from Hayden Valley when snow became too deep there, staying put for the rest of winter in the Firehole Valley. Meanwhile, a herd of 500 or 600 elk never bothered to leave because they found the valley suitable for year-round occupancy, making the herd one of the few anywhere that didn't migrate. Even some plants found the conditions to their liking, making the dead of winter an anachronism. The star among them is Ross's bentgrass, a tiny plant found only in the Firehole Valley geyser basins and Shoshone Geyser Basin to the south (Figure 3.4). Growing only near thermal vents, the grass germinates in early winter, blooms in late winter, and sets seed in May or June, finally withering away in the heat of summer (such as it is). I actually found one blooming in January, though it probably wasn't successfully pollinated. I also found other plants prospering in winter in that amazing valley, all of them hugging the ground in thermal areas for warmth or, in one exceptional place, clinging to the side of a three-foot-deep ravine—and growing six or eight inches tall—with a hot creek below creating a natural greenhouse. Masters of survival in what is otherwise a forbidding time of year, such plants were a diminutive but loud illustration that winter in Yellowstone is many things: contrasts, harshness, beauty, surprises, and even life.

Something else was evident in my experiences there, something that was common to all of them. Sometimes overwhelming, sometimes subtle, it was perhaps most palpable on foggy mornings. On clear and calm nights, steam from geyser eruptions and hot springs produced a fog so thick we couldn't see Old Faithful Geyser from the visitor center where I worked. Such thick fog could make predicting Old Faithful's next eruption difficult or impossible, for the longer the geyser erupted,

Figure 3.3: Ghost trees in Upper Geyser Basin, 1990s. The trees are caked with rime from nearby Oblong Geyser and the Firehole River. On mornings following clear, subzero nights (when the coating happens), the landscape near open rivers and geyser basins is transformed into a winter Wonderland—and the colder the overnight low is, the thicker the rime and the greater the beauty. AUTHOR COLLECTION.

Figure 3.4: Ross's bentgrass (*Agrostis rossiae*), 2001. This grass, only three or four inches tall, is found nowhere else in the world. Native only to some geyser basins in Yellowstone, it has altered its life cycle and stature to benefit from the unique conditions found in the thermal areas. NPS PHOTO BY JENNIFER WHIPPLE; COURTESY OF NPS, YELLOWSTONE NATIONAL PARK (HTTP://WWW.NPS.GOV/FEATURES/YELL/SLIDEFILE/INDEX.HTM, ACCESSED MAY 30, 2017).

the longer it would be until its next eruption, and we couldn't very well get an eruption duration if we could not even see the geyser—or so I had thought before the winter began. Life at Old Faithful revolves around those predictions, so there is some pressure to produce a reliable prediction, or shame could befall you (while I write this somewhat tongue-in-cheek, we actually did have to take a ranger off that duty one summer—when such predictions really are important—because she couldn't master them). However, I soon found that there was a way to derive the prediction on foggy mornings. We had an infrared monitor on the geyser, so by examining it we could see when Old Faithful last erupted, along with the approximate length of its eruption. Using this information, we could get a general idea for when it would next erupt. At that time, I would step outside and, since the fog was too dense to see the geyser from any safe distance, tune in with my ears. In the silence afforded by frigidity and the associated absence of people, I could easily hear the famous geyser, including the splashes when it was warming up, the increasingly powerful roar as it grew into an eruption, and the gradual return to quiescence as its energy subsided. When I could no longer hear water splashing (that winter did not get cold enough—-40°—to freeze geyser water before it hit the ground), the eruption was done, and I had the duration I needed to calculate a reliable prediction.

Standing in the arctic air and listening for signs of geyser life was a profound experience. Other than my sense of touch telling me that I should have been dressed warmer (I would not be on a snowmobile when I worked the visitor center, so I had put on a more humane amount of clothing), I needed only my hearing. I could see nothing but a dimensionless gray fog, and nature's aromas and tastes were in hibernation (except for a hint of sulfur in the air). With few vehicles out that early, there was little vehicle noise, and the rare visitor who came by then usually joined me in the experience. Despite the lack of sensation, the experience filled the senses, flooding the mind with the knowledge that something powerful, much stronger than a person, was there. It was humbling and overwhelming, subtle and seething, roaring and trickling all at the same time. And an hour or two later, when the fog began to lift, nature's power came to full display, with ghost trees by any geyser or hot spring being unveiled and the air practically sparkling with translucency and clarity. Sun dogs would cradle the frosty sun, frost crystals would float in the air, and geysers would attempt to keep the fog from leaving with more eruptions. It was magic, power palpable enough to feel in your soul.

Although I spent many more winters in Yellowstone, I never again spent one snowbound at Old Faithful. It was by far the best, the standard against which I compare all the others. Only one other winter came close, one that presented me with almost as many opportunities to do what I had done that snowbound season: immerse myself in the wonders of a snow-covered, frozen Yellowstone. Two of the remaining winter tales are from those two seasons; the third is an amalgamation of experiences from many of my Yellowstone winters. Through them all ran Yellowstone's power, sometimes obvious, sometimes hidden from sight, but always palpable, as it was on those foggy mornings at Old Faithful.

Shoshone Geyser Basin

In a place full of wonders, there are some that stand out from the crowd, that seem to be made of pure magic. They are not found along the roads that most visitors never leave; rather, one has to work to get to them. One such wonder is south of Old Faithful, reachable only by hiking, paddling, or cross-country skiing for at least a long day: Shoshone Geyser Basin, fronting the western end of its namesake lake. Home to a few geysers, including the frequent performer Minute Man Geyser, the basin is home to dozens of colorful hot springs and thermal vents. No road has ever gone to the geyser basin, so it is better preserved than those in the Firehole Valley, where extensive, illegal souvenir collecting resulted in widespread destruction of delicate hot spring and geyser deposits in Yellowstone's early years. Shoshone (as the geyser basin was known to overwintering Old Faithful employees, pronounced with just two syllables, not the three when paired with "Geyser Basin") is also home to Ross's bentgrass as well as the sagebrush lizard, the only four-legged reptile found in Yellowstone. Like the bentgrass, Yellowstone's sagebrush lizards can be found only in some widely separated geyser basins, though unlike the grass, it ranges widely outside the park. At the cold and snowy climes found throughout most of the park, it is remarkable that any reptile gets by, let alone thrives; warm ground in the geyser basins gives the cold-blooded animal the edge it needs to survive. With its multi-colored springs, Minute Man eruptions, and lizards scurrying about, Shoshone is the stuff of indelible memories for those expending the effort to visit it.

Always wonderful, Shoshone becomes truly remarkable in winter, as I discovered when I was snowbound. Sometime that January, I made my first trip there, a full-day, 19-mile skiing adventure. Watching the weather forecast for a clear day, I saw one predicted for my next day off. I made plans for an early departure, putting my pack together and waxing my skis for the subzero conditions I would find at dawn. With a thermos of hot tea, extra clothing, a good first aid kit, and ample food, I stepped out into the morning's arctic air and into my favorite skis (Landsems, the direct descendants of the best touring ski ever made, Epokes, with their trademark "Torsion box" construction that provides great maneuverability in soft backcountry snow). Leaving the housing area, I quickly found the trail, crossed Zipper Creek, and began the climb up to the plateau 500 feet above Old Faithful's south side. Alternately sidestepping and herringboning, depending on the slope angle, I made steady progress on the popular, hard-packed Howard Eaton Trail, which would lead me to the less-traveled trail to Shoshone. The exertion of climbing quickly displaced my shivering. Soon I reached the top—time for a sip of water and a glance back to Old Faithful. Through this burned forest, I could see the geyser's fog catching the first rays of the cold early morning sun. Shouldering my daypack, I resumed the trek, moving faster in the flatter terrain. The trail took me through a finger of trees the '88 fires had missed and then back into burned area, but then left burned forest for good fifty yards further. From here on, I would be passing through a Santa-land of snow-covered trees and whitened meadows.

Before long, I was at the top of my first descent, where I paused to strategize how I would avoid smacking the trees on either side of this short luge run. Although previous skiers had been this way, there was enough untracked snow off to the side to keep my speed under control until I reached the long, straight runout zone at the bottom. Keeping one ski dragging in the powder on the side and using the other as a snowplow on the trail, I had a few seconds of controlled panic followed by a longer hail-Mary zoom down the straightaway. A few more strides and I was at the first meadow, which was my cue to depart from the more popular trail. The meadow and I looped around a stand of trees, depositing me at the jumping-off point to Shoshone, a footbridge over the Firehole River. The snow coverage on both sides of the bridge was thin, thanks to warm ground, while the bridge was no warmer than the frosty air, so it was mounded high with snow. Sidestepping up and back down off the bridge and then moving carefully around some thermal vents on the other side, I quickly found the trail that other park employees had broken out a few days ago. This was my route into the Shoshone winter Wonderland, and I could not have been happier.

Leaving the river for now, I followed the trail through some trees and reached another bridge, again piled high with snow. Ordinarily this one provided safe passage over a thermally influenced marsh, but that day a furry troll was guarding it: a bull bison, enjoying the easily accessible forage in the wetland, about twenty feet from the ski trail. For a moment he and I eyed each other, neither one wanting to give up their coveted resource. Knowing how precious energy was to overwintering animals, I reasoned that he wouldn't mind a temporary invasion of his personal space if it were clear that I was not going toward him or his food. With that as my hypothesis—and hope—I skied to the bridge and sidestepped up, facing him so I could see him if he came my way. I don't know what I would have done if he had done so, but I may well have slipped into the muck, giving the troll some goring and stomping practice. Apparently, he preferred to satisfy his hunger, for he watched the funny-looking human climb up the mound of snow, half fall down the far side, and slip away. My hypothesis was confirmed, and we were both the better for the peaceful outcome.

With adrenaline lending speed to my strides, I skied up and over the next hill, dropping back down to the banks of the Firehole River. Even this close to its source, the river was open, belying the presence of more hot springs upstream. I kept skiing, leaving the river for the next several hours. Soon, I emerged in the corner of a large meadow, which extended a mile or so to my right. Another solitary bison was in the meadow, several hundred yards away (he apparently was not on troll duty). Cutting across the corner and reentering forest, I shifted into low gear, for the trail immediately began the second major ascent of the day. The forest shifted gears too, becoming a mix of fir, spruce, and both lodgepole and whitebark pine. Because fir and spruce don't shed their lower branches as they grow (as the two pines do), falling snow is shunted away from their trunks, forming cavities or depressions in the snow around them. Known as tree wells, they could be a problem for a fast-moving skier, as I would be this afternoon, returning down this same hill. For that reason, I took a mental note of their location, and continued climbing. After four hundred feet of elevation gain, the trail slipped into a forested ravine that led to Grants Pass and the Continental Divide. I tried to discern the actual spot where the trail crossed the line dividing Atlantic Ocean snowmelt from the Pacific's, finding several possibilities. Perhaps with more time and effort I could eliminate the look-alikes, but I was on a mission to get to Shoshone, so I moved on.

Skiing down into the Pacific Ocean drainage, I arrived at the next trail junction, at the edge of Shoshone Meadows. The sign marking the location was buried, which meant the snow was at least five feet deep. From the meadows, Shoshone Creek would lead me to the geyser basin, but first I had to find the stream. I had actually skied this far a few weeks before, but lost the ski trail there because wind had filled it in with more snow. There are two crossings of a smaller stream in the meadows, and with the snow so deep, I had spent a lot of precious time trying to find the buried bridges. Not that day, though: the ski trail was easy to see, proceeding straight to the first bridge, through a copse of trees, and then down to the second bridge. I gleefully followed, memorizing the location of the two so I would not be turned around again. A third bridge was more obvious, for it crossed Shoshone Creek, a much larger stream with banks less hidden by the deep mounds of snow. Stepping carefully across that narrow bridge, I turned right and began to head downstream.

Skiing along Shoshone Creek was a delight (Figure 3.5). About ten feet wide with a steady current, the creek was open and green, vibrant with aquatic plants, another oasis of life in the midst of winter. Here and there a dollop of snow rested on the water, seemingly warning the vegetation below not to get too exuberant, lest it discover what the time of year was for plants not sheltered by warm water. Liquid gave way to solid above the creek: solid ground, sloping gently upward, and solid H2O, blanketing the earth with white. The snow-covered ground continued sloping up fifty or sixty feet, defining a partly forested valley about two miles long. Through the crystalline beauty led a pair of ski tracks, an invitation to explore. I took the invitation, discovering new arrangements of beauty round every bend. Occasionally a warm seep would guest star in the show; in other scenes, it would be a tributary or a thicket of trees. Complementing the visual feast was the trickle of water and the zing of cold, sharp air. It was pure ambient, auditory, and visual pleasure, a prelude of winter beauty for the magic around a few more bends.

When the valley began to open up and the creek to slow, I knew I was getting close. Rounding one last bend, I saw a landscape that could only be Yellowstone: a broad, flat plain with a scattering of trees and steam columns, and one or two small forested hills. The ski trail left the creek, going straight toward one of the largest steam columns. It ended where the snow ran out, near the base of one of the hills. I had arrived at Shoshone Geyser Basin and would no longer need skis, for there was enough subterranean heat that I could connect bare patches with thinly covered ground to explore the place on foot. My first destination was Minute Man Geyser and the hot springs near it. The geyser played several times for me, the eruptions only minutes apart and ten or twenty feet tall. Much of the water thrown by the geyser was lost in the instant fog produced when scalding

Figure 3.5: Shoshone Creek, 2008. The stream is a corridor of life through this winter wilderness and a fitting introduction to Shoshone Geyser Basin. AUTHOR COLLECTION.

water meets super cold air. The foot path I was on continued past Minute Man, so I followed it to Union Geyser, which was once the star performer of the basin, erupting from three different vents to heights of 50 to 100 feet. Dormant since 1976, the geyser was the last thermal feature accessible from the foot path, so I returned to Minute Man and took another footpath toward the shore of Shoshone Lake. It went through a small bowl of sizzling and bubbling hot pools and fumaroles, nestled between a forested hill on my right and a lower hill to the left. Looking for a lunch spot with a view, I climbed the left hill and found a site overlooking Shoshone Lake. I cleared some snow from a spot by a small tree, put a foam pad on it, and sat down. It was about eight degrees.

That is the literal description of my activities there; the sensory experience was full-bore and incredible. Shoshone was a place of color and contrast, life and dormancy, frost and heat. Trees in the basin were caked with all things frozen: snow from the heavens, ice from geyser spray, rime from drifting fog, and hoarfrost from the stars. Some trees bowed over with the weight, some were festooned with draperies of crystalline frost hanging six inches from their branches, and some stood above the others like guards in uniforms of white (Figure 3.6). Snow engaged in a perpetual battle with the hot ground, the white stuff disappearing entirely in the hottest places, melting more slowly from cooler zones, and piling up on rocks and cooler ground. Melt patterns produced canvases of whimsy: an abstract of doodles here, Picasso in snow there, complete with off center mouth (Figure 3.7). Rocks resembled ice cream cones with scoops of vanilla atop them; the larger the rock, the bigger the treat (Figure 3.8). Slopes that were warm but not hot grew green moss, whole hillsides of the color that had disappeared from the surrounding landscape months ago. Hot springs and their runoff channels featured rainbows of colorful cyanobacteria, streamers of life defying winter. Wisps of steam and vapor

Figure 3.6: The five frosty guardians, 1995. A prolonged cold spell led to exceptional rime coating these trees in Shoshone Geyser Basin. AUTHOR COLLECTION.

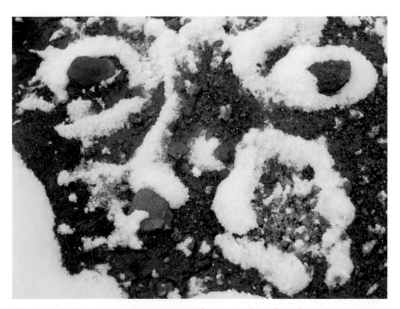

Figure 3.7: Picasso in snow, 2008. The ground in this photo is just warm enough to melt snow, producing this Picasso-esque likeness of a face, complete with out-of-place mouth. AUTHOR COLLECTION.

Figure 3.8: Snow cones and green moss at Shoshone Geyser Basin, 1990s. Warm ground shelters a field of bright green moss through the coldest nights while rocks and boulders provide insulation from that heat, allowing snowcaps and cones to grow atop them. AUTHOR COLLECTION.

circled about on the whims of nature's fancy. This was indeed a winter fantasy land.

From my lunchtime lair the whiteness seemed to go to infinity (Figure 3.9). I looked out over the lake, its frozen surface almost mirroring the wispy cirrus clouds above. Above the dark forest on the opposite shore rose the distant peaks of the seemingly misnamed Red Mountains, the range that spends far more time annually being white than any shade of rust or crimson. It is the snowiest place in Yellowstone, with over 500 inches annually in at least one alcove. Framing my view was an entire family of ghost trees, the elders seeming to teach the seedlings how to look the frostiest. With so much soft snow absorbing the few sounds present, deep and exquisite silence accompanied the visual feast. Puffs of polar air hit me in the face, more felt than heard. From behind me came an occasional whisper from a fumarole, the sizzles and bubbles reserved for explorers stand-

Figure 3.9: A landscape in ermine, 1995. Ghost trees, a frozen lake, and wispy white cirrus clouds make for a field of white infinity at Shoshone Geyser Basin—as well as a memorable lunchtime view. Author Collection.

ing within a few feet. From the distance in front of me came a soft serenade of trumpeter swan notes, the out-of-view musicians confirming the presence of open water, probably where the creek joined the lake. From a little further right came a solitary coyote yip, the sole accompaniment to the swans, and an indication that a whole food chain existed there, all made possible by the thermal activity in that remarkable place. For most of the hour, utter quiet prevailed, a heart-thumping, ear-ringing absence of sound and noise that is as precious as platinum in America today. Shoshone was indeed an oasis of life, a place of rare beauty, and a land of winter magic.

With my lunch now a memory, shivers setting in despite the hot tea, and the time approaching two o'clock, it was time to get skiing toward home. Standing, I exulted in the landscape and soundscape serenity for a minute more, trying to imbibe the experience deep into my being. Satisfied that I was infused with the experience and its energy, I turned and retraced my steps through the bowl of sizzles and bubbles. Coyote the trickster had not touched my skis, so I applied a wax suitable for the not-quite-so-polar afternoon conditions, strapped the skis on, and took off. I skied back along Shoshone Creek, through the meadows of the same name (confirming the geography of the crucial bridges as I did so), and ascended Grants Pass. The approach to it is easier from Shoshone Meadows than from the north—a good thing for this well-traveled skier. Skiing through the forested ravine on the other side, I marveled at the orange trail markers, already just knee high; in summer, they are eight or ten feet off the ground. Continuing, I zipped down the slope I'd climbed that morning, successfully avoiding the tree wells. When I crossed the corner of the large meadow at the bottom, I saw that the resident bison had company; hopefully the bull that had joined him was the furry troll, now off-duty. In another hour I found the bog bridge unguarded, so I didn't wait for him to reappear. Soon I crossed the Firehole River and was approaching the luge run, now the last climb of the day. This hill seemed a nuisance to me, coming as it did at day's end, when I was pretty spent. But it was the price of passage, so I put it behind me and enjoyed the final descent to my dumpy but warm trailer home.

In taking this journey, I got a small taste of what park photographer Frank J. Haynes and arctic explorer Frederick Schwatka experienced on their winter expedition to Old Faithful and some of the park's other attractions early in January, 1887. Intrigued by the wonders produced by the clash of temperature and H2O extremes, the two embarked on the first known winter expedition into the park—in one of the harshest winters on record throughout the West. For transportation they used skis, eight- or ten-foot-long hand sculpted boards that were about four inches wide and an inch thick, a good four times the mass of today's backcountry ski. They were the most advanced technology of the era, and their large surface area would keep the skiers afloat in Yellowstone's soft and deep snow. Skiing south from Fort Yellowstone at Mammoth Hot Springs, the two men and eleven other guides took two days to ski the 21 miles to Norris, a decent pace. There, though, the party fractured, with Haynes and three others continuing on while the remainder traveled back to Mammoth with Schwatka, who had collapsed of exhaustion. Haynes and his partners made it to the famous geyser, taking the first photographs of the area's wonders in winter. Trees so laden with hoarfrost and rime they looked like ghosts, billowing clouds of steam, and temperatures topping out at -10° F—and bottoming out at -52° F—greeted them (Figure 3.10). Retracing their strides to Norris, they then crossed over to Canyon, visiting the Lower Falls, whose spray builds up an ice cone 150 feet tall, half the height of the waterfall. The four then turned north, hoping to finish the expedition with a few

Figure 3.10: Haynes party in the Norris Geyser Basin area, 1887. Trees caked with rime drifting from nearby thermal features, rocks and small trees pillowed over with snow, and ethereal lighting through subzero fog were some of the visual rewards awaiting Haynes and his companions. The ground in this photo is probably thermally warmed, given the much deeper snow to the right. Note the length of the ski. NPS PHOTO, PHOTOGRAPHER UNKNOWN; COURTESY OF NPS, YELLOWSTONE NATIONAL PARK (HTTP:// WWW.NPS.GOV/FEATURES/YELL/SLIDEFILE/INDEX.HTM, ACCESSED MAY 30, 2017).

more days of skiing. Instead, they were treated to another side of the Yellowstone winter as a blizzard forced them to bivouac for three days and nights, with no shelter. They survived, but just barely, and finished the trip after 29 days. For their effort, Haynes got 42 prints, which doesn't seem like much until you realize that each one was from a glass plate that he lugged with him, along with a bulky camera and other gear, over some 150 miles of trackless, uninhabited wilderness. Yellowstone's winter allure was strong indeed.

The allure is still strong. Thousands of people travel into the frozen Yellowstone every winter now, most of them in a Bomb or one of the many other kinds of "snowcoaches" (multi-passenger, enclosed, oversnow vehicles) developed in recent decades. Others take guided trips via snowmobile, the vehicles having been cleaned up and quieted significantly from the noisy, polluting machines that so dominated the park's roadways and frontcountry in the 1990s and early 2000s (how that situation arose and the political posturing it engendered is a story I tell in my first book *Yellowstone and the Snowmobile)*. As for me, I attempted the trek to Shoshone two or three more times that winter, succeeding but for the last time, when I came across grizzly bear tracks near the Firehole River bridge. Grizzlies are not known for their gentle dispositions at any time, least of all when they have just finished their five-month fast, so I thought better of the day and found a different destination. I lived to ski another winter and completed my seasonal assignment (with considerable food to spare). That spring I attempted the trip again, but lost the trail in the forest near Grants Pass, where there was still so much snow that the trail markers were completely buried. Life's twists and turns did not bring me another snowbound season at Old Faithful again, but I never forgot the beauty and peacefulness of Shoshone. I was able to visit several more times, including one in which the high for the day was 0° F. Snow sculptures, pristine whiteness, and the paradox of life amid death and dormancy captivated me every time as much as they did the first. I sat at the very same spot to eat lunch every time, always savoring the continuity of the landscape and its winter beauty. Small changes would be evident, from differences in the ways trees were frosted to the opening of new fumaroles or sizzlers, but the landscape was always familiar and enchanting. Each trip was a retreat and homecoming, a return to a sacred place, one that would energize far more than the caloric cost of skiing there. It was not just geothermal power enabling life to exist in a forbidding time of year, it was salve for the soul. In multiple ways, it was—and still is—power both sustaining and renewing.

Pelican to Lamar
by Cross Country Ski

Lying on the upper bunk at the Pelican Springs Cabin that February night in 2006, I was roasting. I had no blankets on me, no sheet, not even a shirt, and still I was burning up, unable to sleep. My friend Steve Swanke had kindled a fire in the wood stove when we had arrived earlier that day, but by bedtime the heat was unbearable—and a little unbelievable, since it was at least 120 degrees colder outside. When we had left his home on Yellowstone Lake that morning, Steve had stuffed more wood in his woodstove there than I believed possible. The self-professed pyromaniac had done the same thing here at bedtime, but he had evidently forgotten to cut the damper back. With his wife Denice and our friends Kerry and Stacey Gunther, we had skied in from the Pelican Valley trailhead on the north shore of Yellowstone Lake that morning. It was a brutal ski, with the high for the day below zero and a headwind and corresponding wind chill cold enough to freeze any exposed skin. Donning all our clothing, balaclavas, and whatever face shields we had with us, we made the eight-mile forced march in a little over four hours, stopping only long enough to gobble a handful of trail mix and sip a few swallows of water. We were beginning a four-day trip from Pelican Valley to Lamar Valley, a route of about forty miles featuring three patrol cabins, each a day's travel apart. Much like the scouts who skied this way long ago, we would connect the cabins, staying in them, shoveling snow from their roofs, and taking note of anything that looked awry along the way. Arriving at the Pelican Springs Cabin around one o'clock, we had opened the cabin and let Pyro (Steve) do his thing with the fire. Before long he had a fire going, but it would be a while before it would warm up the cabin and its contents, which were no warmer than the arctic air we had been enjoying. So, we decided to eat lunch outside, using the cabin as a windbreak (Figure 3.11). Thankfully, that put us on the cabin's south side, so we had the sun in our faces and could take the face protection off—but not the down parkas, stocking caps, gloves, and other winter attire suitable for a Norwegian solarium.

Yellowstone has a long tradition of rangers patrolling the park's backcountry trails by ski and using the patrol cabins for shelter, as we were doing. Indeed, the cabins were originally known as "snowshoe cabins," for that very reason (skis were called snowshoes in the army era). Army scouts and, after 1918, NPS rangers took to the trails in winter because they knew poachers preferred to take wildlife then, when the animals' fur was the longest. In fact, one of the most infamous poacher ap-

Figure 3.11: Lunch at the Pelican Springs Cabin solarium, 2006. From left are Stacey and Kerry Gunther, the author, and Steve Swanke. Note how much winter clothing we are wearing, despite the solar exposure. AUTHOR COLLECTION.

prehensions took place in Pelican Valley in 1894, when civilian scout Felix Burgess and Army Sergeant Troike caught poacher Ed Howell in the act of killing and butchering some of Yellowstone's last remaining bison. Believing Howell might be in the valley doing his misdeeds, the two had made the three-day ski down from Fort Yellowstone at Mammoth Hot Springs. Skiing into the open valley, they saw Howell in the distance and split up, to approach him from different directions. Howell was known to bring his dog along with him, so getting the benefits of surprise would be difficult. Compounding the danger was that Howell had a repeating rifle, while the scouts had only one side-arm between the two of them, an Army revolver useful in only close situations. Jumping a ravine with his long skis, Burgess approached Howell, who was intent upon butchering a bison carcass. The wind was in the scout's face, so neither Howell nor his dog knew someone was there until it was too late. Burgess and Troike had caught Howell in the act, so they ordered him to cease his activities and to accompany them back to Mammoth, where he would receive his punishment. That meant that the three of them got to be skiing partners for the return trip, an uncomfortable arrangement made worse by the fact that the scouts had to keep Howell away from his dog, which he wanted to kill for letting the scouts apprehend him (Figure 3.12).

Three days later the party arrived safely at Fort Yellowstone, including the dog. The scouts soon discovered that there would be no trial, though, because there was actually no federal law prohibiting the killing of park wildlife. The scouts and their undesirable companion had all known this and that the Army's hands would be tied, but the scouts were duty-bound to protect the park and its denizens, or at least do their best. Still, they would not let Howell off scot-free; rather, they put him in jail for a month, then expelled him from the park and told him that he could retrieve his belongings from the park's most distant

Figure 3.12: Army scouts skiing with their prisoner Ed Howell, 1894. Howell is probably at far left, farthest from the dog (which is the dark lump in the snow) he wanted to kill for failing to alert him to the scouts' presence in Pelican Valley. The identity of the fourth person is not known. Note the single, long pole they used for forward movement; contemporary Nordic skiers use two considerably shorter poles—and much shorter skis. NPS PHOTO, PHOTOGRAPHER UNKNOWN; COURTESY OF NPS, YELLOWSTONE NATIONAL PARK (HTTP://WWW.NPS.GOV/FEATURES/YELL/SLIDEFILE/INDEX.HTM, ACCESSED MAY 30, 2017).

entrance. Such creative justice was little more than a slap on the wrist for Howell, for a single bison head was worth ten times the value of the gear he would lose by abandoning his confiscated gear. There were more bison in the park, and as big as the park was, he would just take his chances on being caught and return for more the next winter.

However, this time would come to be different. As it happened, Emerson Hough, a writer for *Forest and Stream*, a national conservation journal, was in the park and witnessed the proceedings (or the lack thereof). He wrote an article about the travesty and wired it to his editor, George Bird Grinnell. The two had been trying to address this problem for years and realized immediately that this story could be the ticket to congressional action. They were right; the resulting public outcry over the Yellowstone situation sped legislation through both houses of Congress in only six weeks, getting the president's signature just a few days later. The law prohibited the hunting of park wildlife, and is still the law under which park authorities prosecute poaching (along with a companion law passed a few years later). And, in more than poetic justice, Howell became the first person prosecuted under the act prompted by his wretched actions. Finding him violating his expulsion the following summer, the Army gave him another month behind bars, along with a sizable fine. Justice was slow in coming, but it must have been sweet nonetheless.

Back in the twenty-first century, my skiing companions and I found our own satisfaction in the relative warmth of our solarium. Our faces and digits thawed, our internal furnaces were stoked with food, and our interest in continuing the journey renewed. Discussing our options for the afternoon, Kerry expressed concern about the next day's ski, which would be the longest. To boot, that day's route featured the only significant climb of the trip, 1300 feet up to Mist Creek Pass, which divides the Pelican and Lamar drainages. To take some of the edge off that lengthy ski, he suggested some of us break out the trail to the pass that afternoon, which would make the climb up to it tomorrow—with full packs on our backs—a little easier. We liked his reasoning, and knew the forest we would soon enter would break the headwind that had made the morning so challenging. Pyro offered to stay behind and get the cabin warmed up while the rest of us skied to the pass. Two hours later, we were there, looking up to the frosty Absaroka peaks and down at the terrain we would be traveling through the next day. It was a wild and white delight to behold, one that we might not enjoy again in winter. Exulting in the landscape but knowing the daylight was waning, we turned around and schussed back to the cabin, the adrenaline from the exciting descent providing an internal shield against the self-generated wind chill. We arrived with an hour of light to spare, and joined Steve in the now cozy cabin. The skiing was done for the day—but not the encounters with temperature extremes.

The Pelican cabin is cozy in the best of circumstances, but more so with five people and their gear. As we opened our packs and changed out of our skiing clothes, the cabin acquired the look of a teenager's bedroom, with clothing and assorted backpack contents strewn on every bed. Cross-country skiing burns calories and generates sweat, especially when a person is breaking trail, so more clothes were hung to dry from every hook and interior clothesline. Boots were propped up by the stove to dry, their inserts removed to speed the process. Skis stood in every corner to melt the snow and ice that accumulates on the bindings; iced bindings—and, therefore, the ski—can be impossible to use if left alone, on the next day. The five of us had all brought freeze-dried meals, so water was heating on the propane stove to reconstitute the food. Another large pan was on the woodstove, full of melting snow, to refill water bottles. The net effect of all this heating, drying, and melting, plus the five of us exhaling warm and moist air, was humidity, and lots of it. Even though the cabin was probably in the 70s by this time, the air was saturated. It was so humid that any time the cabin door was opened, a knee-high stream of fog blew in. Subzero air streaming in was flash-freezing the humid cabin air, immediately condensing its high moisture load and giving the appearance of fog. The contrast with the world outside could hardly have been more dramatic, as I ruefully discovered in the upper bunk when we turned the lanterns off. I laid there for a while, hoping the temperature would drop or that sleep would come. When it became clear that neither would happen soon, I called down to my fellow skiers, who had wisely taken lower bunks or spread their bedrolls on the floor. They told me that there was room for me on the floor, so I slithered down and found a more conducive environment for sleeping. Pyro, of course, was closest to the stove, to stoke the fire as the flames got low.

The next morning, we turned on the two-way radio we were carrying to call the park dispatch and check for messages. When we turned it on, we happened to catch the Lake area ranger reporting the weather observations, something rangers from each ranger station did in winter. Lake was the closest station to us, and our cabin did not have a thermometer, so we listened with anticipation. We knew it was very cold, but were still surprised to hear that it was -30° F! About this time, it was time for some men in the group to experience the call of nature as women do every time nature beckons. Thirty below makes everyone reluctant to use an unheated outhouse, especially those of us who have, shall we say, external plumbing, but sometimes nature's call is more of a demand, as it was for me that morning. Someone suggested we light the outhouse itself on fire and use it while it was burning, gambling that the frosty air would keep us from being burned, but we—that is to say, we men—doubted even that would keep us warm. With no better ideas being offered, I gathered my courage and went out into the freezing wilderness to meet my fate. My outhouse experience was brief but memorable, and I gained a new respect for the rangers who overwintered at some of the remote ranger stations in the park interior (as several did in the 1920s and 30s). None of those stations had running water or electricity, so the dedicated rangers faced the freezing outhouse—and many other deprivations and challenges—every day. We modern day rangers might think we are participating in the long tradition of winter trail patrol, but in reality, we are just touching the tip of the iceberg (to use a common, but fitting, expression).

Once we had our packs together and the cabin tidied, it was time to retrace our steps to the pass. With the trail already broken, we made good time, completing the climb in a little over an hour (Figure 3.13). The rest of the day would be downhill or flat, but still a challenge given the mileage and need to break trail. The skier in the lead does the lion's share of the trail work, using his or her skis to pack the soft snow down. The person immediately behind has the next hardest job, packing down the snow more. By the time the third skier comes along, the trail is generally made. Typically, ski parties rotate through the lead position, with the leader moving to the end position after fifteen or twenty minutes of breaking trail, and then moving up in line as the other skiers take their turn. Wilderness patrols also usually travel in groups, so no one gets too fatigued. With gravity

Figure 3.13: Denice Swanke and the view south from Mist Creek Pass, 2006. To the right of Denice (the expedition's fifth member) can be seen Pelican Valley, which we traversed the first day. In the distance is the frozen Yellowstone Lake and the Red Mountains. AUTHOR COLLECTION.

now on our side, we dropped down into the Mist Creek Valley, descending through forest and then entering a long meadow. The temperature was no warmer than the first day had been, but there was no breeze, so we stayed warm and enjoyed lunch on a sunny south-facing knoll in the meadow. Our hunger sated, we resumed skiing through a forest burned in 1988—Mist Creek is the partial namesake for that year's Clover-Mist Fire—and found an abundance of lodgepole pine saplings almost tall enough to obscure our view of the Absaroka peaks hemming the valley. This was a quintessential Yellowstone experience, with cold, beauty, and evidence of extraordinary natural forces defining the journey.

As the afternoon began to wane, the valley began to open up, an indication that we were approaching the Lamar River. We dropped down one last slope, after which the terrain was flat. Soon we were next to the river and following it downstream a half mile. With only an hour of daylight left to the day, we found the cabin, at the edge of a streamside meadow (Figure 3.14). Steve, who was midway through our strung-out party, signaled the good news to the two of us in the rear by turning to face us and lifting his ski poles above his head in a salutation of joy. It had been a long but excellent day, and the late arrival at the cabin made the wisdom of breaking out the trail to the pass yesterday clear to all. Had we not done so, we would have been still skiing and facing an after dark arrival or even a night out, bivouacking in twenty below temperatures. While each of us was carrying a sleeping bag for that unwanted possibility, the best a bivouac would have given us was survival; restful sleep would have been nearly impossible. Thankful that we would not be suffering that fate, we let ourselves into the cabin and let Pyro at the woodstove. Part of the responsibility that comes with using a patrol cabin is to leave the woodstove with a ready-made fire in it, so that rangers who arrive exhausted can light a

Figure 3.14: Arriving at Cold Creek Cabin, February, 2006. The cabin is nestled in some trees at right, while three skiers approach it, one behind the other, just left of the cabin and in front of a live pine tree. AUTHOR COLLECTION.

fire with one match and collapse on a bed. The fire, therefore, was easy to light, but warming the cabin was not. For the next hour, we waited and watched the fire take and then grow, all the while seemingly giving off no heat. It was a visual trick, looking at flames and expecting to feel warmth, but finding none. It was as though the flames themselves were frozen, except that they were the colors of the real thing, not the blues and white one would expect of frozen flame. In reality, it was evidence of how cold the cabin and its contents really were, for the fire had to raise the temperature some fifty degrees before anything could even begin to thaw. This cabin's name—the Cold Creek Cabin—pretty much summed it all up; this was a frosty place in a vast frozen wilderness.

And frosty it was, with well below zero temperatures overnight again, but probably about ten degrees warmer than the previous night (again, the cabin lacked a thermometer). This cabin was larger, and Pyro restrained himself with the wood-stove, so we had no blowing fog or sleep-depriving heat. The cabin also had several more windows, which enhanced the openness and which looked out on one of the wilder settings in Yellowstone. The snow-covered meadow extended a half mile to the north, where the five-hundred-foot-tall ridges bordering the valley pinched close, leaving room for only the river. The ridges were partly forested and partly burned, with occasional trees highlighted against the sky, their branches turned up to the heavens, as if celebrating their wild home. Cold Creek is as geographically wild as it is visually, lying within two miles of the remote point I had approached on my Mirror Plateau hike a few years earlier. Here, we were close to thirteen miles from the nearest road, but considerably more by trail. Three different trails converge at Cold Creek; all of them take close to twenty miles to deliver the wilderness traveler to a road. In short, Cold Creek was a second Thorofare, not quite as remote, not quite as difficult to reach, but every bit as beautiful and wild.

We longed to linger in that enchanting place with the relax-ing cabin, to recuperate and enjoy the primitive ambiance. We hadn't foreseen its calming beauty, but we had commitments at work in three days, so we reluctantly continued our trek the next day. Across the meadow we skied the next morning, then onto the frozen river. The trail paralleling the river climbs over some hills while the river does not, so it was the easier route, even though following it took us through some twists and turns that the trail climbed above. I was initially skeptical of skiing on the frozen river, fearing a wet and cold accident if we found thin ice, but soon realized it was both safe and enjoyable. The cold weather had produced thicker than normal ice, our skis distrib-uted our weight, and the river was only the size of a creek in this headwaters area, so breaking through would likely only wet our feet and shins. In fact, we had to ford the river halfway through the day, and the water was so shallow that it did not overtop our boots (the river was open there because it was downstream of Willow Creek, whose thermally warmed waters joined the river and kept it from freezing for a couple miles).

As the miles on the river added up, the sensory experience became an intimate counterpoint to the arctic vastness of the last two days (Figure 3.15). Even away from Willow Creek's influence, we occasionally heard gurgling water and saw water movement in places where the current prevented ice from completely encasing the river. But for the water and us, this was a world almost bereft of sound—and this was about the noisiest landscape we were to pass through. The sights were equally lovely, with the river forming a serpentine trail through the whitened world, a pathway of snow-covered ice. Ten or twenty feet wide, the river maintained a consistent gradient with almost no rapids, so it was a broad ski trail when not thawed by Willow Creek (we took the trail paralleling the river in that zone). Here and there, rocks poked above the ice, sometimes as frozen mounds of snow, sometimes as snow cones of white atop a dark gray boulder. Complementing the river's delights were cascades of translucent gray icicles on the steeper banks, giving away the location of seeps and small springs. Where the banks were not so steep, lodgepole pines lifted our eyes to the pale blue sky above, their needles holding on to the dusting of snow that fell when this arctic air moved in. Willows lined the frozen river, their red branches providing the only native color besides the pine needles. With the sun still out and the temperature around 5° F, it was a unique day of skiing, an intimate encounter with nature's beauty.

We arrived at the Calfee Creek Cabin with plenty of daylight to spare. It was similar in size to the Pelican Springs Cabin, so we enjoyed one more cozy evening together. As I waited for sleep to

Figure 3.15: Life and death on the Lamar River, 2006. Two of the skiers make their way down the frozen Lamar River while an elk antler frozen into the snowy riverbank suggests a grimmer side of winter in the northern Rockies. AUTHOR COLLECTION.

come that night—in more comfortable sleeping environment—
I thought of a winter ski patrol that ours, even with the brutal
first day, paled in comparison to. Almost exactly fifty years before our trip, rangers Harry V. Reynolds, Jr., Nathaniel Lacy,
and Delmar Peterson embarked on a two-week patrol through
the Thorofare region. Reporting on the trip afterwards, Reynolds (who authored the formal report of the trip) wrote that
temperatures never got above freezing, varying from 28 above to
39 below zero. Snow fell every day but one, snow depths ranged
from 42 inches to 95 (that's almost eight feet!), and they skied a
minimum of eight miles every day but one, with one day being
16 miles and another 18. Impressive statistics those may be, but
the really memorable events happened on their way out of the
Thorofare. Their route into the wilderness had brought them
along the east shore of Yellowstone Lake and then up the upper Yellowstone River Valley, which is all flat terrain. From the
Thorofare Ranger Station, though, they turned west, skiing the
South Boundary Trail to the South Entrance. This is the same
trail Carla and I hiked (in reverse) when we saw the red fox, so
the three men had two significant climbs, the first over the Two
Ocean Plateau and the second over Big Game Ridge and Mount
Hancock. About a day's travel apart—in good weather—were
two patrol cabins where the men would seek shelter. Good
weather, though, was something in short supply for those three.

Departing the ranger station at dawn on March 4, 1956,
Reynolds, Lacy, and Peterson began the first climb, up and
over the Two Ocean Plateau. Ten inches of heavy new snow
made trail breaking difficult, so much that one of Lacy's bindings broke, delaying them an hour while they repaired it as best
they could. Underway again, they continued climbing while the
storm intensified. By early afternoon, there was so much new
snow that they were sinking in above their knees, making forward travel next to impossible. They were soaked to the skin

with sweat and snow, and they had more than six hours to go. Recognizing the futility and danger of going on, they turned around at three p.m., heading back to the cabin they'd left that morning. Even with the trail being broken, their return took six hours, demonstrating they made the right decision. They had planned to resume forward progress the next day, but with snow still falling, they laid over for the day, repairing Lacy's binding more securely and resting up. Their second attempt the next day at crossing the plateau was successful, but it was still long and arduous. They didn't arrive at the Fox Creek Cabin until an hour after dark, and then had to dig their way in, the building being buried to the eaves. Still, they had the first major climb behind them.

As difficult as Two Ocean Plateau was, it was but a warm-up for Big Game Ridge. Underway again shortly after dawn the next morning, the three rangers enjoyed something new for the journey: clear skies. With good weather seemingly on tap, the skiers decided to forego easier but longer routes around the ridge, going instead up and over it (which is what the South Boundary Trail does under all that snow). Delayed a little by muscle cramps in one of Lacy's legs (small wonder they didn't suffer more health problems from the trying conditions), they topped out on Big Game Ridge at two o'clock. From there, it was just an easy mile and a half across the flat ridge—or so they thought. For them, it would be a trek taking the rest of the day, and then some. Barely had the men caught their breath from the climb when they noticed clouds moving in from all directions. Not wanting to be caught out in the open on the exposed ridge, they started across it. They soon realized that crossing it quickly would be difficult in the best of circumstances—and that they had a new blizzard to contend with. Rather than finding a smooth field of snow on the ridgetop, they found that wind had scoured and drifted the snow into a series of lateral snow ridges ten to twenty-five feet tall, some of which were more than a half mile in length. Oriented perpendicular to their intended route and nearly vertically sided, the ridges of snow presented a route-finding challenge in good weather—and worse, much worse, in their situation. The men spent all afternoon trying to find a way through, following the couloirs between the parallel drifts of snow, all while being pelted with snow fired into their faces and eyes by hundred-mile-per-hour wind gusts. In the blizzard's flat light, they struggled to see where they were going; some couloirs brought them under deadly cornices, others terminated in cliffs hundreds of feet tall, yawning over abysses obscured by wildly swirling snow. The men knew that even a minor misstep could be deadly, but they had little choice but to go on, for backtracking promised the same dangers.

Darkness fell while the rangers were still in the labyrinth of peril. Their objective now became finding the shelter of the trees they knew clothed the sides of Big Game Ridge. Feeling their way forward with an extended ski pole, they finally dropped off the west side of the ridge and found a group of firs on a steep slope. They were out of the screaming wind, and could turn their attention to constructing a shelter for the night. They kindled a fire on some green logs (to keep the fire from melting its way downward into the snow) and tunneled into the snow above the trees for a snow cave (planning to sleep in cabins, they had foregone carrying a tent). By the time they crawled into the snow cave, it was 2:00 a.m. Setting up the shelter had taken five hours, crossing the ridge had taken six, and the morning's ski eight, for a combined total of more than twenty hours that day, all with little rest—and they weren't close to finishing their ordeal. Conditions did not improve overnight, so the next morning the three decided to descend the slope below and follow the drainage out to more level terrain. That route took them along the west slope of Big Game Ridge and out of the park, a circuitous route that demonstrated how disorienting the drifts and couloirs on top were. Finally on flat ground, the rangers got back on track and resumed skiing toward the Harebell Cabin, their last. With snow still falling and fatigue setting in, they saw darkness fall again without the cabin in sight. Nonetheless, they kept moving, each man hoping against reality to find the cabin but resigning himself to spending another night out. But at 9:30 p.m., three hours after nightfall, they found it—by stumbling on the top of its stovepipe. The cabin was completely buried, but they didn't care. Shelter, warmth, beds, and hot food were just a few dozen shovels-full of snow away.

For those three rangers and for us, the last day of skiing was easy and almost boring, with our temperatures soaring into the twenties after a final night below zero. Reynolds, Lacy, and Peterson finished their epic journey with just some frost-nipped toes and fingers (frost-nip is not as serious as frostbite, for the person recovers full use of the affected digits, though the digits may be unusually sensitive to cold for years or even decades). We don't know what weather the three rangers had on their last day, but it was not worth a comment in Reynolds' report. For us, clouds entered our sky for the first time, signaling the return to warmer weather. We continued skiing down the frozen river for the morning, but left it where the valley opened up downstream of Cache Creek. The final leg of the trip was a quick ski across the now wide valley to a bridge over Soda Butte Creek, on the other side of which was the car. Our journey into the wild, into winter extremes, and into the past was over. We had seen some of Yellowstone's wildest scenery, passing through one of the park's remotest places and seeing no one. We had experienced some bitterly cold temperatures, conditions made worse by severely cold wind chills. And, we had taken shelter in three of Yellowstone's historic patrol cabins, buildings that have sheltered rangers on such trail patrols for more than a century.

From the wildness to the winter severity to the need to take shelter in cabins, it had been a tour of nature's forces, especially the primacy of winter. As cold and lonely as it had been, though, it was just a glimpse of what winter could really be like in Yellowstone. Temperatures colder than thirty below still occur, blizzards with wind chills approaching triple digits below zero still rage, and rangers still take shelter in patrol cabins. Rangers Reynolds, Lacy, and Peterson would still recognize winter in the grand old park, the time when nature's power is raw, biting, and in your face.

Winter's Limitations

For most of the plants and animals inhabiting Yellowstone, winter is the ultimate litmus test of survival: if they can make it through the season of extremes, they will probably prosper there. All of the park's native residents have evolved to handle subzero cold and deep snow in various ways. Trees and shrubs harden their tissues against the damaging effects of frost and ice crystals by converting water in their cells to sugars that act as antifreeze. Grasses, forbs, and deciduous trees pull their energy into their root systems. Some smaller plants adopt an annual life cycle, dying out completely in fall and gambling that their seeds will germinate the following spring. Firs and spruce assume their conical shape to shed snow outward while pines are flexible enough to bow down under the weight of snow and spring back when the weight falls off or melts. Some conifers and quaking aspen even make hay while the sun shines, turning on the chlorophyll in their needles (conifers) and trunk (aspen) to photosynthesize on warmer days in winter and especially in spring. And as mentioned earlier, Ross's bentgrass takes an entirely different approach, altering its life cycle and stature to take advantage of the unique conditions present in Yellowstone's geyser basins. These are just a few of the ways that plants make it through a season that easily comprises half the year or more.

Animals employ a similar range of adaptations to winter. All put on longer fur and most put on fat, to get through the cold and lean times to come. Elk, deer, pronghorn, and bison migrate to lower elevations where snow is less and temperatures milder. Grizzly and black bears hibernate, along with some rodents, while moose stay put or go up in elevation to browse on fir and spruce needles, striding through the snow with their long legs. Some rodents stay active under the snow, burrowing through it as they do through soil and eating the dried grasses they encounter in their tunneling. Others harvest the fruits of their summer labors, such as pikas, who consume the grasses they gathered and dried in the summer sun. Beaver and red squirrels do likewise, the former gnawing on the branches they waterlogged and sank in the ponds they created, the latter feasting on the pine nuts the grizzly bears didn't eat from their middens. Clark's nutcrackers mimic the squirrels, retrieving the cones they stashed while chickadees do like elk, grouping together and, in the birds' case, shivering controllably to stay warm. Whatever the plant or animal, you can be sure they have some adaptation—often multiple ones—to winter in Yellowstone.

Successful these adaptations may be, but winter is still the season of limits, so sometimes even adaptations that have served the animal well come up short. Perhaps the best example of this is the non-migratory Madison River elk herd, which was already living on the edge when wolves arrived there in the late 1990s. The predatory pressure of the large canines was more than that elk population could bear; within five years of wolves' arrival, the herd was wiped out. With wolves reinserted to the mix, the valley's rules of survival changed enough that elk could no longer persist in that already marginal winter habitat. The animal's adaptations to winter could only do so much; with wolves now present, putting on fat and clustering in the thermal areas were no longer adequate to persist in that range.

These are the exceptions that prove the rule, though, for most of the time, the winter adaptations found in Yellowstone's native inhabitants function well, enabling the plants and animals to survive and prosper in a forbidding climate. The adaptations do the job, and they do it well. The limits of winter do not just apply to wildlife and plants, though; they also apply to the humans who choose to venture forth into the Yellowstone made white and cold. Beyond dealing with the cold, there are many ways we have bumped up against, and continue to discover, winter's limits. Sometimes the encounter is with a known and predictable limit, and other times it is with something unexpected. Usually the encounter is recognized in the here and now, but sometimes it is visible only in hindsight. Most of the time, the encounter is benign, but sometimes it has more significant consequences. Finally, most of the dangers are avoidable, if we choose to learn from our shared experience, but sometimes they are not, especially when we forget the things we have learned or ignore obvious warnings. Everyone who spends a significant amount of time in the Yellowstone winter has had some encounter with winter's limits, as the Reynolds party found in the Thorofare. Here are three of my own encounters with the limits of winter in Yellowstone, experiences in which I came to understand that nature's power is as evident than when snow is on the ground as not.

In the mid-2000s, my ski buddy Jim Williams and I took off on an overnight trip across the Gallatin Mountain Range in the park's northwest corner. Hopping a ride on a snowcoach to West Yellowstone, we spent a night in a hotel there and watched a movie on television, a novelty for two guys who spent most winter evenings absorbed in their books. Unfortunately for me, the movie hit on some emotional baggage I was carrying at the time, so I spent much of the night tossing and turning. At least that's what I thought had caused the restlessness, but hindsight would suggest it was worries about something potentially more dangerous than emotional wounds. Catching a ride north to the trailhead the next day with a friend, we began skiing east on the Fawn Pass trail. Our objective was to get to the patrol cabin with the mythical bruin tree, some ten miles away and 1,500 feet up. The first four miles were on a relatively flat trail that was part of an eight-mile loop popular with local residents. Passing through open forest and small meadows, the trail began to climb after about three miles. Skiers had already been that far, making the ascent easy even for a sleep-deprived skier like me.

At the four mile mark, our route diverted from the broken hard-packed ski trail and started to climb more steeply. Breaking the trail for ourselves now, I realized how tired I really was. I could barely keep up with Jim, even though he was doing the hard work in front. Carrying a forty-pound pack, the smallest hills were exhausting, and we still had well over a thousand feet of climbing to go. Hoping for a second wind, I continued following Jim, who was motoring onward and upward. Soon we left the trees and began angling steeply up an open slope dotted with sagebrush. Most of the shrubs rose above the snow, but here and there one was buried. Sage often holds onto pockets of air when it gets snow-covered, pockets that collapse under a skier's weight. Repeatedly, our snowpack collapsed to the ground as we tried to ascend the hillside, forcing us to back up, angle our skis up, and climb out of the hole. It didn't take long before I could only move a foot or two forward before I had to stop and rest. I was having serious doubts about my ability to do this trip.

The weather was not helping matters. It was about 30° F. (above zero, not below), a temperature at which snow seems to get heavy. The sky was thickly overcast and spitting graupel, snowflakes that are coalescing into quarter-inch pellets of softening ice that is close to melting. A gusty southwest wind was blowing, and the cloud ceiling was low, obscuring any view of the mountains we were heading toward. Higher up, the air was probably cold enough that snowflakes were not coalescing, and it was likely snowing hard enough to accumulate. That snow was falling on a snow layer that was itself getting heavy as it absorbed water vapor from the relatively warm and humid air. Underneath all of this was a layer of depth hoar, snow that had had much of its moisture and cohesion sucked out by the upper layers of snow and, ultimately, by dry, cold air (colder than what we were experiencing at that moment, such as subzero nights) in a process known as sublimation. The net result of putting heavy snow on depth hoar that resembles ball bearings is instability and avalanches on steeper slopes. In fact, as this weather system had intensified over the last several days, the warnings of the local avalanche forecast center had followed suit. By the time we had left home, their warnings were the most dire I'd ever heard, strongly recommending skiers to stay well away from any steep slope or, better yet, to stay home. The collapsing snow on that hillside resembled what we would find up higher, except that it would be deeper and on a slope steep enough to slide. We also might not even know when we were entering an avalanche zone due to the low clouds and poor visibility. In short, one or both of us could easily be killed by an avalanche that we caused but which we never saw coming.

As the weaker one of us, I could no longer ignore the signs that we should abort the trip. Even if I had the energy to complete the trip, and even if we had had another skier or two to share in the trail breaking work, the wisdom of undertaking that trip in those weather and avalanche conditions was fast becoming dubious at best. So, I stopped my partner and told him I was too exhausted to go on. He responded by saying he felt strong enough to break trail all the way (an unlikely feat, as another ski tour with Jim would soon show), but I stated I could not make it even under those circumstances. I don't remember if we discussed the avalanche conditions then, but I know we had previously. Hindsight suggests we may have reached differing conclusions, his more positive than mine—and perhaps more immutable than mine, less influenced by on-the-ground conditions. Perhaps I should have been more assertive with my concerns about the trip before we had left home, but I had been as excited about the trip as he was, and as ignorant of actual field conditions. Regardless, it didn't matter anymore, because I could not go on. Reluctantly, we turned around and skied out. Vexed by conditions for which Yellowstone was *not* known— who would have thought to expect such warmth and associated conditions—we avoided a situation that was fraught with uncertainty and possibly danger. In the end, I think I lost sleep the night before not so much because of the movie, but because of anxiety about doing the trip at all. It was a trip that defied expectations in more than one way.

The next winter, Jim and I embarked on another memorable and long sought ski tour, one that would demonstrate the wisdom of having turned back from Fawn Pass. It was a twelve-mile day trip down the Pebble Creek Valley in the park's northeast corner with our mutual friend MacNeil Lyons, a partner to share in the wild and the trail breaking. We zipped up a thousand-foot ridge that guards the valley from casual interlopers, then dropped down into the large meadow gracing the creek's headwaters. The field of white is a high elevation fortress, nearly surrounded by Absaroka peaks lifting one's eyes to ten thousand feet and beyond. We paused there to soak up the silence and beauty, and to have a snack. Satisfied we had stoked stomach and soul, we pointed the skis down valley and toward Cutoff Mountain (so named because the park's generally linear north boundary slices the summit out of the park). Arriving at the mountain's foot in just twenty minutes, we left the meadow behind and entered the snowy forest that would embrace us for the rest of the day. We had skied three miles in about ninety minutes, a good pace.

As we soon discovered, the forest more swallowed than embraced us, for our pace slowed to barely half the morning's. Forest floors receive less sunshine than open meadows, making the snow in forests less capable of supporting a skier (until more snow accumulates, collapsing the depth hoar). Every ten or twenty strides in the forest, the snow under the trail breaker collapsed to the ground, making that person do the same maneuver Jim and I had done on the slope the year before: back up, ramp the skis up, and climb out of the hole. It was not as bad as the year before, and we had another person to share the work, so we continued skiing. Sometimes we'd go one or two hundred yards without the snow collapsing, but other times it collapsed every other stride. We were making progress, though, so on we went.

After a couple miles of this physically demanding travel, we stopped for a well-deserved lunch. Like most winter lunch breaks, filling the stomach redirected the blood away from the internal furnace, so we ate quickly. As we were downing the last bites, we were astonished to see another group of skiers approach. The Pebble Creek Trail does not get much use in the winter, and the few people who do ski or snowshoe it usually stop at the meadow and retrace their steps back out over the protective ridge, as I had done in years past. Yet here they were, eight in all, one or two of whom I recognized. We chatted briefly, and then left them behind to eat their own lunch. We continued breaking trail, our slow and plodding pace the antithesis of motion on skis. I kept expecting to see the other group catch up to us, since their pace on the broken trail had to be considerably faster than ours, but they were nowhere to be found. After an hour of increasingly faltering forward movement, we stopped for another break, resting muscles and eating power bars. While we were stopped, the other party caught up to us. At least that's what our ears told us, for we heard some shouts but didn't see anyone. I had actually just had that same experience before we stopped, but had seen no one, so I had assumed it was some trick of geography bringing their calls to my ears. Looking up the trail this time, though, I did see movement, but it seemed like one of them was gesturing to the others to stop and stay out of sight. In fact, we soon heard someone saying as much.

Backcountry skiing, like most activities, has an unwritten but generally understood code of conduct. One of its concepts is that there is no free lunch: if the trail is not already broken, you should offer to take your turn if you catch up to the lead party. That group can refuse your offer, but you should at least offer to help, especially if the breaking is difficult or your party is larger. Yet here they were violating not only that code, but also common human decency and courtesy. They were strong and experienced skiers, they knew that code, some of them even recognized me, and they had to know we were quite tired. I looked at my two fellow skiers, who seemed as bewildered at the situation as I was. Having little patience for freeloaders, I soon called out, "We know you're there, and we are exhausted, so it's time for you to break trail." No response. I repeated myself. Still no response. I repeated myself again, with the same result. Jim and MacNeil were silent, as befuddled as I was. Finally, I got the other group to do something when I told them that the only direction any of us would go was toward them. Still they said nothing, but soon began to ski toward us. As they passed us, they smiled and said hello, but not one of them apologized or even bothered to thank us for breaking out the majority of the trail.

With eight fresh trail breakers, they zoomed ahead and were

not to be seen again, even though we were then moving almost as fast. We reached the trailhead two hours later, tired and approaching exhaustion. Had the other group not come along when they did—with or without the guilt trip they deserved—we would still have made it, but just barely, and probably close to sundown. It's debatable whether we could have or should have foreseen those snow conditions, for I had gone skiing many times in similar situations (such as the Pelican to Lamar trip) without encountering such collapsible snow. We were wise to bring another person along, and had done everything else to prepare ourselves, but still pushed the limits. What's more, we were confronted with a situation wherein some people overstepped the limits of common decency, acts of rudeness and selfishness that I have seen neither before nor since on the trail. Those skiers made a difficult situation worse, and demonstrate in a most unfortunate way that winter's limits are not the only ones winter travelers must be prepared for. We were fortunate that we had enough stamina to get through on our own, but the situation could have been quite different. Had we not had the energy to complete the trip, their childish actions could have meant an unexpected night out, hypothermia, and potentially worse. Sadly, sometimes nature's limits are not the ones with the most potential harm.

Thankfully, most of the time, we humans cooperate in facing winter's limits, as I experienced about ten years before these two incidents. It was not in the backcountry, but it easily could have been. I was working as a snowcoach driver / guide and had picked up some passengers at Old Faithful to bring them to Mammoth Hot Springs. A winter storm was moving in, and I knew that conditions could be dicey later in the trip, based on past experience. So, I briefed my passengers on the situation, explaining that snowcoaches might be nifty vehicles, but they needed to remain on hard-packed snow-covered roads. If I lost visibility and managed to drive the vehicle off the snow-packed road into soft snow, we would be stuck. With the wind we were seeing that afternoon, whiteout conditions could prevail on Swan Lake Flats, which we had to cross late in the trip. If blowing snow made it impossible for me to see the next reflective snow pole on the roadside, I would have to ask for volunteers to get out and walk in front of the vehicle. With their feet, they would be able to tell where the hard-packed road ended and the soft stuff began, and I would follow them close behind. In this manner, we could safely inch our way through the whiteout, which I said would probably last less than a mile.

If I thought my passengers would accept this news with concern and open minds, I was quite wrong. They looked at me as though I had just told them that Santa and Rudolph would ferry us through the whiteout. But two hours later, they grew increasingly quiet as we left the sheltering forest behind and crawled onto the flats. The sun had set and the wind was from behind, so the view out the front was of snow wildly swirling away from us. It was as though a giant abominable snowman was yawning, pulling us irresistibly toward him with the air he was inhaling. Gradually, the wind intensified and the blowing snow shrank our sight distance. The headlights illuminated three reflective poles ahead of us, then two, then only one. It stayed that way for a few minutes, but we soon lost sight of even one snow pole. The coach by then was dead quiet, the passengers no longer doubting my word. That's probably why three of them practically jumped out of their seats when I asked for volunteers to walk the road in front of us. I cautioned them to remain abreast of each other so no one got beyond hearing range of the vehicle horn, which I would sound when visibility improved enough for me to drive safely. They hopped out and led the way through the whiteout. Despite my warning, two of them started to leave the third one—and the snowcoach—behind, so I blew the horn and corralled them back to safety. Visibility had improved by then, so they climbed in and we went on our way. The whole incident lasted less than fifteen minutes, but it left all of us with an indelible impression of what blindness by whiteout was. More to the point, I had a personal glimpse of how dangerous it would be to have that happen in the backcountry, where headlights, reflective snow poles, vehicle horns, and heated vehicles are not to be found (Figure 3.16).

Whiteouts, bitter cold, unsupportive snow, avalanches, deep snow, and unusually warm weather are just some of the limits of winter in Yellowstone. Such limits have many incarnations, combinations, and degrees of clarity, all with which the plants, animals, and people of Yellowstone must contend. In some ways, they may come to depend on such limits: extreme cold keeps many pests away; deep snow is a landscape-wide reservoir

Figure 3.16: Poor visibility on Shoshone Lake, 2008. Two skiers make their way through near-whiteout conditions on Shoshone Lake. Barely visible above and to their right is the forested shore. AUTHOR COLLECTION.

of water nourishing countless streams and organisms, including humans; and unsupportive snow gives some animals the isolation they need to reproduce and successfully raise offspring. But more commonly, winter's challenges keep many other organisms away: ponderosa pine, Gambel oak, and mountain mahogany are absent from Yellowstone, even though they are all widespread throughout the West; white-tailed deer, raccoons, and skunks are all rarely seen on the Yellowstone plateau, but are common outside the park; and people still prefer to visit the park in summertime, not the season that dominates the park more than half the year. Instead, lodgepole pine is by far the most common tree, hibernating and migrating animals the most widespread native residents, and displaced Norwegians the prevailing biped—all of them organisms that are adapted, or that adapt themselves, to the extremes and limits of winter. The season of snow and struggle, cold and challenge, and darkness and death is, for the majority of organisms, the most influential season in Yellowstone.

Reflections

In the last fifty or sixty years, Americans have discovered winter sports. Ski resorts have blossomed throughout the country, ice skating rinks have opened in most major cities, and the outdoor sporting equipment business has mushroomed into a multi-million dollar industry. People pursue dozens of different winter sports, finding fun and enjoyment during the time of year that was once no more than a season to endure. The seemingly endless months of darkness have become a time some anticipate with excitement and joy. Indeed, winter for many is *the* time of year to be out and about—but only to a point. If the temperature drops into the single digits or below, if the wind picks up, if the snow falls too hard, we retreat to the warmth and security of our homes and ski lodges. We identify with winter, but not if it gets, well, too wintry, too much like the real thing. We want a sanitized version of winter, with temperatures in the twenties, no wind, and plenty of sunshine, much like the idyll that upscale ski resorts market to their wealthy patrons. We shiver at the thought of sixty below, we shudder thinking about being lost in a whiteout, and we cringe contemplating what it must be like to break trail through knee-deep snow for miles.

But for all that, the limits and extremes of winter still fascinate us. Outside of Alaska, Yellowstone National Park is one of the few places Americans can experience winter's extremes, in person or, better yet for most of us, in narrative form. We have long been drawn to see the park's winter wonders, so we have willingly subjected ourselves to the vagaries of cold, snow, and darkness. We have found that where there is extreme cold, there is also extreme beauty (Figure 3.17). But along with that discovery, we have also had a direct view of nature's power. That power brings struggle, morbidity, and death to some creatures, while others endure, survive, and even prosper. Those events are part of the cycle of life, multiples of which interconnect with those of the past and future to form a never-ending continuity of life, existence, and energy. Yellowstone in winter exposes this continuity to full view, demonstrating that the companion to summer's explosion of life is winter and its challenges and mortality. The thermal basins add nuance, interweaving oases of life with the sea of dormancy surrounding them. Wonderland in winter, then, is a grand tapestry of life and death, existence and rebirth, beauty and extremes. Whether we immerse ourselves within that tapestry or admire it from afar, we see and feel the natural, eternal power in it.

Figure 3.17: Osprey Falls, 2008. Some waterfalls freeze entirely, encasing the moving water in ice—along with most of the sound.
AUTHOR COLLECTION.

CHAPTER 4

Journeys of Immersion

From high, high above,
the raspy calls of cranes—
We watch in wonder.

—David Kirtley

The morning dawned foggy on Heart Lake that July day in 1987, with Mount Sheridan, which overlooks the lake, nowhere to be seen. With four or five other employees from Canyon Lodge, I had spent the night at the lake after hiking in from the South Entrance Road the day before. It had been a lovely, easy seven miles through a lodgepole pine forest lush with grasses and grouse whortleberry, the trees giving way to meadow and wetland after five miles. Once at the lake, we had set up camp and explored the thermal area at the base of the mountain. Rustic Geyser and Columbia Pool were the star attractions there; the geyser didn't perform for us, but the pool was a penetrating blue rimmed with delicate white sinter. We then returned to the lakeshore for dinner, enjoying a serene evening with a moving cloud show over the lake and some gentle, passing showers that didn't even justify rain jackets. We turned in early, the better to get a pre-dawn start on climbing the mountain.

Rousing ourselves at first light, we emerged to a scene that was dark and chill, the moisture from the evening rain having condensed into thick fog. Undaunted, we gathered our packs and some food and water and began the four-mile, 2800-foot climb to the summit. I'm not sure what we expected to find in that fog, but what we received I never forgot. The trail ascended straight up for the first half mile, whereupon the slope became steep enough that it began to switchback. We were in the fog still, but somewhere in the next mile or so, the light started getting brighter. Soon we were breaking out of the fog, rising above it as we gained elevation. The experience was dazzling, transforming from cloistered gloom to a world of glitter and color. As we continued climbing, the land around us slowly emerged from the fog. The strengthening sun reflected off the fire lookout on the summit above and highlighted the top of the cloud from which we had just emerged.

With the sunshine adding zip to our step, it wasn't long before we arrived at the summit and fire lookout. Mountains and volcanic plateaus stretched out in the four cardinal directions, a view limited only by mountains and earth's curvature. To the south, practically at our feet, rose the Tetons, their jagged peaks rising abruptly from another fog bank, that one shrouding Jackson Lake. Peaks gave way to plateaus as our eyes turned west, the lava flows and ash falls of the Yellowstone hot spot. Turning north and then east, mountains resumed their roles as guardians of Yellowstone and its treasures, the Gallatin, Madison, and northern Absarokas standing fast. Every lake we knew to exist in the area was shrouded in fog, blankets of clouds that burned off two hours later (Figure 4.1). It was a huge, wild country almost unmatched in America, outside of Alaska.

Once we had admired the view and snapped the obligatory

Figure 4.1: The view from Mt. Sheridan, 1987. Fog shrouds Heart Lake (foreground) and Yellowstone Lake (background). AUTHOR COLLECTION.

photos, we sat down to eat a second breakfast. It was about this time that the man staffing the lookout came out to visit with us. Jim McKown, we learned, had been the Mount Sheridan lookout for over twenty years. Interspersed with his fire watch duties, he enjoyed writing; he spent winters writing as well, intentionally forgoing a career position to make his summers on the remote mountaintop possible. That must have struck more than one of us as notable and out-of-the-ordinary, for we then asked him what kept bringing him back to a post with no running water, electricity, or telephone. He was already a person to remember—or even, perhaps, emulate—but his answer made an indelible impression on me. Gesturing toward the fog-shrouded lakes, he said simply, "mornings like this."

After a couple hours soaking up the view and contemplating the experience—natural and social—we began the hike back to camp and then to our cars and summer jobs. Jim's simple, yet profound statement gradually sank in as I continued exploring Wonderland the remainder of that summer, and then another summer, and eventually, well over half as many summers as McKown (when combined with his summers atop Mount Washburn, to which he soon moved, at least thirty-one summers). I came to understand and embody his coda, sacrificing permanence and security to more deeply explore Yellowstone and the West while I was young and fit. As I did, I found myself more and more tightly bound to Yellowstone, its landscape and animals, and the natural forces that energize that landscape. More than most bonds to a native landscape, I think, the bonds to a place like Yellowstone can be quite powerful, even life-changing. Perhaps that's because the landscape is so unaltered and primeval, and the natural forces so obvious and integral; whatever the case, the connections seem, to me, to be unbreakable, maybe even as strong as life itself. The stories that follow illustrate the rich variety of ecological, geological, historical, educational, social, and emotional bonds possible between and among us and Yellowstone. In addition to the breadth, they also show the depth of such bonds—and that anyone can form them.

A Memorable Hike
on the Bechler River Trail

Winter's biggest storms arrive in Yellowstone from the southwest, blowing across the plains of southern Idaho before crashing into the Madison and Pitchstone Plateaus, and then into the rest of Yellowstone and its protective mountains. Rising to nine thousand feet and more over the two plateaus, the storms drop their loads of moisture, leaving feet, even yards, of snow by April and May. Melting slowly and percolating into the gravelly soil, the meltwater comes out in springs—both hot and cold—as the plateaus give way to canyon and plain. Tumbling over cliff and precipice, the streams those springs nourish delight us with waterfalls by the dozen in Yellowstone's southwest corner, known as the Bechler region or, more descriptively, Cascade Corner. Roads don't go where the falls are most concentrated, but trails do, with perhaps the best of them being the Bechler River Trail. Twice in the 2000s, I had the pleasure of hiking that trail from Old Faithful to the Bechler Ranger Station, a distance of thirty miles. Both times I went with a group from the Yellowstone Institute, a nonprofit organization (now part of Yellowstone Forever) sponsoring educational field trips in the park. The first time was the more memorable experience, largely because the connections we made included a most unexpected corporate sponsor. Here is that tale, one that featured every phase of H2O.

We met at the Lone Star Geyser trailhead near Old Faithful: six or eight participants, Tim Hudson the backpacking guide, and myself, the geographer along to spin some yarns about the area's cultural and natural history. I may not recall the exact number of trip participants, but I can't forget two of them: a two-hundred-fifty-pound man and his wife. Introducing themselves, they told the group that they were from Texas and were celebrating their twenty-fifth wedding anniversary by doing something completely different, this backpacking trip. However meritorious their motivation may have been, his weight was cause for some concern, since he was already carrying an extra fifty pounds without his pack. On a lengthy backpacking trip like this into one of Yellowstone's more remote regions, the readiness of every participant is crucial, for if anything should befall a person, medical help can be several hours or even days in coming. However, we knew that the route was pretty friendly to first-timers, that our intended pace would be easy, and that nothing about his medical information had caught the registrar's attention, so we left it at that for the moment. I have long since forgotten their names, so for reasons that will soon become clear, I will refer to him as Phil and her as Mo. With the introductions complete, we finished the last-minute preparations and embarked on a journey that promised plenty of rewards for all.

The first two miles were on a former road that parallels the Firehole River. Flat and wide, the trail made walking abreast of each other possible and conversation easy. It was probably there that we learned that Phil had quit smoking a week before the trip (Mo had never smoked). Additionally, he must have been loyal to the cigarettes produced by Philip Morris, for he had accrued enough loyalty points to buy the backpacks he and Mo were carrying from the tobacco giant (not the company that first comes to mind for provisioning a first-time backpacker!). "Backpacks" is a generous term for the bright red things, formless duffel-bag-like blobs that had little suspension or contouring to the human form. They were huge, big enough to store the gear for three hikers—a good thing for a duffel, but not for a first-timer's backpack, where space limitations reinforce the need to pack only the essentials, thereby minimizing the weight being carried. The blobs would have to do, though, so we kept hiking.

After lunch at Lone Star Geyser, we found the trail I loved to ski, the one to Shoshone Geyser Basin. We crossed the bridge over the Firehole, the jumping-off point for wilderness adventures as much in summer as in the snow season. Thus far, Phil and Mo had kept up with the group, but that was about to change. Before we had even arrived at the base of Grants Pass (one of the trip's two significant hills), the trail went over a small hill, practically halting Phil (and Mo and Tim, who stayed with him). The others in the group went ahead but waited at the top, finding it to be a surprisingly long time before Phil and his group caught up. I was with the faster hikers, and conferred with Tim when he arrived. We agreed that Phil was so slow that trying to keep the party together would be frustrating for, and unfair to, the others. So, I would go ahead with the faster hikers while Tim stayed with Phil and Mo. We would rendezvous at the campsite in Shoshone Meadows, just on the other side of the pass.

Our plan succeeded without a hitch, with Phil and Mo arriving an hour after my group. In camp, we learned that nicotine was not the only explanation for Phil's slow pace. He had indeed fallen victim to his pack's size, packing camp chairs (small, but stout), a full-size tent (in which he could almost stand up), and a hatchet (for pounding the full-size stakes into the ground). This was gear suitable for car camping, not wilderness travel, where one is carrying the pack for miles. His pack must have weighed 70 pounds—and it would get heavier, not lighter, as the trip went on, as we also saw that evening. When it came time for dinner, he was too tired to eat; after eating a few bites of his rehydrated meal, he put it back in the pouch from which it had come, a pound or two heavier than it had been before. In the backcountry, wilderness travelers must carry out everything they bring in, lest the place become trashed. Burying leftover food is not an option, for animals like grizzly bears may smell the food, exhume it, and eat it. If they do, they can learn to associate food with people, losing their fear of us and becoming a danger to future wilderness travelers. For these reasons, then, Phil's pack became heavier as the trip went on, probably topping 75 or 80 pounds by trip's end, about twice the weight of the typical hiker's backpack. Phil was indeed the archetypal Philip Morris victim, an addict who may have just quit the habit, but whose lungs would never regain the vigor they once had—all made worse by the heavy gear he was toting.

Away from the group, Tim and I discussed the situation. Phil was obviously out of his league here, yet here he was, on a silver anniversary trip that would certainly be memorable for him and his wife (we could only hope it would be for the intended reason). They had survived the first significant climb, and if they could make it up the other hill tomorrow, the rest of the hike should be easier for them. We decided that Tim would tell them what to expect tomorrow and thereafter and let them decide whether to go on. If they chose to continue, Tim would suggest that they get a jump on the climb while the others took a morning side trip with me to Shoshone Geyser Basin. That would enable them to tackle the hill on their own pace, while the others could experience the fantastic geyser basin.

Phil and Mo were not to be dissuaded from continuing on and liked the idea of getting a head start on the climb, so the two groups went their separate ways after breakfast the next day. The faster hikers and I enjoyed the greenery along Shoshone Creek, arriving in the geyser basin in an hour. If the winter there was notable for all things frosty, the summer was color gone wild. Hot springs painted the colors of the rainbow on their surroundings, with their waters blue, green, or clear and their runoff channels yellow, orange, and red, colored by cyanobacteria that crave hot water. Wildflowers bloomed on nearby patches of meadow, and sagebrush lizards scurried about, happy to show us their unique home (Figure 4.2). Some danced across the open, white sinter, while others skipped across the moss that was such a bright green in winter. The warmth of summer had dulled the green and dried the ground cover somewhat, but the lizards didn't mind. We found logs that bridged the creek, enabling us to see more thermal features on the other side. In the cool morning air, steam columns gave away more of Shoshone's secrets: hot springs tucked into the trees bordering the basin. It was a landscape of charm and character, a year-round oasis of life. We left reluctantly.

Back at camp, we ate lunch and threw our packs together. Before long, we were climbing through thick forest, on our way

Figure 4.2: Sagebrush lizard, 2001. The only legged reptile in Yellowstone, this lizard uses the geothermal heat of some geyser basins to survive Yellowstone's cold climate, including Shoshone Geyser Basin. AUTHOR COLLECTION.

to our highest campsite. Well before we arrived there, we caught up with the others. Phil did not look happy, with exhaustion in his eyes. Tim must have thought the same thing, for he took me aside and asked for the CPR mask I was carrying. I gave it to him, but not before I asked if I should stay with him, to do what I could to avert a situation necessitating its use. He declined, saying that given the circumstances, it just made more sense for him to have it. Additionally, Phil was still moving, practically willing himself to put one foot in front of the other. Backpackers don't ordinarily offer to help carry a group member's personal gear or unnecessarily heavy gear, but several people asked anyway. By this time, the group was gelling, with everyone hoping all would complete the trip, so no one took offense when Phil said no. With Mo and Tim following, Phil soldiered on, along with the Philip Morris blobs.

After another hour or two, we arrived at the camp, on a knoll overlooking a large meadow. Bridging the gap between the 9000-foot Madison and Pitchstone Plateaus, the meadow showcased grass and sky, the one curing in the late summer sunshine and the other turning dark with clouds in the southwest, portending the storm forecasted for the next three days. Everything about that place spoke of its high elevation—8,400 feet—and its dominant season, from the whitebark pines sheltering the campsite to the stunted, twisted, and gnarled saplings trying to take over the meadow (Figure 4.3). In addition to contending with the crushing snow, saplings must also deal with the frequently waterlogged soils in the meadows. They can't effectively do both, so they remain as saplings, always looking as though a yeti twisted them as it sat on them. And, as we found the next

Figure 4.3: Stunted saplings in high elevation meadow, 2006. Trees cope with heavy snow on the well-drained soils around this meadow (such as those on the far side), but not in the meadow's frequently waterlogged soil, which stunts their growth, making them repeatedly bent over by the snow. AUTHOR COLLECTION.

morning, snowfalls in September also bespoke a high elevation, for two inches of heavy wet snow greeted us when we emerged from our tents. With more snow falling lightly, we warmed our hands and hearts with steaming cups of coffee. Phil and Mo had the biggest smiles I'd seen since we left the trailhead, and the mood all around was light. The trials of the first two days were in the past, and Cascade Corner was beckoning with promises of downhill gradients and hot water warmth.

We were underway quickly, keeping one eye on Yellowstone's meteorology and turning the other to its geology. Soon we were hiking past Douglas Knob, a small forested hill that is Yellowstone's smallest lava flow, erupted about 120,000 years ago. It is neighbor to the park's youngest lava flow, the much larger one that created the Pitchstone Plateau some 70,000 years ago. The Pitchstone is an immense high elevation grassland with outcrops of lava poking above the thin soils, seventy-thousand years too little time for complete soil development. While we would not be seeing that grassland or lava, we were about to enter an equally marvelous result of Yellowstone's volcanism. On its western flank, the Pitchstone lava flow abuts the Bechler River lava flow, one of the many flows making up the Madison Plateau. The margins of lava flows are often shattered and easily eroded, so valleys and canyons typically form in such volcanic intersections. Happily for us, one such drainage yawned in front of us, the Bechler River Canyon, a fifteen-mile-long parade of waterfalls, lush forests, and hot springs. Almost immediately after passing the knob, we started dropping into the canyon. As we did, the snow turned into rain, a drizzle that dampened our packs and rain covers, but not our spirits.

The first indication that we were arriving at something special was Twister Falls, a small cascade whose face turns and twists as the water drops. Just beyond it, the trail began descending steeply, losing a thousand feet of elevation in just over a mile.

Emerging into a small meadow, we reached a trail junction, the sign there marking the way to the Ferris Fork. We would go that way the next day, our layover day. Continuing on, we soon passed Three River Junction, where the Phillips, Gregg, and Ferris Forks join within a hundred yards of each other to form the Bechler River. A confluence of waters warm and cold, the junction was also a union of beauty and magic, as we were already beginning to see. For the next 36 hours, we would immerse ourselves within that natural paradise, a celebration for all the senses. Hiking toward our campsite a mile down canyon, we rounded the bend and entered a larger meadow, a place where the nascent river slowed to a limpid crawl between canyon walls five hundred *feet* tall and the same number of *yards* apart (Figure 4.4). Fir and spruce trees climbed the walls here and there, yielding to grasses and flowers where the slopes steepened, and eventually to cliff and dark volcanic rock before reaching the canyon rim. The meadow was carpeted with grasses of various hues, punctuated by an occasional patch of yellow monkey flower or small hot spring, the steam rising into the cool and humid air. The trail wound through this serene place, kissing the edge of a hot spring or warm pool, and hugging the rock talus that marked the foot of the canyon wall. It was an intimate landscape of beauty and promise.

Leaving the meadow, we walked a short distance through forest and found our campsite for the next two nights. It featured a private waterfall, Albright Falls, tumbling down from the canyon rim. Nearby was Batchelder Column, a solitary rock pillar standing guard over the falls. The vegetation was lush, making the selection of tent sites simple: go where others have cleared suitable ground, for everything else was thickly vegetated. Fir and spruce trees provided shelter from the intensifying drizzle, so we ate lunch under them and discussed options for the afternoon and layover day. I don't really remember what we did for

Figure 4.4: Three River Junction area, 2006. The Bechler River winds through this lush meadow, while the spires of fir and spruce dominate the forest, an indication that snow falls heavily here. AUTHOR COLLECTION.

the rest of the day; most likely, we took our cue from Phil and Mo and climbed in our tents for some deserved rest. Indeed, the mighty blobs—and their tired but happy porters—had arrived in the heart of Yellowstone's Bechler region, and we were being lulled to slumber by that which makes it so lush: precipitation in the form of rain, the pitterpat on our tents.

Morning dawned overcast and wet, little changed from the day before. Rain or not, we had a day to take in the area's hot waters, falling waters, and raining waters. Retracing our steps to the trail junction, most of the group began hiking up the Ferris Fork. The intersection of volcanic geology and hydrology is always interesting, but on the Ferris Fork the results are particularly spectacular. Hot springs big enough to warm the entire stream, cascades and waterfalls strung like freshwater pearls, and the park's best hotpot are all there, on the lowermost two miles. One notable hot spring sits astride a mound four feet above the stream, steaming and roiling in a cauldron twelve feet wide, continuously cascading gallons of boiling water into the stream every minute (Figure 4.5). Another bubbles up right in the stream, mixing with cooler water and giving backpackers a hot tub in the wilderness. Most of the group went there to enjoy the contrast of a steam bath with cold drizzle, but a few group members joined me on a bushwhack to Quiver Cascade, an hourglass-shaped falls on the Philips Fork. In the rain and cloud cover, the cascade appeared to fall from the clouds, a gift from the watery heavens (Figure 4.6). Our wanderlust satisfied, we explorers retraced our steps back to the Ferris Fork and joined our hotpotting friends, who were well into some memorable in-body experiences. We could hardly have been more connected to

Figure 4.5: Hot spring on Ferris Fork of the Bechler River, 2006. In the summer months, the influx of hot water to the Ferris Fork from this and other hot springs can be enough to make the entire branch comfortable for dipping. AUTHOR COLLECTION.

Figure 4.6: Quiver Cascade, 2003. The waterfall is sometimes called Hourglass Falls, for obvious reasons. Note the plunge pool at the bottom. AUTHOR COLLECTION.

Yellowstone's power and geology than we were that day—as well as to each other, fellow travelers in the Yellowstone wilderness.

Once we were all sufficiently pruned, we dried off and began the return trip. I had been to the Ferris Fork several times previously, but that day I noticed something I had overlooked before, something unusual about the already unique stream. From the two large hot springs down to Three River Junction, few mature trees grew close to the fork (Figure 4.7). Here and there one did, but otherwise the only trees within twenty or thirty feet were small spruce and fir, and they were as battered as the saplings in the high country meadow we'd camped by two nights ago. The trees back from the stream were dominated by spruce and

Figure 4.7: The lower Ferris Fork, 2006. With a few exceptions, no mature trees line the riverbanks because, in winter, so much rime from the warm water cakes them that, in combination with the heavy snowfall, they topple. The cliffs of the Bechler River Canyon can be seen downstream. Note again the preponderance of spire-shaped spruce and firs. AUTHOR COLLECTION.

fir, an indication that plenty of snow accumulated here (no less than ten *feet* of it on the patrol cabin near our campsite a few Februarys before). With the benefit of my winter experiences in the park, I realized that the warm waters of the Ferris Fork caked nearby trees with so much rime in winter that, in combination with the heavy snowfall there, they were continually being flattened, crushed, and smashed to the ground. Even though I had hiked almost every mile of Yellowstone trail by that time and been a continual student of the park for more than a decade, there was clearly still much more to discover and experience there. Pointing this out to my fellow prunes, I joined them in marveling at the forces that interweave to create this landscape. It was the capstone to a day that was filled with wonder and awe, another strand in the web of connections we were forming to the place called Yellowstone.

The next day dawned overcast but dry, perhaps with the promise of clearing skies. It was time to move on, down the canyon of imagination and dream. Water was the theme uniting our experiences that day—water and beauty. The forest through which we hiked was exceptionally lush for Yellowstone, rich with fir and spruce, thimbleberry and huckleberry, marsh and greenery. The river we followed and forded twice was endlessly fascinating, a perpetual cascade, then a stair-stepping plunge, lastly a quiet meander. Even the nomenclature evoked aquatic fantasia: an island named Treasure with a jewel nearby named Iris Falls, both guarded by another waterfall named Colonnade (Figure 4.8). Turning unwanted intruders away at the canyon mouth were more things water: a large swamp at our elevation, and above, two sentinels looking out over the meadows beyond, Ouzel Falls and Ranger Lake (perched just beyond the canyon rim). Around every bend in the trail were watery surprises, cold water springs gushing forth the snowmelt from plateaus above, seeps sheltering plants like bog orchid and elk slips, and wet meadows purpled with elephanthead

Figure 4.8: Colonnade Falls, 2006. Both the upper (33 feet) and lower (67 feet) falls drop over the edge of lava flows, which are resistant to erosion. AUTHOR COLLECTION.

and camas. Even the soundscape was aqueous, with gurgles, drips, and frothy roars dominating. Rising above the world of water, though, were the canyon walls, cliffs, and talus piles of lava, reminders that the watery delights have foundations of fire. It was a place and time that would be hard to match, a dreamscape of water, fire, and beauty.

We made our last camp among some open pines looking out over Bechler Meadows, which extend three or four miles to the south (Figure 4.9). The meadows are wet in spring and early summer, too wet for the trees that grow in Yellowstone, which prefer well-drained soils. Some years the meadows are *really* wet, as I told the group, relating the experience of US Army Scout Peter Holte and an unnamed companion on a spring trip through Bechler Meadows more than a century before us. The two had left the Snake River Soldier Station at the South Entrance on May 12, 1902, arriving in the meadows the next day. There was still snow on ground, so the two were skiing, but melting snow and rain were not making the travel easy. The snow was slushy and heavy, and even small streams were swollen with runoff, forcing them to find alternate ways to cross. On small streams, they felled nearby trees and crossed on them, but on the Bechler River, they had to make a small raft, paddling across and landing on the other side some distance below. Bechler Meadows had become a lake two miles in diameter, so they skied where possible and waded in other areas. When they got within five or six hundred yards of the now-gone Bartlett Patrol Cabin near our campsite, they had to detour two miles to get to it, the cabin being almost surrounded by the lake—and the only dry route to it was a narrow isthmus just a few inches from going under.

Things didn't get any easier once the two scouts finally made it to the cabin. The building itself was falling apart, the roof having collapsed in two places and leaking everywhere else as though the rest of it were about to finish the destruction. Over-

Figure 4.9: Bechler Meadows from near Ranger Lake, 2003. The Bechler River meanders through the meadows as storm clouds exit the skies. Our last campsite was at the right edge of the lower right meadow. AUTHOR COLLECTION.

night, it rained heavily, raising the lake level two or three feet and inundating the isthmus, leaving them and their pseudo-shelter on an island of questionable aridity. Holte and his companion realized their adventures with a raft were not over, so using some nails from the cabin and some logs from a nearby corral, they built a new raft and prepared themselves for a second—and much longer—voyage the next day. The rain again continued all night, expanding the lake to three or more miles across and within ten feet of lapping on the cabin door. Putting their now-useless skis on the raft along with their packs, they launched their ship of salvation and poled their way across the lake. Soon enough, they found the Bechler River, the only moving water in the vast snowmelt lake—and the only clue they'd reached the river. They floated down river, watching beaver splash around them and six elk swim across the river (forlorn both species probably were, evicted from their homes by the rising floodwaters). When they reached the trail back to the Snake River Soldier Station, they disembarked, tied the raft to a tree, and took off on a wet hike home, frequently wading above their knees in frigid snowmelt. Once they reached the station, Holte and his partner had to spend an extra day there before proceeding back to Mammoth Hot Springs while Holte recovered from his aggravated rheumatism, three days of wading through cold water being not what the doctor ordered.

Holte's account shows how wet Bechler Meadows can be, under natural conditions. We found them dry and lovely, the more so as the evening progressed, because the sun finally emerged from behind the clouds. But, as I also told the others that evening, were it not for equally gallant efforts by Holte's successors, the meadows might have become a whole lot wetter, permanently—and, in a big way, unnaturally. The trouble started in 1919, when potato and sugar beet farmers in southern Idaho suffered widespread crop losses from a crippling drought. Wanting more irrigation water to prevent future losses, they looked around for potential reservoir sites and found a good one on the Fall River (into which the Bechler flows), in the very meadows we were camped on. This may have been the same topographic feature that had created Holte's lake, a pinch point on the river where it exits the meadows. Approaching Secretary of the Interior Franklin K. Lane with their proposal, they found him receptive to the idea. That was not surprising, for Lane had successfully lobbied for the Hetch Hetchy impoundment in Yosemite National Park six years earlier. Indeed, Lane quickly ordered NPS Director Stephen Mather to both allow a survey of the proposed reservoir (and Yellowstone Lake, which a similar group of farmers in Montana proposed to deepen), and also to author a report favoring both projects. Mather refused to write the paper, and

Yellowstone Superintendent Horace Albright tried to stymie the surveys, but the surveyor nonetheless reported favorably on the two proposals. While the Bechler reservoir would have been modest by today's standards—maybe 25 feet deep—it would have flooded all of Bechler Meadows, backing water up well past our campsite, almost to the foot of Colonnade Falls.

The National Park Service was the new kid in the neighborhood, having just been created in 1916, and with the dam in Yosemite on its way to reality, things were not looking good for Yellowstone. But conservationists nationwide realized the situation's difficulties and import, and went to work throughout 1920 to defeat the proposals, relentlessly organizing support among the park-loving public and like-minded politicians. They argued that reservoirs had no place in national parks, where their wildly varying water levels would destroy important wildlife habitat, expose ugly mud flats, and severely tarnish the natural beauty. New Jersey conservationist William C. Gregg (for whom the fork of the Bechler is named) explored Cascade Corner, finding a wealth of waterfalls and cascades, more than in the rest of the entire park. Furthermore, conservationists argued the dams would second the dangerous precedent set in Yosemite, effectively opening all national parks to commercial exploitation, to the detriment of the American people. Finally, there were better, more functional reservoir sites outside Yellowstone. By year's end, conservationists and the NPS had turned the tide, and both proposals fell to ignominious deaths early the following year, failing to advance to floor votes in Congress. It helped that secretary Lane had moved on by then and that his successor, John B. Payne, was as much a park defender as Lane had been a reclamationist. The Bechler proposal resurfaced five years later with the reservoir site to be excised from Yellowstone, the excision to be compensated by a larger park addition to the north. That proposal suffered another justified death by a government committee investigating several proposed boundary adjustments at the time; it was unimpressed by the proposal's merits. Cascade Corner's protection has not been threatened since, thanks to the tireless efforts of many farsighted defenders generations ago.

Relishing our view of the intact meadows, we watched the shadows lengthen and turned in for the last time. Our last day dawned clear and cold, with frost on the tents. Before we could begin the hike out, we had to ford the Bechler River. This final encounter with it was freezing, a painfully cold farewell kiss from the river that had brought us so much pleasure (Figure 4.10). Three miles of hiking across the meadows awaited us on the other riverbank, a ninety-minute walk with the new snow on the Teton Mountains shining to the southeast. Beyond the meadows was another three-mile walk through a lodgepole pine

Figure 4.10: Drying off from fording the Bechler River, 2003. Phil and Mo are at right, sitting on the blobs (perhaps the best use for the ungainly backpacks). From here it was a quick six miles to the trailhead. AUTHOR COLLECTION.

forest, an anticlimax to the wonders we'd been immersed within
for the past several days. And at the end of the trail, our vehicles awaited us, ready to whisk us away to home, hot showers,
and relief for aching muscles and tired backs. We were done
with the hike—including Phil and Mo and the blobs—and
with Yellowstone's Bechler area, but it was not done with us.
The experiences we had and memories we'd made would sink
into our hearts and minds in the following weeks and months,
becoming part of our persona. Vast and indomitable geologic,
atmospheric, and ecological forces had set an impressive stage
for us. Spending a week in the essential Yellowstone, we came
face-to-face with those forces, an encounter made the more indelible by the social and emotional bonds we had made. The experience was humbling, awesome, and intimate, a direct view of
the real Yellowstone, a place of beauty, power, and community.
Moreover, we saw that Yellowstone has long moved us to embrace and protect it, as it will probably always do. Yellowstone
is a living reminder of the natural beauty that once surrounded
us everywhere but which we have too frequently eliminated or
tarnished. Indeed, Bechler's history shows us that we can do
better—much better—at inhabiting and stewarding our world.

An Autumn Hike
Through the Thorofare

When a geographer plots all roads in the contiguous 48 states
and then looks at the results, the American West practically
jumps off the page (Figure 4.11). Almost all other regions of
the country are thick with roads, their density thick enough to
color the states east of the Rockies solid gray, with cities easy to
discern as nodes and strips of black. The west coast is similar, a
thin strip of gray and black extending from Canada to Mexico.

Between that strip and the plains is the West, its road density too thin to color the map darker than a blotchy light gray. Denver, Phoenix, and Salt Lake City appear as islands of black in a sea of comparative roadlessness. Here and there the shading disappears entirely, islands of a different kind. These are the completely roadless areas, places of nothingness if your objective is to drive somewhere. To me and many other wilderness fans, though, these blank spots are the places of greatest interest. Most of them are the wilderness areas protected in perpetuity under the 1964 Wilderness Act, or other roadless chunks of land in the national parks, forests, and other federal lands.[1] They are the places of remoteness, the most evocative hidden gems. They conjure images of solitude, wilderness, wildness, freedom, openness, and beauty. They are the stuff of imagination and desire, places that salve the heart and mind, places that stimulate wanderlust and longing, places that challenge and create. Far from being empty lands, they are the most cherished and powerful, places without which we would be less as a society.

And they are scarce. If you define remoteness as distance to the nearest road and compute the most remote points of the blank spots, you may be disappointed to learn that in all the contiguous states, only fifteen of the blank spots contain a point more than ten miles from the nearest road. Four of those places are in or near Yellowstone: the Bechler, the Mirror Plateau / Upper Lamar area, the Absaroka / Beartooth Wilderness just north of the park, and the Thorofare, containing the country's most remote point outside of Alaska. In the fur-trapping era, a foot route within this sprawling wilderness was an easy way to get on the Yellowstone plateau from the Jackson Hole area, providing it with its somewhat anachronistic name. Today, the

---

1   Some of the others are military installations and bombing ranges, wildlife refuges, and desert lands.

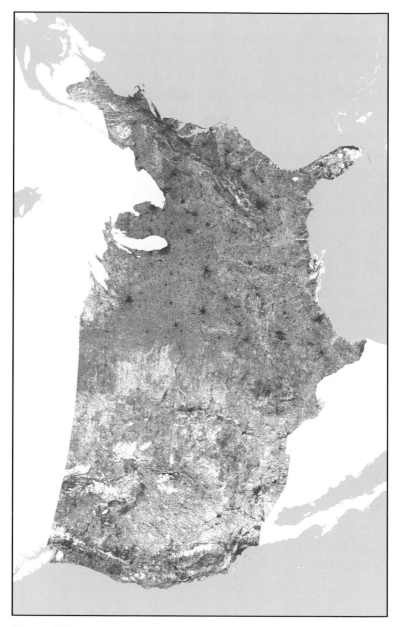

Figure 4.11

Figure 4.11: Map of US road system, by Eric Compas. Each road is a thin gray line, and all roads are shown, regardless of level of improvement. Black areas are places with a high road density, such as cities, while white areas are places with no roads, such as national park backcountry. Dark gray areas are places with a moderate road density, such as farmland, while light gray areas have a low road density, such as national forests. Roads not only delineate the level of overall development and, in their absence, the National Wilderness Preservation System (federal lands preserved as wilderness pursuant to the Wilderness Act), but also other geographic features of interest, including the large agricultural valleys of the West (Idaho's Snake River Plain and California's Central Valley are particularly evident), some state boundaries (because definitions of what constitutes a road differ by state, notably in North Dakota), and other protected lands (Adirondack Park in New York, and the mountains of the Pacific Coast states and New England).

Thorofare is anything but a thoroughfare, a 2,600-square-mile wilderness consisting of Yellowstone's southeast corner, the Washakie Wilderness in the Shoshone National Forest, and the Teton Wilderness in the Bridger-Teton National Forest. With only foot paths and trails for routes of travel, the Thorofare is big and remote, its remotest point almost nineteen miles from a road. To get there, you must shoulder a backpack weighing over fifty pounds or hire an outfitter to take you in on horseback. Either way, you're in for a weeklong journey, a trip few people undergo. The Thorofare's wonders are indeed well guarded— but lavished upon those who make the effort to get there and experience it.

Once I obtained maps that did not depict the Thorofare as a blank spot, I started to plan a hike through it. I was stymied for a few years by a lack of hiking partners, by injuries in those would-be hiking partners, and difficulties getting a week off in the summer / fall hiking season, which was also the busy summer tourist season. The stars finally aligned in 1993, an October trip that brought Carla and me scurrying out earlier than planned when a powerful storm besieged us with a full day of rain and a chaser of snow. That abbreviated sample of the Thorofare was still enough to bring me back for more two years later and many summers thereafter. Some years I didn't get there, but other years I had the good fortune to get there twice. Both 2002 and 2003 featured multiple trips; this story is from the first of those fulfilling years, and the next story is from the second one. The 2002 hike was with two former roommates of mine, both named Mike. With me bearing the same name, we were the three Mikes, each of us bearing a nickname for this trip: Elder Mike (Stevens), who was a generation older than the other two of us; The Imp, a fitting descriptor for the youngest and shortest group member (and who usually preferred to go by his middle name, Sean [Miculka]); and Yogi, a nickname Sean had given me years earlier, cueing from my last name (an experience on the hike would provide a different, perhaps more fitting inspiration for my moniker).

With these ways of distinguishing between us, we set off on a nine-day, 90-mile hike that, owing to our personalities and group makeup, included more moments of levity than most of my hikes. The first happened just five miles in on the trail to Heart Lake, the same trail I'd taken fifteen years earlier to climb Mount Sheridan. The three Mikes had stopped at Paycheck Pass, the high point of land the Heart Lake ranger has to climb to get to his hard-earned pay, to admire the view and eat lunch. The land at our feet dropped off to the Witch Creek Valley, ending at the lake two miles away. It was a tranquil scene, the quintessential Yellowstone: mountains, meadows, a lake, and steam rising from hot springs here and there. The September sunshine was warm, so we sat in the shade of some trees the '88 fires had missed. Chatting among ourselves, Elder Mike gradually became somewhat difficult to understand because he had stuffed most of his lunch in his cheeks, much like a chipmunk. I wondered if, given our late September start, he was stocking up on food, fearing a replay of the blizzard that had stranded early park explorer Truman Everts in the very geyser basin we were looking at, in 1870. Or maybe his food caching was part of his grizzly bear survival strategy, where if he was treed by a bear, he would have a meal with him. However amusing those scenarios might have been, I knew the real reason was that "men are pigs," as my mother says after raising four boys. Having shared a room and many meals with Elder Mike, I had become accustomed to his habits and gently correcting him when needed. He was a loveable and funny guy, so I told him I couldn't understand him when he was mimicking a chipmunk. He got the hint, swallowed the food, and didn't repeat the charade for the rest of the hike. Evidently, he decided that, for all its merits, oral food storage was best left to the perky, furry experts—or he didn't want to chance acquiring a certain two-syllable nickname (maybe both).

Our lunch and laughs done for the moment, we descended to the lake and walked partway around its north shore before making camp. The site featured a commanding view of Mount Sheridan rising mightily up from Heart Lake, the mountain's face covered with landslides old and young and in various stages of revegetation. Numerous faults crisscross the face, shattering and pulverizing the bedrock and leaving unstable slopes that slide with fault movement or excessive soil wetting. We enjoyed a tasty dinner, broke out my mini cribbage board, and played a couple games. Elder Mike and Yogi duked it out with cards and pegs while The Imp looked on, learning the game. Before sunrise the next day, we rose to frost on the tents and watched the rising sun light the mountain on fire, a show that was perhaps the inspiration for the range's name, the Red Mountains. Warming his hands on his coffee mug, The Imp asked Elder Mike for a word of wisdom to start the day off well. Without hesitation, Elder Mike quipped something like, "What did the mama buffalo say to her baby buffalo as he left for his first day of school? Bison!" The Imp and I groaned, and recognizing an opportunity for some daily levity, The Imp repeated the request every day thereafter, always with an impish grin. Elder Mike obliged every day, always with a groaner, some memorable, others less so. The third morning, recognizing the same impish grin, Elder Mike bestowed the name The Imp on him, an indication that the three Mikes were gelling into a convivial group.

Hiking again, we left the lake behind and began ascending the open and intimate Outlet Creek Valley. At its head was a small lake of the same name, where we stopped for lunch. It was a peaceful place, the lake the size of a large pond and backed by a forest of mostly burned trees (Figure 4.12). The setting was a little different when I passed through nine years earlier, when Carla and I were hustling out of the Thorofare in front of that winter storm. The storm had hit with a full day of rain, the cold and steady kind that seeps through the best rain gear and leads to hypothermia. We had eaten lunch then at Outlet Lake as well, hunkered down under a spruce tree, the last dry spot we saw until we let ourselves in the patrol cabin at Heart Lake hours later. It was one of the wettest days of hiking I'd ever had—but even that was nothing compared to what this place was like in the glacial era some ten or twelve thousand years ago. That ice dam had formed in the center of Yellowstone, preventing the Yellowstone River from draining to the north as it does today. Yellowstone Lake rose until it found a new outlet, that which bears the name now. Roaring down the 200-foot-tall hill we were about to climb, the lake waters hit bottom and turned southwest, carving out the valley we'd just hiked up, before emptying into Heart Lake. It must have been a sight to behold: the river that was quite a bit larger than the modern-day Yellowstone, thundering down the steep hill and swirling in an

Figure 4.12: Outlet Lake, 2002. This peaceful pond has a far different past, for not only did the 1988 fires burn the forest around it, but the lake itself was scoured out by the glacial Yellowstone Lake outlet river, crashing down a 200-foot cascade that hit bottom here. AUTHOR COLLECTION.

aquatic maelstrom at the bottom. Outlet Lake owes its existence to that maelstrom, the falling torrent churning and scouring out the bottom as if in a rage that something had dared cut short its appointment with gravity. It was hydropower on steroids, quite the opposite of the quiet experience the three Mikes enjoyed.

Departing the lake with a turbulent past, we shifted into low gear for the climb up the once-great cascade. That was a small hill by Yellowstone standards, and Elder Mike motored right up it, but not without introducing us to a mantra he would repeat on every climb thereafter. It was short—just two words—but it succinctly expressed his opinion of backpacking: "the weight!" He never inserted an epithet between the two words, but I had the sense that he was doing so in his mind. Mike was known for his ability to hike twenty miles or more in a day, but he rarely shouldered a full-size backpack. Even so, he would tote his weight the full ninety miles without a hitch, two spoken words at a time, plus an unknown number of unspoken ones.

Elder Mike's experience on that first hill was, perhaps, not unlike that of a certain fish in Yellowstone Lake: Yellowstone cutthroat trout. The fish is a west-slope species, found primarily west of the Continental Divide, in rivers and lakes that drain to the Pacific Ocean. Yet they are native to Yellowstone Lake, whose waters end up in the Atlantic Ocean. Fish cannot swim over the divide, but if the divide shifts on them, as it would have when the ice dam formed (sending the lake's water to the Pacific Ocean via the Snake and Columbia Rivers) and again when it broke (sending its water back to the Atlantic Ocean via the Yellowstone, Missouri, and Mississippi Rivers), the cutthroat may have been able to colonize the lake. By swimming and jumping up the 200-foot cascade, they would have been in Yellowstone Lake, and by remaining there when the ice dam broke and the glacial lake drained to its present level, they would have been in for good. That's if they could overcome the raging torrent that created Outlet Lake. Cascading waterfalls sometimes have slack water and pools off to the side where fish can rest before resuming their attempt to surmount the falls, so it's possible they stair-stepped up that way, but I have my doubts. There would have been a tremendous volume of water pouring over, and the slope was steep. For these reasons, the glacial outlet has mostly been dismissed as the likely colonization route. There must have been another way—and indeed there was, and still is, as we would see on our way out of the Thorofare.

After another two hours of hiking down a valley similar to the one we'd just traveled up, we reached our campsite for the night. It was another lovely site, at the very southern tip of Yellowstone Lake's South Arm. If the previous campsite's view was mountain glorious, this one's view was landscape moody (Figure 4.13). A shadowed foreground of grasses cured by frost and sun gave way to a narrow finger of lake, scattered pockets of darkened pines kissing the shore. Beyond the finger, a strip of fire-killed forest stretched across the mid-ground, practically glowing in a shaft of sunlight breaking through the atmospheric armor above. That strip was almost white, the trees having shed their bark long ago, leaving the naked trees to bleach in the summer sun. Shadows resumed beyond the finger of light, continuing to the distant Absarokas, their slopes competing with the clouds in a contest of the blues. The mountains, which looked like a high bumpy ridge at that distance, were in the lead, the dark forest-cloaked slopes approaching indigo. It was a scene of brooding power, slowly growing darker as we supped, transfixed by the unfolding landscape drama. It was hard not to be impressed with this celebration of life, human and natural.

Figure 4.13: Sunset at the end of the South Arm, 2002. A nearby cement monument, two feet tall, has the initials "S. P. Y. L.," which stand for "Southernmost Point of Yellowstone Lake." As specified in Yellowstone's 1872 enabling legislation, the park's south boundary was to be the parallel ten miles south of that point. AUTHOR COLLECTION.

Underway the next morning, we traded one arm of the lake for another (South for Southeast), and were about to leave it behind when we were stopped dead in our tracks by a local resident. I was in the lead when I—that is, Yogi—looked up to see a lone grizzly bear walking toward me, about a hundred yards away. I stopped abruptly, grabbed my bear spray from the holster, and began backing slowly to the relative safety of the other two Mikes. They arrived in less time than it seemed, pulled out their bear spray cans, and clustered together with me, all of us moving slowly backwards and watching the bear to see what it would do. Once it saw that there were three of us, it stopped and left the trail, walking calmly away from us and the lake, but standing up once to look at us, as if it had second thoughts about giving way to mere humans. The bear's attitude said it all: this was its home and we were uninvited guests. We meant nothing to it, and it would avoid direct conflict for now, but we had best be moving along. We decided not to argue and were on our way quickly, Yogi hoping his nickname did not somehow predispose him to more ursine encounters.

Before long, we left the lakeshore and arrived at the delta, the utterly flat plain where the Yellowstone River slows, meanders, and drops some of its sediment load before entering Yellowstone Lake. Initially, our trail paralleled the delta for a couple miles, going upstream to avoid the extensive marshes and willow bottoms near the river's mouth. Once we reached *terra firma,* the trail struck out across the flats. There the delta and river valley are two to three miles wide, with the river at the far eastern edge. We stopped for lunch partway across, a stop made memorable because it was chilly even with the sun shining. Another hour of hiking warmed us up again, preparing us for the Yellowstone River ford at the far side. That time of year, the crossing is only knee-deep, but the water was icy. We forded easily and continued to our campsite at the base of Turret Mountain, an aptly named rock sentinel 10,000 feet high with nearly unscalable cliffs all around (Figure 4.14). It was another premier site, made the more special because it could have been under water or at the edge of a smelly, ugly expanse of mud had reclamationists succeeded in raising the level of Yellowstone Lake at the time when the Bechler dams were proposed. In fact, everything we had hiked that day (except for some of the higher land between the two arms) would have been under water. Adding 25 or 30 feet to the lake level would have given the farmers in Montana (where the Yellowstone now flows upon leaving the park) far more water than the proposed Bechler reservoir, because the lake is many times the size of Bechler Meadows. So much, in

Figure 4.14: Turret Mountain (right) and Colter Peak above the Yellowstone River delta, 2002. This meadow and all the land extending to the base of the peaks would have been under 25-30 feet of water had Montana reclamationists succeeded in raising the level of nearby Yellowstone Lake. NPS leaders and conservationists nationwide joined together to successfully defeat several dam proposals in the 1920s and 30s, and again in 1991. AUTHOR COLLECTION.

fact, that the idea of raising Yellowstone Lake's level came up two additional times, as recently as 1991! Thankfully, the NPS and its conservationist allies prevailed in those assaults on Yellowstone Lake's integrity, as they had with the Bechler. One of those conservationist friends was Franklin Delano Roosevelt, who visited the park in 1937. Upon seeing Yellowstone Lake and learning of the reclamation proposal being debated then, the President told park superintendent Edmund Rogers, "You do not need to worry, Mr. Rogers, no one will ever be permitted to touch that lake." We do indeed stand on the shoulders of visionary heroes, those who sacrificed their time and energy to give everyone the unsullied national park we have today.

That night was the coldest of the trip: 22° F., a second indication that a cold front had blown in that day. It was autumn in the Thorofare, a time of crisp nights, glorious sunny days, bugling elk, and color. Once we thawed and broke camp, we had an easy day of hiking up the Yellowstone River Valley. This was the trapper's thoroughfare for good reason: it was almost flat for the next fifteen miles, and when the route leaves the Yellowstone and climbs up to the Continental Divide, it barely ascends 200 feet. Elder Mike had little reason to express his two-word opinion that day or the next, following the Thorofare. Flanking the Yellowstone River Valley are two high plateaus, the Two Ocean on the west and the Trident on the other. Both names reflect their geography, the one bisected by the Divide and the other splitting into three ridges on its western face, much like Satan's lance. Both plateaus end abruptly in thousand-foot cliffs above the Thorofare, their feet shorn off by the mighty glacier that once occupied, sculpted, and deepened that valley. Melting away ten or twelve thousand years ago, nature's sculptor transitioned from solid to liquid, and the Yellowstone River began depositing sediment, enough to turn the glacial U-shaped valley into the pancake-flat and vertically sided corridor we have today. Surrounded by 10,000-foot plateaus and higher peaks, the Thorofare is indeed a natural route through the mountains, as much for fur trappers two centuries ago as for the three Mikes and other wilderness explorers today (Figure 4.15).

Walking the fur trapper's thoroughfare was a delight, an ever-changing tapestry of life and color. Forests burned and unburned, meadows moist and dry, and vistas near and far greeted us around every bend of the trail. Thorofare vegetation was already a patchwork of meadow and forest when the 1988 fires moved through, making the mosaic even more diverse. Other smaller fires since then have furthered the mix, so that today the wilderness traveler passes through stands of green trees (their cover holding on to the night's chill), bright green sapling lodgepole pine (some thickets too dense to walk through,

Figure 4.15: Yellowstone's Thorofare, 2001. The northern and middle prongs of The Trident rise above the Yellowstone River Valley. This broad valley was part of the fur trapper's thoroughfare, a natural route of travel from Jackson Hole to the Yellowstone plateau. Colter Peak is in the distance. AUTHOR COLLECTION.

others quite open), and burned openness (the ghostly silver snags whistling in the afternoon breeze) (Figure 4.16). Fireweed graced the more open stands of burned trees, the very name confirming the plant's importance in revegetating burned areas and stabilizing the soil. The pink and purple flowers were gone a month ago, their color migrating to the senescing leaves and evolving to crimson and yellow. Meadows broke the forest into patches large and small, the largest openings concentrated in the southern part of the valley. Sedges, still holding on to some chlorophyll in late September, dominated the wetter meadows, while grasses, cured to golden by the autumn sun, prevailed in the drier ones. Waist-high willows, their leaves a frosted yellow, displaced the sedges from the wettest habitats. Towering above

Figure 4.16: Two Ocean Plateau and the upper Yellowstone River Valley, 2006. A diversity of vegetation greets the Thorofare traveler today, just as it did for the trappers two centuries ago: forests and meadows, large and small, burned and unburned, wet and dry, old and young. Nature's forces dominate in this huge wilderness. AUTHOR COLLECTION.

this land of plenty were the ramparts of the Trident and Two Ocean, their escarpments dusky red in sun and dusky brown in shadow. Afternoon breezes carried the sounds and scents of autumn: the rustle and rattle of leaves already gone dry, the squeals of distant bull elk bugling, the aromas of warmth and grass. We were charmed by that journey, one that still evokes feelings of excitement and promise, connecting us to the Thorofare and its wonders today as surely as it did for trappers two centuries ago and Native Americans for millennia before them.

Like the rising sun at Heart Lake, the setting sun set the landscape on fire that night, turning the meadows into fields of gold and the cliffs into fortresses of ochre. We camped at the north end of Yellowstone Meadows, which sprawls southward to the base of Hawk's Rest, the rounded mountain that brings together the waters of the Yellowstone River and its largest wilderness tributary, Thorofare Creek. After a night that was not so cold, we resumed our journey, hiking through the meadows, exiting Yellowstone Park and entering the Teton Wilderness, and fording Thorofare Creek and the outlet of Bridger Lake, a scenic jewel nestled between the Yellowstone and its tributary. On an earlier trip through the Thorofare, I had camped by the lake and saw what appeared to be a log floating across it. Doing a double-take, I realized it was a bull moose swimming across the lake's narrow mid-point. As I saw then, moose are excellent swimmers—and they are not the only mammal that likes the Thorofare's aquatic habitats, as we soon discovered after leaving the lake and crossing the Yellowstone. Not ten minutes later, we had to don our stream-crossing sandals again, for the trail had become part of a beaver pond. For at least a quarter-mile, the trail was under icy cold water, as was everything around it. Our toes going numb, we trudged through the shin-deep water and made it through. Along with the grizzly we'd bumped into and the elk that continued to serenade us, there were abundant signs that the Thorofare is an inhabited landscape, populated with wildlife as diverse and dynamic as its vegetation.

The beaver had impounded Atlantic Creek, which was our pleasure to follow beyond the beaver pond. It meant, though, that we had to part ways with the Yellowstone and its magnificent valley. Pausing at the last vista, we savored all that we had seen and experienced. That morning, we had traversed the vicinity of the most remote point, the place farther from a road than any other in the contiguous states. There are other definitions of remoteness to be sure, other places equally difficult to reach (perhaps more so), places without maintained trails, places that require specialized climbing or boating skills and equipment, places that demand bushwhacking through scrub, poison oak, and thorns. True enough, but few of them have the extent and diversity of wild country, wildlife, and wild forces creating and changing the land as the Thorofare. That land is indeed one of riches, a sea of wildness, a place of beauty, a landscape for the soul and the spirit.

With a final look, we turned and began ascending Atlantic Creek. It treated us to another ford, one that evoked the earlier beaver pond splash dance. This one was aligned with a bend in the stream such that we had to walk in the forty-degree water for about fifty yards, a second price of admission to the upcoming landmark, the Parting of the Waters. Not another Moses reenactment, it is the place where a fish can cross the Continental Divide without leaving water. Picture a flat, linear valley about 500 yards wide, its floor covered in grass and willows, its forested sides partly burned. Halfway through the valley, one crosses an imperceptible high point, a crown of land that sends the two streams draining the valley, Atlantic and Pacific Creeks, flowing in opposite directions. To this point, the valley could be any Rocky Mountain valley bisected by the Continental Divide, but this valley contains something unusual and probably unique.

At the crown of land, North Two Ocean Creek falls down the valley's side, right on the Continental Divide. On reaching the valley floor, the creek splits, the two halves never to rejoin. One half becomes Atlantic Creek, the other Pacific Creek. This is the Parting of the Waters, as a rustic sign on a tree between the two forks, known as distributaries, announces (Figure 4.17). The same sign gives the distance the two waters must flow before reaching their ultimate destinations: 3,488 miles for Atlantic Creek and 1,353 miles for Pacific Creek. Were a certain fish to swim up Pacific Creek to this point in spring (when small North Two Ocean Creek is full with snowmelt), the fish would only need to turn right to be in Atlantic Creek, which becomes part of the Yellowstone River and soon, Yellowstone Lake. This geo-

Figure 4.17: Parting of the Waters, 2002. View is downstream and to the south, showing the split in North Two Ocean Creek. Sean Miculka (The Imp, at left) points to Atlantic Creek, while Mike Stevens (Elder Mike) does the same for Pacific Creek, the two distributaries that will never meet again. In spring, when the stream is full with melting snow, fish can cross the Continental Divide here. AUTHOR COLLECTION.

graphic exception is almost certainly the route cutthroat trout took to colonize Yellowstone Lake, across the Continental Divide, a barrier ordinarily impassable for fish. In recognition of its unique geography, the Parting of the Waters is a National Natural Landmark, a site of outstanding national geological or ecological interest.[2]

The first time I visited this place was with Carla, ten years earlier. Unbeknownst to us at the time, we had made camp right between the two distributaries. We soon realized the significance of that campsite, and I wanted to give The Imp and Elder Mike the same experience, but the site was occupied (an unusual occurrence). So, we backtracked a quarter mile to another campsite, saving the visit for the next day, when I knew we would hike right past the landmark. After another night of cribbage and good-natured banter, we awoke to more frost and blue sky. We were underway quickly, Elder Mike anxious to see a place he had long waited to experience. Photographing the two of them pointing to the two distributaries, I wondered if the Parting had ever been so endeared, so treasured as it was that morning. Regretfully, we soon left it and the trapper's thoroughfare, climbing 2000 feet to the South Two Ocean Plateau. By the time we reached the top, I could have sworn I heard a perceptible pause in Elder Mike's refrain, as in, "the … weight!" Whether he was interjecting a silent expletive or just gasping for breath in the thinning air, I don't know, but once again, he didn't let any distance develop between himself and his two younger hiking partners. At the top, we paused for lunch and the view, a 360-degree panorama of mountains, grassy plateau, and beauty. The breezy prairie was auburn in the autumn sunshine and dot-

---

2 There is a South Two Ocean Creek, but I have not been able to visit it. The USGS topographic map does not show it splitting like its equal across the valley.

ted with azure ponds and scattered clumps of trees, near perfect elk habitat. The Tetons punctuated the western horizon while the Absarokas did the same on the eastern one. It was a sky parlor of life, color, and remoteness, a culmination of sorts for an exceptional wilderness tour.

Crossing the plateau and descending its northern slope, we turned west and made camp for the night in Fox Park, another large meadow. The remaining three days put an exclamation point on the themes we'd been experiencing: life, beauty, remoteness, connection. I told the other two about the griz I had seen the year before in Fox Park just as I unzipped the tent to start breakfast. It fled the scene, but not before I had jolted Carla from her slumber and scrambled to find my bear spray. We saw no bear this time, but we did see another beaver dam and regular indications that this is a home for many. We struggled together to get through a two-mile stretch of trail obliterated by fire-killed trees that had fallen on it and that had not been cleared, walking on and hopping from log to log, sometimes five feet off the ground. We got pelted with graupel one evening and later awakened by our neighbor's horses walking through our campsite, the bells on their necks tolling their location (and coming dangerously close to Elder Mike, shivering in his bivouac shelter). We laughed at Elder Mike's words of wisdom, his lack of them the last two mornings, The Imp's bantering with the elder. We shared more campfires, more cribbage games, more communal meals, more camaraderie. We reentered the park, spending our final night at a park campsite. And on the last day, we sauntered through old-growth spruce and fir forest for the final four miles, and then took our boots off for one more ford across the Snake River, just a hundred yards from the car.

With that, the journey was over, but it would never disappear from our lives and personal experience. The Imp became one of my best friends, Elder Mike a good friend (who surprised Yogi with a heartfelt letter as I was writing this very story). Both of them soon married, their life experience taking new and wonderful turns; I did not, though I did find love. All three of us maintain residence of one kind or another in or near Yellowstone. We can't get Yellowstone out of our lives; it has touched us deeply, permanently, profoundly. The Thorofare hike was in many ways the deepest immersion in the essential Yellowstone for us, a deep dive that I repeated several times (once with Sean the Imp, but not again with Elder Mike). More than most other places in Yellowstone, the Thorofare illustrates the ecological, geological, and atmospheric forces that create Wonderland and the vibrant tapestries that result from them and their interconnections. The area's size and level of protection makes these forces and connections obvious, but its remoteness brings them into sharper relief than elsewhere in Yellowstone. By immersing ourselves within that world for over a week, we were obligated to center ourselves in our surroundings, to see, sense, and focus on the world through which we hiked. To do otherwise would have been to invite injury, accident, and even ruin, as the grizzly bear encounter demonstrated. By exercising restraint and humility, we both traveled safely and also opened ourselves to rewards of insight and emotion. Not only did we come to understand some of the innumerable forces, bonds, and connections that innervate that land, we formed powerful connections to it and to each other. We also realized that, no matter how much we know— or think we know—nature will always hold more secrets, more insights, more depth. Some call this wonder, others mystery; I call it wildness. Whatever the name, it may well be the most wonderful thing about the Thorofare and places like it, for it shows us that we are not even close to understanding nature and we probably never fully will, so there will always be magic in it. The Thorofare teaches us, then, that if we observe and reflect, if we incorporate restraint and humility into our interactions with nature both in the Thorofare and beyond, and if we preserve the vast wilderness for future generations, nature's world of life, connectivity, and beauty will be ours to thrill ourselves within, now and in the future.

Absaroka Journey

Shouldering our packs that August 2003 morning at the Isha-wooa Trailhead in Wyoming's South Fork Valley, I had more than the usual number of butterflies in my stomach. I had long been accustomed to doubts and worries at the beginning of a major expedition, doubts about the risks inherent in wilderness travel (such as a grizzly encounter) and worries that I forgot something important (like the cooking pot on a hike in Zion National Park a few years earlier, which forced me to backtrack a mile to get it). This time, though, the risk seemed more palpable, as a giant forest fire was putting up a massive smoke plume across the valley. The fire itself was out of sight, in another valley beyond the three-thousand-foot-high ridge that looms over the South Fork. My friend Josh Becker and I had climbed that ridge the year before, camping just over the crest on the stream draining Boulder Basin. We had not explored the basin further, leaving it for a future trip. Clearly, the basin would be much different now, making me regret that decision a year ago, even though I knew the fire was renewing the forest there. Today, I knew the fire would not affect us, constrained as it was by this deep, open valley. Fires don't generally burn downhill unless pushed by wind, which was unlikely here, and if that somehow did happen, the fire would stop once it ran out of fuel at the lower treeline. So, with the butterflies assuaged for now, we turned our backs on the fire and started hiking.

That fire was a good allegory for the hike Josh and I were

embarking on, for it was to be a tour of forces big and powerful in the Yellowstone region. The hike itself was to be big
and brawny: a ten-day, one-hundred-mile hike through the
Thorofare (Figure 4.18). More than just a wilderness odyssey,
the hike would put us face-to-face again with the immense,
landscape-scale forces creating and shaping the region. I have
discussed these forces already, along with their immense scale
in the Thorofare, but this hike will also demonstrate the tight
connections Yellowstone has with the wilderness lands around
it, bonds that link Yellowstone inextricably to the ecosystem
of which it is the core. Yellowstone may be the star attraction
there, but it would be nowhere near as wild without the wilderness lands bordering it on all but its western side. The geologic

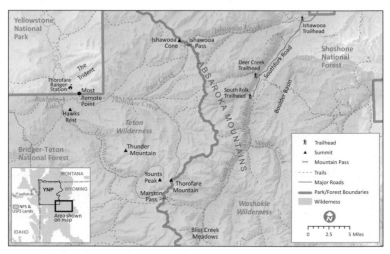

Figure 4.18: Map of Thorofare hike, by Eric Compas. The hike went in a
counter-clockwise direction, beginning at the Ishawooa Trailhead on the
South Fork Road in the northeastern corner of the map. One hundred
miles long, the hike took us through the Washakie Wilderness in the Shoshone National Forest, the southeastern corner of Yellowstone, and the
Teton Wilderness in the Bridger-Teton National Forest, finally ending
back in the Washakie Wilderness.

and atmospheric forces would be little changed if the park stood alone, but the ecological processes, the wildlife, and the sense of wonder those evoke would be seriously compromised without the embracing wilderness areas.

The first four days were a good introduction to these attributes, as we put forty miles of trail between us and the Boulder Basin Fire. That inaugural day was hot, which helped the fire explode, but the evening brought some light rain, which may have put it down some. The second day brought cooler temperatures as we crossed over Ishawooa Pass ("Ishawooa" is a Native American word meaning wet—as in fresh—wolf droppings) and made camp on a knoll above Pass Creek, whose waters we would follow to the heart of the Thorofare. For entertainment that evening we watched a quick shower move across the face of Ishawooa Cone, which towers above the meadow-strewn, flower-filled valley (Figure 4.19). By this point, we were settled into the pleasant wilderness routine that defined our days: warm up with coffee and breakfast in the dawn chill, break camp, hike for a while, take a break for a late morning snack. Hike some more, then have lunch with a view. Hike further, find a place to camp, hop in the creek to clean up, and relax with hor d'oeuvres and a shot of Southern Comfort (or "Soco"). Finish the evening with dinner, lengthening shadows, and sunset, while being serenaded by bugling elk, as we were that evening. Repeat the next day and for the next week, enjoying the amenities of the different campsites, like the swimming hole by our third campsite (if one can call a forty second micro-dip in freezing water "swimming"). It's a comfortable routine, one that centers us in, and binds us to, the wilderness landscape.

On day four, we followed Thorofare Creek (which Pass Creek joins) to the Thorofare Ranger Station in Yellowstone, which is within shouting distance of the most remote point. The ranger there, Brad Ross, invited us to spend the night in a wall tent

Figure 4.19: Ishawooa Cone and the upper Pass Creek Valley, 2003. Most of the trees across the meadow are dead, victims of beetles that invade older forests and that burrow into the cambium of weakened trees. Fires will renew such forests, clearing dead trees and beginning a new forest by opening the serotinous lodgepole pine cones. AUTHOR COLLECTION.

behind the cabin, elevated to keep bears out. We accepted his offer, as well as the hot shower included in the four-star accommodations (the water heated by a campfire kindled within a coil of copper pipe). Brad and I knew each other through work, and we passed the afternoon and evening discussing park and wilderness management. At one point, a grizzly bear walked by, two hundred yards away on the main trail. We watched it amble along, blissfully unaware that we were watching or that the boundary between park and national forest wilderness is nearby. The bear is a good indication that Yellowstone is the center of a much larger ecosystem, for it's unlikely that grizzly bears would persist without the surrounding wildlands. Yellowstone may be a big park, but it is not big enough to sustain a healthy griz population, where every bear needs a hundred square miles or more to forage within. The fire-dominated landscape we'd been hiking through is another example of the park's connections to its neighbors: just as the bear doesn't recognize an arbitrarily drawn boundary, fires don't either. The fire that burned through the Thorofare in 1988 hopped back and forth across that boundary, making a mockery of the two agencies' efforts to administratively "accept" or "refuse" the fire (the fire started in US Forest Service wilderness, was accepted into Yellowstone, but was refused entry when it turned back to the wilderness, all the while doing whatever nature wanted). Even the remotest point depends on the contiguity of park and forest land, together making a much larger piece of protected land than either would possess without the other. In multiple ways, then, Yellowstone and the surrounding wilderness lands are one ecological whole.

Moreover, this is a grand scale ecosystem, with those ecological forces operating on a landscape-wide basis across millions of acres. Fires may be the best example we encountered on that hike, for the only time we were not in fire-dominated vegetation was when we went above treeline later in the trip. As we had seen in the first forty miles, fire is everywhere in the Yellowstone ecosystem, even in the unburned forests of Ishawooa and Pass Creeks. Many of the trees in those two drainages were dead, victims of beetles that tunnel through the cambium, the layer of a tree that brings water and nutrients to its needles. The trees ordinarily defend themselves by flooding the insects out with sap, but as they age, that defense gradually weakens. With so many trees senescing simultaneously, it's possible that they are all the same age, germinating together following a fire that burned much of the drainage(s). Whatever the past history, it's definite that those forests are now ready to burn with so much dry fuel, just as those in the Thorofare Creek Valley did in 1988. We would continue to find fire's signature throughout the Thorofare, from more burned forests to senescent ones wait-

Figure 4.20: Bridger Lake and the slopes of Two Ocean Plateau, 2003. This scenic gem is within a mile or two of the most remote point in the contiguous states, almost nineteen miles to the nearest road. Moose have been seen swimming across the lake. AUTHOR COLLECTION.

ing for a fire, young trees trying to become a forest, and more smoke plumes belying a fire starting a forest anew.

We left Brad and the Thorofare Ranger Station the next morning to follow the Yellowstone River to its source, high in the Absaroka Mountains. We soon got our feet wet crossing Thorofare Creek, and then parted ways with that companion to the Yellowstone River, which the creek joins a couple miles down from the ford. Shortly thereafter, we passed Bridger Lake, the lake I had passed almost a year earlier with the two other Mikes (Figure 4.20). The lake is unusual for the Absaroka Mountains in that it's not up high, at or above treeline. That's because the andesitic lava that comprises most of these mountains is cobbled and fragmented, making it easily eroded. Streams and rivers carry a high sediment load in the Absarokas, especially in spring and early summer when snowmelt brings eroded materials down. When the streams and rivers flow into a lake, they slow, losing the kinetic energy necessary to keep the sediments suspended and moving. Consequently, they drop their sediments, filling the lakes in over time. Bridger Lake survives because it is orphaned from both Thorofare Creek and the Yellowstone River, so it receives very little sediment input. Nestled in the crotch between the two, it is probably a kettle pond, formed when the glaciers receded about ten thousand years ago, leaving a large block of ice that the meltwaters flowed around. Sediment deposition from the meltwater built up the land on either side of the block of ice, which eventually melted into the depression left behind, producing the peaceful lake we have today. Most other lakes in the Absarokas are near the headwaters of their drainages, where the input of eroded sediments is not large, allowing them to persist. Elsewhere, the lakes have been filled with sediments, producing the meadows that pepper the river valleys, like the one we were soon hiking through.

For close to seven flat and scenic miles, we hiked along Yellowstone Meadows, finally reaching its upper end just shy of the 8000-foot elevation mark (Figure 4.21). As it happens, that is the same elevation where we first encountered large meadows hiking down Thorofare Creek the day before—and of Yellowstone Lake's former outlet at Outlet Lake. This continuity of elevation means that, when glacial Yellowstone Lake was higher and flowing out via Outlet Lake, the Southeast Arm probably extended all the way to here. Just as the Yellowstone does today, the meltwater Yellowstone River and Thorofare Creek would have slowed upon flowing into the lake and dropped the sediment they were carrying, creating a marshy wetland similar to today's delta. This deposition may have pushed the Southeast Arm some, or even all, of the distance from the former delta to the current one, a distance of thirty miles. The erosion and deposition continue today (if at a much reduced level, since

Figure 4.21: Thunder Mountain (at right) and the meadows of the upper Yellowstone River, 2003. The vertical, craggy face of the mountain at left was formed in the glacial era; first, the glacier occupying this valley deepened it, to the extent that mountains on either side came to be held up by the glacier. When the glacier melted away, the mountain no longer had its icy footing, so the entire mountainside collapsed, sliding down to the valley floor. Several such landslides (known as "mass wasting" to geologists) occurred in the Thunder Mountain area. AUTHOR COLLECTION.

the runoff now is just a fraction of that produced by melting glaciers), as we soon saw. Above the meadow's upper end, we crossed the dried and hardened remnant of a debris flow (Figure 4.22). Sometime since 1995, when I had last hiked that trail, a thunderstorm had deluged that area, dropping more rain than the burned slopes above the trail could absorb. The waterlogged, destabilized soil began to move downhill, picking up speed and more soil, along with logs, rocks, and whatever other materials were on the ground. Moving as a muddy, liquid mass, the debris flow continued flowing downhill until the slope began to level out, causing the flow to fan out, pushed by the material still coming down. Eventually, the flow stopped, there being no more loose material to move. It was good evidence that nature continues to sculpt and create the Thorofare, that it is still a dynamic, evolving landscape.

The continuity of the Yellowstone landscape was especially evident the next day, when we took a layover day and climbed nearby Thunder Mountain. From its 11,623-foot summit, we took in half of the Greater Yellowstone Ecosystem (Figure 4.23). The glaciers of the Wind River Mountains glinted in the sunshine a hundred miles to the south, while the Tetons serrated the horizon fifty miles west. To the north, Yellowstone Lake mirrored the sky above it, while the Absarokas surrounded us, their tundra bright green in the sparkling summer sunshine. Extending from the north end of the Wind River Mountains clear to Livingston, Montana fifty miles north of Yellowstone, the Absarokas are the 180-mile-long backbone of the ecosystem geographically, geologically, and ecologically. No other mountain range comes close to constituting as much of the ecosystem (between a fourth and a third of it, depending on how the ecosystem and mountain range are defined). Geologically, the Absarokas wrap around the Yellowstone hot spot on the three sides fronting the volcanic plume, much like a wave be-

Figure 4.22: Remains of a debris flow, Thunder Mountain area, 2003. Fires often destabilize mountain slopes by killing trees and their root systems. This debris flow obliterated the trail, so we walked across it, finding it quite hardened and difficult to walk on. AUTHOR COLLECTION.

ing pushed up by an approaching submarine. And ecologically, the Absarokas contain some of the best wildlife habitat in the ecosystem, including some of the most productive grizzly bear terrain—so good, in fact, that more than half of the bear's range expansion since the 1990s has been in that mountain range. As if to illustrate the Absaroka's centrality and vibrancy, Thunder Mountain gave us views of a smoke plume in the distance, perhaps the Boulder Basin Fire, still burning. Meanwhile, in the foreground were old, now-vegetated landslides, whole mountainsides that collapsed when the glaciers melted away, leaving the slopes without the footing once provided by the ice. With the debris flow continuing the mountain reshaping, these evidences of continuing change were clear illustrations that the Absarokas are very much alive, evolving both ecologically and

Figure 4.23: Josh and the author on Thunder Mountain, 2003. This easterly view takes in the Absaroka Mountains and, in the center horizon, a smoke plume from the Boulder Basin Fire, which drifts to the right. Everything in the view is part of the Thorofare Wilderness Complex, protected in its native condition. AUTHOR COLLECTION.

geologically. Moreover, no boundary lines were evident anywhere in the mountaintop view, reemphasizing the connections between and among Yellowstone and its neighboring national forests. Greater Yellowstone is indeed one ecological, geological, and geographical whole, a homeland of nature, its forces, and its denizens.

That evening was a pleasant one, made the more special because we enjoyed our Soco on the rocks (snow from a mountaintop drift that I had packed into one of my water bottles). The next morning dawned overcast with light rain falling, a promise of coolness for the day's hiking, which featured a climb of almost two thousand feet. Breakfast consumed, we resumed hiking up the Yellowstone, turning south where the river's two forks join and heading for the two meadows that grace the river's South Fork. The trail to the emerald twins had not improved in the eight years since I'd been that way previously (the worst two miles of the trip), but the reward was still worth the sweat and effort. We made camp on a knoll overlooking the upper meadow, one of my favorite campsites anywhere. Under a dramatic sky of dark but broken clouds, the South Fork of the Yellowstone—just the size of a small creek there—wended its way through a subalpine patchwork of knee-high willow, sedge, and grass, their complementary shades of green a verdant quilt of summer exuberance (Figure 4.24). Pulling the departing storm hither and yon were Younts Peak and Thorofare Mountain, both rising half a mile above the meadow, catching the clouds and wringing moisture from them to nourish the fledgling river. The shoulders and slopes of the two guardians were clothed with vertical strips of forest and avalanche path, the one barely persevering in a climate not really meant for trees, the other the paths of snowslides that make it totally impossible for any trees at all to grow. Landslides created both meadows, creating lakes that the South Fork filled with sediment, producing the two

Figure 4.24: The upper meadow on the South Fork of the Yellowstone, 2003. Younts Peak (at left) and Thorofare Mountain rise above the meadow and capture the clouds. Both mountains are easily climbed, allowing one to be temporary lords of the wilderness, source of the longest free-flowing river in the 48 contiguous states. AUTHOR COLLECTION.

serene fields of green. It was a wild splendor of land and sky, one that embodied nature's forces, past and present, as much or more than any western landscape.

The Yellowstone's two forks cradle Younts Peak, surrounding it on all sides and receiving all of its runoff. Doubling their force at their confluence, the two forks assume one name and flow north and a little west through Yellowstone and for another fifty miles north of the park. When the Yellowstone reaches the northern end of the Absarokas, it turns east, not to waver from that direction until it ends in the Missouri River, just over the state line in North Dakota. All told, the river flows more than 670 miles without a single dam impeding its flow, making it the longest free-flowing river in America, outside of Alaska.[3] Two other major western rivers also get their start in the Greater Yellowstone Ecosystem: the Green, one of the Colorado's largest tributaries, and the Snake, also a major tributary, this time for the Columbia. All of these rivers are heavily utilized for recreation, freight shipment, power generation, irrigation, and drinking water, by tens of millions of people from Washington State to Louisiana and from California to North Dakota. It is easy to see the many connections, in places quite distant from the Northern Rockies, we have to the rivers of Greater Yellowstone. The entire American West is, to some extent, dependent on the clean water the Greater Yellowstone Ecosystem provides—without the reservoirs proposed in days gone by.

Late August at almost ten thousand feet can be cold, as the frost on the tent the next morning attested. Breakfast may have been hot, but we were not, the sun slow to rise above the ridge on the meadow's south side. We departed in the frosty shadows, wearing rain pants as insulation against the frost-covered willows overhanging the trail. Soon, we were past the meadow and climbing again, this time to the very headwaters. The trail was rocky, but soon the headwaters began to come into view, a wide and wild alpine basin between Younts Peak and Thorofare Mountain (Figure 4.25). A meltwater creek tumbling down the mountainside opposite us marked our entry into the gathering place. Other rivulets emanated from residual snowbanks, trickling downhill and coalescing in the basin to form one fork of the Yellowstone. Here and there a clump of wildflowers still bloomed, in defiance of (or denial about) autumn's imminent arrival. The basin, too, was still green, the tundra plants seemingly unwilling to stop photosynthesis this early, still trying to

---

3 There are a few weirs that divert some of its flow for irrigation, but these are not considered impoundments.

Figure 4.25: Thorofare Mountain and the very headwaters of the Yellowstone River, 2003. The South Fork is in the ravine in the foreground, small enough for almost anyone to hop. The basin is at 11,000 feet above sea level; the mountaintop, above 12,000 feet. AUTHOR COLLECTION.

bank a little more energy for the following summer growing season. The air was crystalline, the atmosphere practically glittering with clarity and purity. The soundscape was also pristine, with only the distant frolic of water, puffs of warming air, and our boot footfalls. We had that world to ourselves, passersby in a place that has never seen long-term human habitation, perhaps only a seasonal camp of Native Americans or wilderness travelers like us. It was a place as wild as one can find in the contiguous states, without human development, alteration, or activity. It seemed appropriate for the Yellowstone to arise in that basin, a place every bit as unshackled as the river itself.

Once we had sufficiently regaled ourselves in that special place, we turned to what awaited us: an afternoon of hiking downhill. We crossed out of the headwaters to Marston Pass, from there dropping into the South Fork of the Shoshone River drainage (not to be confused with the South Fork of the Yellowstone we had just left). Sometime that afternoon, we crossed paths with a man on horseback leading a pack string of mules, the first human we had seen in three days. We made camp in a small meadow with a big view, and took a side trip the next morning to a big meadow with a bigger view, Bliss Creek Meadows (another creation of a post-glacial landslide). From there we turned around and followed the rugged South Fork down and out of the wilderness, which took a day and a half. Clouds began building that afternoon, with rain developing overnight. It was the season's first major autumn cold front, which often waits until September, but not that year. Our entire last day was rain-soaked and cold. The worst of the day was fording three or four creeks plus the river, because the absence of sunshine kept them as liquid icicles. If the day was cold (so much so that we skipped lunch, inhaling some power bars instead), the crossings were colder and Needle Creek coldest (perhaps because we had just forded another creek, so our feet were pre-chilled). The best of the day, though, was the vividness the rain gave to the landscape, with deeper, richer colors and clouds occasionally parting to reveal glimpses of the peaks rising thousands of feet above us. We didn't see any snow, but driving home the next day I could see the storm had whitened the highest peaks. The storm ended up reminding us that atmospheric forces unite Yellowstone with the surrounding forests and wilderness areas in one continuous landscape of the northern Rockies, a land whose climate is cold, with fleeting summers and long, cold, snowy winters. We certainly bonded with that climate throughout the trip, but all of us who visit the Greater Yellowstone Ecosystem connect with that climate every time we step or look outside, whether we ski or cozy up to the woodstove, hike or go by horseback, canoe or fish from shore, geyser gaze or skinny dip in a secret hideaway.

With that, our wilderness odyssey came to an end. Today,

when I think back on that trip, many different impressions flood the heart and mind: The immensity of the Thorofare … A landscape without borders, contiguous and continuous … Our smallness, mere specks in a landscape of vastness … Summertime heat to autumnal chill … Landscape of fire … Tempestuous beauty of upper meadow … Glorious beauty of the headwaters … Solitude, many days with no other people … Odyssey into the wild … Immensity of time and space … Soco on the rocks, river flowing by below us … Peaceful meadows rooted in glacial ice dams and cataclysmic landslides … Ruggedness of the South Forks … Wildness of that wilderness … Camaraderie, shared struggles and successes … Landscape of power … Connectedness within and among us and nature's many forces and resources. If I had to choose three or four words to capture the essence of that journey through the Thorofare, they would be massive, odyssey, power, wild. For all of its resources, forces, interconnections, and ongoing creation, the Thorofare's ultimate value can only be sensed. Beyond the lessons of the other places in Yellowstone and the other stories in this book (which the Thorofare also imparts), I think the Thorofare whispers that one of the most important reasons to have wild places on its scale is to stir heart, mind, and emotion in a grand and penetrating way—in other words, to experience awe. We come to understand that, as powerful as the forces creating the Thorofare are, there is an essence, a unity, a presence more powerful, more all-consuming and all-encompassing, that is the underpinning of all. Some call this Gaia, some their God of choice, some love; however we reference the essence, it's best glimpsed—and sometimes only glimpsed—in the big wild, in places like the Thorofare.

Slough Creek
in All Four Seasons

In Yellowstone's northeast corner lies Slough Creek, a broad and open valley that is serenity molded into a landscape. I first ventured into Slough Creek in 1992 as part of a weekend hike, spending a day and night there. That encounter became the first of many, as I grew evermore enchanted with its graces and brought friends and family there to form their own memories. For a while, my trips there were almost annual, pilgrimages of sorts to a kingdom of nature. They became less regular as time went by, though I continued taking day trips there, often on cross-country skis. A few of these journeys stand out from the others, but the valley's riches and sense of place took many, if not most, of my trips there to understand (if anyone can ever

Figure 4.26: The view up valley from Elk Tongue Cabin, 1992. The northern Absarokas appear through a notch in the ridges framing the Slough Creek Valley. Cutoff Mountain is to the right, out of view. AUTHOR COLLECTION.

truly grasp all the meanings of a place as rich as Slough Creek). The story that follows is a melding of several experiences with its wonders, encounters with nature's power over the course of time and season, all in one place of beauty.

That first encounter with Slough Creek brought Carla and me to one of the two patrol cabins in the valley. Unlike most of Yellowstone's backcountry cabins, the Elk Tongue Cabin was not built of logs, but rather of frame construction. Still quite rustic, it had the typical assortment of wood-burning and cooking stoves, basic table and chairs, and cabinets containing canned goods and simple dishes, utensils, and pots and pans. Those occupied the three walls with windows, with two sets of bunk beds filling out the fourth, windowless wall. That same wall hid the best view from those inside, one that is exceptional Rocky Mountain tranquility (Figure 4.26). Slough Creek lazily winds its way through a large meadow with Cutoff Mountain looking down from on high and the northern Absarokas filling the distant horizon up valley. I've often wondered why the cabin's builders designed it to exclude that charming view; while the cabins generally place function over form, it's no secret that enjoyment of form (in the natural beauty there) could inspire the cabin's occupants to perform their protective functions better. Be that as it may, the cabin did have a broad covered front porch framing that view, so we cooked, ate, and otherwise spent the evening there. The valley was in its summer exuberance, green and full of life and energy. We watched the shadows lengthen and take over the drainage, at which point they began to move up the face of Cutoff, transforming the reddened rock to darkened brown. Time has erased the memory of what we may have heard, but it's a good bet that we heard the prehistoric cries of sandhill cranes, or the yips of coyotes playing with their young, or the gurgles of the stream as it flowed past, or all the above. The warmth we'd enjoyed earlier that day began to give way to the coolness of evening in the mountains, sending us in search of fleece and jacket. It was an evening of beauty, natural quiet, and serenity.

Before hiking out the next morning, we hiked three miles north to the park boundary. There sits Silvertip Ranch, a guest ranch sandwiched between Yellowstone and the Absaroka-Beartooth Wilderness. The ranch is the reason the trail through Slough Creek is actually a wagon road, for the valley is the ranch's access route for supplies. Everything from propane to run the ranch generator to food for the cook's imagination is freighted eleven miles up the valley on a wagon drawn by two horses. The ranch's clients travel through the valley as well, on the wagon or on horseback. Once there, the guests fish, go on trail rides, and take in the ranch's glorious wilderness setting. The ranch manager showed us the main lodge, which was comfortable but not ostentatious. Still, we knew staying there was a luxury we could only dream of affording, given our reality of seasonal employee wages. Our curiosity satisfied, we retraced our steps to the much humbler lodging we had enjoyed and had lunch on the porch. The eight-mile hike out that afternoon brought us through meadows green in the summer sun, past anglers enjoying some of Yellowstone's best fishing, and alongside a creek whose water had the clarity of glass. As we could see, Slough Creek was in its summer prime, with exuberant life everywhere we looked. Moreover, it was egalitarian, its delights available to anyone who can walk. Yellowstone and the surrounding national forest wilderness are all public land, owned by all Americans. This amazing birthright, surely America's best idea, means that anyone who has the means and ability to travel to this area can partake of its wonders. Not everyone can make it into Slough Creek, but almost everyone can experience Yellowstone and its neighbors as most people do, from their vehicles and on the park's boardwalks. That experience may not be the

Figure 4.27: Tony Britten savors the view from the Elk Tongue Cabin porch, 1992. Bears have broken into many of the patrol cabins, so they all have heavy-duty shutters (visible to his right) that unlock from the inside. Note the snow shovel, hung above the typical snow depth, so rangers on winter patrol can shovel their way in. In snowier locations, the shovel is hung right below the roof crown. AUTHOR COLLECTION.

same as a wilderness hike or a stay at Silvertip Ranch, but it is still something extraordinary, an upfront, personal encounter with nature's world. One of the real values, then, of places like Slough Creek and Yellowstone and the Absaroka-Beartooth Wilderness, is their absolute democracy and freedom, available and open to all, no matter their class, race, creed, nationality, experience, or gender.

After that visit to Slough Creek, I entered the pilgrimage phase of my relationship with it. Just two months later, I was back in the enchanted valley, this time with my college buddy Tony Britten (Figure 4.27). Retracing the steps Carla and I had taken out of the valley, Tony and I paused at the first meadow two miles in, a round bison pasture with a granite knoll in the center and Cutoff Mountain looming overhead. The mountain was frosty white, already bearing the kiss of winter. The meadow was the first of two that are labeled first and second, numerical designations that seem superfluous in a valley of seemingly endless meadow. Their grasses cured by frost and sunshine into golden flax, the meadows were delineated by forest-cloaked hillsides and tree-lined tributary streams and rivulets. Here and there, yellow and orange quaking aspen gilded the dark forests, touches of contrasts in a valley of gold. We spent the evening on the porch again, conversing in hushed voices, being serenaded by elk bugling, and pausing for amazing silence when the bulls took a breather. We were transfixed by low-angle lighting and elongating shadows, followed by twilight, gathering blackness, and then a view into the star-studded heavens. Dawn brought frost and a moose in the willows by the stream, enjoying the last tender—if partly frozen—leaves for the next six months. We savored the morning light, shafts of gold slowly dispersing the misty tendrils of water vapor, melting the frost crystals, and returning color and hue to the land. Hiking out, we took a side trip to McBride Lake, another treasure in that idyllic valley. The lake was a fitting ending to a glorious fall weekend, a complement of sky blue to the golden wonders we'd been walking through.

For several years thereafter, I took almost annual autumn adventures to Elk Tongue, but didn't get there in winter for more than a decade. In 2009 I finally made the ski trip there with my partner Ellen and her teenage son Ben. That cabin is a ten-mile trek in winter, two more than in summer because the gravel side road to the trailhead is not plowed. We covered the first four miles quickly, the trail broken out by other skiers enjoying a fun day trip to the first meadow and back. The Lower Slough Cabin overlooks that meadow and brought back lots of memories for all of us, good times shared with friends

Figure 4.28: The view from Elk Tongue Cabin in winter, 1992. Cutoff Mountain is at right, its summit just in a cloud. The frozen Slough Creek is in the foreground. AUTHOR COLLECTION.

and family there. In fact, on our way out, we stopped there for lunch and Ben found a Matchbox car of his in the woodpile outside the cabin's back door! A place of memories it was, but we continued the ski trek in to Elk Tongue, anxious to see what the trail-breaking would be like for the next six miles. When we had entered the first meadow, I had seen what appeared to be a set of ski tracks climbing out of it, but I wasn't sure about that. If my eyes were deceiving me and the trail-breaking were to be difficult, we would need all the light left in the day to get to Elk Tongue. My eyes, we soon found, were accurate, and the tracks went all the way to Elk Tongue and beyond, a huge luxury. We practically sailed up the valley, arriving at the cabin with hours of daylight to spare. The skiing was delightful, the snow soft and crystalline, the perfect conditions for enjoyable skiing.

It was a different Slough Creek we looked out on from the cabin porch, one of stark winter beauty (Figure 4.28). Snow embraced the land, a cover of white velvet that heightened contrasts not so evident in summertime. Color was erased from the landscape, replaced with black and white. Burned areas stood out more, the snow turning hillsides into winter's grayscale, with gray fire-killed snags bridging the spectrum between almost black living trees and the background of whiteness. Willows poked above the snow in the foreground, their naked branches seeming to shiver in the cold. To the mountains clung a thin veil of icy white cotton candy, occasionally parting when Old Man Winter took a bite. Winter's silence was deeper, the soft snow a blanket of hush. It was a landscape of crystalline beauty, one that held more memories for me, recollections of colors and companionship, of hikes and journeys through the wild, of life's exuberance and autumn's gold, and of winter's starkness and whitened beauty.

Two years earlier, I had made my only spring trip to Elk Tongue, with my hiking buddy Jared and his girlfriend Jill (who had both skied with me a few months earlier to Cache Creek). We were travelers through a landscape of promise and hope, the land finally released from winter's six-month grip. I remember that trip for wildlife taking advantage of the valley's early thaw (relative to that of the higher terrain surrounding Slough Creek), and for the springtime headiness evident in the pungent aromatics of soils and plants newly unburied and released from dormancy. Those attributes (and others) are evident in Jared's and Jill's separate accounts of the journey, which they graciously provided when I asked what their memories of our journey were:

Jared: "It was a beautiful spring day when we started. Jill and I had never been to Slough Creek. The first open meadow we hit was stunning. It was warm and smelled like spring. The creek was meandering and bubbling. We didn't think it could get better, but it did.

"We hiked far into the second meadow, leaving civilization well behind us. Although we didn't see any elk or moose on our hike in, we did encounter plenty of deer and a bison or two grazing in the meadows. I don't remember how many miles the cabin was, but it felt like it took a long time to get there. There was a trail junction in the second meadow and we had to cross a flooded stream there and took our shoes off to do it. The water was cold as ice but refreshing for sore feet.

"The cabin was near the trail junction and it was late afternoon when we arrived and we wearily threw our packs down onto the porch. We were happy to have made it and hungry! I think we made soup that night. We were tired and we didn't stay up very late."

Jill: "The cabin was small and cozy, we cooked a warm meal, sat in wooden chairs, rocked back as we tasted a little whiskey and told stories. The broad porch was inviting and Jared and I slept outside. It was cold. Rain threatened (I thought it was cloudy). At various points in the night I awoke to animals moving through the brush (the cabin is close to the creek and it was flooded). I remember hoping it was not a bear and wishing the porch was taller. We awoke with cold noses and our breath marking the air. There were moose grazing and Jared and I had front row seats to watch. Mike awoke later. We sat on the porch in the crisp air sipping coffee and absorbing the calm wilderness morning. I think we did some chores before packing up to hike out.

"I remember shouldering my pack for the hike out and thinking that I didn't want to leave, that one night was simply not enough. ... I remember crossing the tributary stream and walking the wagon road paralleling Slough Creek. When we saw the bear my heart raced a little faster, not because he was a bear, but because it was the largest bear I had encountered to that date and he was walking towards us. He was a couple of hundred yards away and I had the thought, 'I wonder how fast he could cover the distance between us if he wanted to?' It was May, he was hungry, and we were three skinny humans with three tiny cans of bear spray that felt entirely inadequate. We all got out our bear spray and undid the caps. We watched as he ambled our way; then, he sniffed in the air and did a 90-degree turn. I can't remember if he crossed the creek to the other side of the valley, but he must have. We continued walking."

Jared, Jill, and I all remember hearing wolves howling on the way out, but our recollections differ as to where we were then. Such is the frailty of the human mind, but regardless, they were a part of the journey, and they furthered the sensation that spring is the season of promise in Slough Creek.

I took many other trips to Slough Creek, mostly just to the first meadow. The cabin there was a good place to bring visiting family and friends who were not accustomed to wilderness travel. It was only two miles from the summertime trailhead, but seemed a world away from civilization to them. The cabin's amenities and rusticity struck the right balance between comfort and its opposite to give them a window into the beauty and serenity of Slough Creek and the wild. There, we made new memories and refreshed old ones. My parents were reminded of the camping trips they took in their younger years, while my twin introduced his new bride to camping with a few luxuries. One friend spent the morning reading by the open door while I satisfied my wanderlust hiking further up the valley (he got the better part of the deal, as I swatted flies all morning, that time being the height of the summer fly hatch). Another friend slipped and slid his way with me all the way into the Elk Tongue Cabin on a warm November weekend, the sun melting the snow enough to make the wagon road a muddy, slippery mess—but keeping everyone else away. On all these trips, Slough Creek's quiet magnificence colored the journey grand, partly because open valleys like this have almost always been transformed into golf courses, strip malls, and starter mansions elsewhere in the West. But, I think it's more because places like Slough Creek are landscapes of memory and wonder: the memory of times past and eras long forgotten, the wonder of incredible, timeless nature.

Indeed, when we journey through a wild place across the seasons and over decades, our bonds to the place acquire the depth of an added dimension: time. Memories and connections possess many dimensions, but time imparts the understanding that wild places both stay the same and evolve, remaining familiar overall while adding layers of complexity and interconnection. Our connections to nature follow a similar trajectory, retaining the same foundation while evolving into something that more resembles a relationship. More than just this realization, we come to understand that nature has many sides, and is more than the sum of its parts. Just as Slough Creek is both color and the absence of such, we see that it is both promise and life. Our connections to nature give us similar rewards beyond mere observation, including solace and wonder, promise and fulfillment, resolve and understanding—again, much like a growing and evolving relationship. Slough Creek, Yellowstone, and surrounding wilderness areas, then, are not just landscapes of memory, but also of possibility, wonder, and even love, for everyone and everybody.

Reflections

As we go through life, most of us search continually for meaning and purpose, or if we have found these, affirmation of them. Some of us find them in the pursuit of knowledge, others in their profession, many in service or family, and a few in drugs, drink, or other addictions (sadly). But most find these at least partly in faith, whether Christianity, Islam, Buddhism, Taoism, Judaism, Hinduism, atheism, or one of the world's other religions. Many faiths look to a higher power(s), beings or spirits that offer guidance, wisdom, and / or eternal life. Some profess to be the exclusive way to a happy afterlife, while others express tolerance and inclusiveness. Virtually all faiths, though, teach us the Golden Rule, to treat others as we ourselves would want to be treated. Most go on to apply that same directive to nature: to treat it with restraint, take only what we need, and shepherd it for the generations to come. Eve's transgression in the Garden of Eden, for example, can be seen as humanity's overreach, and her eviction the result of thinking we know more about nature's workings than we actually do. Many also turn to nature as a venue for spiritual contemplation, insight, and growth. John the Baptist found inspiration in wilderness, Buddhists commonly built their monasteries in scenic locations, and Taoism's yin and yang are often understood to be within nature. Whatever the faith, nature plays a prominent and complex role, one that is benevolent when we approach it with humility and restraint.

Nature's commonality and sometimes centrality in the world's religions should not come as a surprise to anyone who has spent time in the wild, but especially in the Yellowstone wilderness. There, nature's power, forces, and interconnections are on full display, and the presence of grizzly bears and other large animals opens—or should open—our eyes wider to them than in places that lack such creatures. To those of us who enter the Yellowstone wilderness, who take the chance of a bear encounter, who experience Yellowstone first hand, many rich rewards may come our way. We may get to watch a wild creature go about its day, aware of our presence but otherwise heedless of our existence. We may ski past the remains of a bison that stepped too close to the hot spring whose warmth sustained it on a frigid night, an accident that reversed succor for ruin. We may feel the earth shake under our feet, experience a two-hour hailstorm in the height of summer, or feel the call of the wild when a wolf pack howls, all of which remind us that we are not the most powerful force on the planet. Whatever the reward, we come to realize that Yellowstone and other wild places are not the exception, but rather the authentic, the original, the real. We return for more, satisfying a deep-seated hunger within us, and in so doing, begin to connect with something visceral, something we have longed for. Through such experiences, we can be transformed into wiser, more knowing and caring persons, ones that understand that, for many world religions, these connections are ultimately glimpses of the divine.

Yellowstone is indeed a landscape of life, beauty, wonder, and awe (Figure 4.29). It is power and connection, life and love, awe and mystery. If we approach and nourish the natural world with humility and restraint as we have done in Yellowstone—humil-

Figure 4.29: Mount Sheridan and Heart Lake at sunrise, 2002. The sunrise view of the Red Mountains explains the name. AUTHOR COLLECTION.

ity in the face of powers infinitely stronger and wiser than we can ever hope to be, restraint against the urge to squander the untold riches and knowledge we have yet to discover—the rewards can be immense, not only for ourselves but for all future generations. If we exercise these cautions, we may yet understand that Yellowstone and other wilderness areas are places of hope, of promise, of the possible. They are solace for the soul, food for the heart, stimulation for the imagination. They are grist for our sense of wonder, an unending source of inspiration and contemplation. They are all these and more, but perhaps most importantly, Yellowstone and wild places like it are infinite wellsprings of joy. The delights of encountering Yellowstone's wildness, the mindfulness of touching nature's mystery, and the thrill of finding wonder tell us that there is unending joy to be had in nature—deep, penetrating joy, the kind that comes from tasting peace, love, and the divine.

Epilogue

*Long conversations
around the campfire —
trout for dinner!*
—David Kirtley

In 2009, I moved away from Yellowstone, not because I wanted to leave, but because I had to find a new job. The four-year position I had occupied ran out, and park management had lost sight of any organization's most precious resource, its employees. Yosemite National Park's managers didn't share that same shortcoming, could see that I had talents that would benefit the agency, and offered me a permanent position that was a significant promotion. I moved there that fall and spent the next four years developing two major river management plans. As much as I enjoyed the stimulating professional environment there—the peak of my career—and as spectacular as Yosemite is, I did not stop missing the Yellowstone landscape. Rangers who have spent time in both parks agree that if Yosemite is the more spectacular of the two, Yellowstone is the more moving, with a depth and complexity that take more time to appreciate. I would agree, and this is probably why Yellowstone continued to exert a powerful hold on me.

For that reason and many more, and because I still owned a house in Gardiner, I traveled to Yellowstone almost every chance I could get. I also applied to any new positions that came open there but found myself regularly outcompeted, usually by people who were overqualified but willing to accept a substantial reduction in pay to be in the iconic park. I was too new to my position to do the same thing, so I began to look upon my time in Yosemite as more long-term (it was a *permanent* position, after all!) and bought a house in nearby Mariposa, California. Buying a house has long been known to be one of the most stressful things a person can do, which was certainly true for me. When we are under stress, our body's defenses may weaken, making us vulnerable to illness. I had noticed an odd feeling in my throat before I even closed on the house, but it went away after I moved in. No more than two months later, though, I began noticing more strange things about my body, like endlessly twitching muscles just under my skin, the sense that I slurred my speech when tired, and an enhanced tendency to cry. My regular physician ordered a few tests, but when they all came back negative, she referred me to a neurologist. When the neurologist blew me off without even glancing at the two-page patient history I had prepared, I requested a second opinion. My doctor that time didn't mess around and got me into Stanford University Hospital, one of the best in California. By the time I actually saw a neurologist there, six months had passed, and my symptoms had advanced accordingly. Two weeks later—on Friday the 13th of September, 2013—she gave me a diagnosis befitting the day: ALS, Amyotrophic Lateral Sclerosis, sometimes known as Lou Gehrig's Disease. ALS is a death sentence, a malady in which the brain gradually loses the ability to control the body's muscles because the neuronal connections to them are destroyed. Eighty percent of the disease's victims die within five years of diagnosis, usually by respiratory arrest, the diaphragm becoming paralyzed like all the other muscles. Some people live longer, but the disease has a 100 percent death rate. My life, in short, would soon begin changing dramatically.

Over the next year, I went from living on my own and working for the agency entrusted with America's greatest treasures to needing full-time care and taking disability retirement. Without a wife or other partner who could care for me, I ended up moving to Missouri to live with my parents, who became my caregivers. The inexorable progression of ALS has defined our lives since then, as I gradually lost the ability to walk, stand, talk, swallow food, clean myself, turn over in bed, type, breathe fully, swat a mosquito, hold my head up, scratch an itch, sign my name, and the myriad other physical activities most of us do without thinking. To deal with these problems, I transitioned to living in a wheelchair, had a port in my stomach and a permanent catheter put in (the former for feeding, the latter for draining my bladder), donned a face mask attached to a machine that forces more air into my lungs when I inhale (similar to the CPAP that people with sleep apnea use), began using assistive technology that tracks my eyes as I move them about an on-screen keyboard (thereby allowing me to type and, with a speech program, speak), and for everything else, accepted my parents' help. To cope with the isolation and loss, I began writing, as much to stay engaged with the broader world as to reflect on my meaningful life experiences, especially those from the Yellowstone area. I thought I would be fortunate to produce one book, but that was in 2016 (*A Week in Yellowstone's Thorofare,* by Oregon State University Press), and now this one (and I'm working on another about climate change in national parks). Indeed, writing has been my salvation, allowing me to savor the trails and wildness of Yellowstone again and again.

St. Louis is where I grew up, and it appears that it will be where I spend my final days, in the very same house (my folks have been here since 1972). As with any homeland, much has remained the same, but much has also changed since I moved away in 1989. For every new shopping center there is a neighborhood whose only sign of change is its taller trees. The same is true of the climate: while the summers are still hot and humid, the winters are nowhere near as cold as they were in my childhood. This is not just memory creep; it's demonstrable fact. For example, November 2016 was the warmest on record, along with February, 2017, which saw two weeks of seventy-degree weather after Valentine's Day. We opened the windows, birds built their nests, and flowers began to bloom, all at least a month ahead of normal. While a February day or two might have been this warm in my childhood here, such sustained warmth usually didn't arrive until April. The two previous winters here were not quite as warm, but they were again warmer than those two or three decades ago. Winters here are indeed getting both warmer and shorter.

The same is true for Yellowstone and the wilderness areas around it: warmer and shorter winters, with less snowfall. Just since I spent my first summer there in 1986, the yearly average temperature has increased a degree Fahrenheit, with another degree in the three decades before that. Two degrees of warming may not sound like much, but it's enough to shorten the typical winter by a full month. In turn, that means that snowpacks are declining in size and melting earlier. In fact, those in the drought years of the early 2000s—when Eric and I were sitting in normally frigid Yellowstone Lake—are tied with those from the Dust Bowl years in being the smallest snowpacks in the last 800 years. While temperatures forty degrees below zero still occur, they are increasingly uncommon, and temps in the fifties below almost unknown anymore. In turn, the lack of sustained bitter cold means that fewer tree-killing beetles are killed, enabling them to multiply in summertime and girdle entire hillsides of trees, as Josh and I saw in the Ishawooa and Pass Creek drainages. Warmer temperatures and shorter winters are also creating a fifth season of the year: fire season, a whopping 78 days longer than it was previously, if it existed at all. Beetle-killed trees help fuel the fires, as Josh and I saw on the same trip, in the Boulder Basin Fire. Climate change is happening now in the Yellowstone ecosystem, and has been for several decades already. The same is true globally, with seventeen of the eighteen warmest years on record occurring since the year 2000. That this warming is due primarily to human activity is almost certain, according to the Intergovernmental Panel on Climate Change, the United Nations group chartered to investigate global warming. Consisting of thousands of climate scientists and related experts from around the world, the IPCC, in its latest report on the subject, noted that atmospheric concentrations of carbon dioxide and methane, the two most potent greenhouse gases, have been increasing so much since 1750 that they are now the highest the world has seen in at least 800,000 years. That increase is anthropogenic, and almost certainly the cause of the global warming the earth has experienced since about 1950. This human influence is well established and pervasive, detected throughout the world's atmosphere, ocean acidity and level, and icefields and glaciers. It is rare to see such a large group of scientists, all trained to be critical of research and monitoring findings, agree so uniformly, but the group boiled down their conclusion to the simple statement that it's 95 percent sure that humans are *the main cause of global warming.*

Clearly, humans have become another force shaping the Greater Yellowstone Ecosystem and all other ecosystems on Earth. In Yellowstone, we have long been such a force, setting the parks and forests aside in recognition of their amazing resources, eradicating wolves and then reintroducing them seventy years later, managing bears, and taking many other actions in defense of the places and ideals embodied in the parks and forests. Looking back further, Native Americans also shaped the area through hunting and the use of fire, though the extent of their impact is a matter of lively debate among the researchers and natives studying the question. Whatever their impact and the influence of Euro-Americans may have been, though, they are miniscule compared to the disruptions we will cause through continued global warming. Left unchecked, Yellowstone's climate by the year 2100 will warm another 6 to 13 degrees F., fueling more fires, altering forest composition to trees that can withstand frequent fires, converting some forests and grasslands into sagebrush desert scrub, drying streams and reducing rivers to creeks, and eliminating whitebark pines entirely. Animals that need snow or cold, like Canada lynx and moose, will disappear, while generalists like elk and grizzly bears will hang on. Globally, we can expect more severe storms like Hurricanes Harvey, Irma, and Maria, heat waves like the 120-degree one that hit India in 2016, and erratic weather like that which brought spring to Missouri in February. If we continue ignoring the climate change reality—which almost no governing body in the world is doing other than the U.S. Republican party and President Donald Trump—we could easily see the Greenland ice sheets melt away, raising the global sea level by 24 feet, which would flood most of the world's largest cities and displace a billion or more people. Likewise, we could see agriculture become destabilized by recurring drought and severe weather, producing famine and increasing conflict and warfare. The human race is well on its way to being another powerful force affecting not just Yellowstone but the entire globe, and not in a good way.

There are many reasons that explain our reluctance to take action against global warming. The most powerful of them is probably simple greed, especially for anyone who has interests in oil or coal companies and regions and therefore fears their revenues will decline as fossil fuel production is curtailed in favor of more carbon-neutral forms of energy. Another compelling reason is that some might fear freedom itself threatened, as limits on our use of gasoline make it harder to use the most tangible symbol of American freedom, the automobile (especially unnecessarily large pickup trucks, SUVs, and luxury sedans). To these and other explanations, I think, can be added another: that skeptics have become too disconnected from nature, too distanced from a native landscape and the subtle (and sometimes not so subtle) changes therein, too removed from wildness and wonder. They have lost their place in the world, have become more attracted to money, possessions, and power over their fellow humans, and they cannot recognize the signs of an ailing planet—or willingly choose not to see those indications. They do so at their peril—really, society's peril, especially those of meager means—for ultimately, we depend on nature for sustenance and survival, and nature's forces are more powerful than ours. No matter how much control we may think we have over nature, no matter how much insurance and food security we may purchase or achieve, and no matter how good our understanding of natural systems is, we remain forever subject to nature's forces. Nature always bats last, and the more removed we become from it, the harder we will fall.

Feeling somewhat removed myself from the native landscape I had known for half my life and wanting to reap the psychological rewards of experiencing wonder, I spent the summer of 2014 in Yellowstone, after leaving Yosemite and before moving to Missouri. Already struggling to walk, I enjoyed going to my favorite accessible haunts, setting up my camp chair, and absorbing the sights, sounds, and smells of those places. The shore of Yellowstone Lake was my favorite destination, because I had long sensed nature's power to be especially evident there, but there were other places of power and beauty. Two that have stuck with me are a private spot on the Snake River with the north end of the Tetons in the distance, and a pullout on the dirt road from Mammoth to Gardiner with the setting autumn sun highlighting the folds in that post-glacial landscape. I shared those times with friends and family or, in the Snake River scene, two canoeists who passed silently. Equally enduring were the boat trips that friends took me on that summer. The longest was an eight-day canoe trip on the Southeast Arm of Yellowstone Lake, a trip that became the setting for *A Week in Yellowstone's Thorofare.* The other two were both floats on the Yellowstone River, both of them quiet immersions in the seasons of the northern Rockies, the first one summer, the second autumn. All of these experiences were reminders of what is at stake in the Yellowstone ecosystem, of what we stand to lose if we don't get serious about global warming, from the stream flows we depend on for drinking water and many other uses, to the crystal-clear, smoke-free air that provides views of the wilderness framing every landscape in the region. Even the geysers may be adversely affected, dependent as they are on an adequate influx of water from rain and snowmelt. A Yellowstone without a faithful Old Faithful, without the dozens of other geysers all erupting according to the whims of nature, will be a saddened place indeed, because they are for many the park's most tangible manifestation of nature's power.

Of all my experiences in 2014, one at Old Faithful seems the most fitting for the last story, for it was the final vignette in my Yellowstone experience. With my hiking buddy Jared, his wife Christina Mills, and my Yosemite friend Jim Roche, I went there for a day in early October, just before I was to move to St. Louis. We had lunch at the Old Faithful Inn, and then Jim ran to the visitor center to get a loaner wheelchair for me and to see what geysers might be erupting soon. He had worked at Old Faithful early in his career (we had actually met then), so when he returned with the news that Grand Geyser was overdue, we hurried there. Grand is the tallest predictable geyser in the world (if one considers a four-hour window of opportunity a prediction) and puts on a spectacular show. It begins by rippling the surface of the pool from which it erupts, then it explodes into a column of boiling water as much as two hundred feet high, after which it subsides to seven to eleven minutes of powerful bursting from its pool. At the end, the bursting stops, but the pool may or may not drain. If it does, the eruption is usually done, but if water remains, the geyser gazer is in for a treat. The pool seethes and churns as the geyser prepares for a finale. Soon it explodes again into the sky, often eclipsing its initial show. Usually it will play a little longer and quit for good, but on rare occasions it will give a third burst (somewhat confusingly, Grand's first seven to eleven minutes of play are considered one "burst," as are the shorter duration finales). In the past, it would give several such finales, but over time the number has declined to the point that three-burst eruptions are the best to hope for. Whatever the number, Grand is a great show, sometimes even drawing applause from the two-hundred-person crowds that have gathered to see it. Think about that for a moment: where else do people applaud a non-living thing that is part of nature? There are few such places, affirming the sheer power in that geyser.

Grand is also a mercurial geyser, seemingly sentient and determined to defeat the most patient geyser gazer for one eruption, but complying with human impatience the next. Many a time I have sat for two, three, or four hours, waiting for a show that seemed intent on not arriving. Sometimes I was with visiting friends or family, waiting for hours and baking in the summer sunshine, but thrilling to the eruption when it finally came. For all its frustrations, though, Grand Geyser would be surprisingly gracious at other times. One time in the 1990s, a thunderstorm pelted the crowd of expectant observers with pea-sized hail, but the geyser quickly rewarded us with a three-burst eruption, as if to thank its loyal fans. Near the end of the eruption, the sun came out, highlighting the final burst against the dark, receding storm clouds, brilliance against tempest. Another time, Grand gave us an after-burst, a rare spike from an empty pool, ten or fifteen minutes after the main eruption. Jetting almost as tall as the geyser's regular play, it could have been a fourth burst.

Perhaps the most meaningful time for me was that day in October 2014, when the geyser erupted after just two minutes of waiting. We had walked up to see the pool already pulsating, the subterranean, superheated water beginning to give way to steam. What's more, Grand gave us three bursts, rocketing into the cobalt Indian summer sky three different times. It was a scene of electric excitement among the crowd gathered there, the highlight of the day for many of them. For me, it was a farewell tiding, a send-off from my favorite and most fickle geyser. Yellowstone, the landscape of power, still moves and inspires, as it has for more than a century, and as I hope it does for many centuries more.

Yellowstone Lake at sunset, 2000. AUTHOR COLLECTION.

Acknowledgments

When Lou Gehrig was diagnosed with the disease that bears his name today, he gave a farewell speech that has become legendary. After referring to the recent press about his diagnosis, he said, "Yet today I consider myself the luckiest man on the face of the earth."[1] He attributed his feeling to his good fortune to playing major league baseball, to his teammates, and to his wife and family. Two years later, he succumbed to the disease, at age 37. In the almost eight decades since then, researchers have made some progress in understanding the disease, but it is still 100 percent successful at claiming the lives of those afflicted with it. There are but two modestly effective remedies to slow or halt its progression, the better of which slows it just 33 percent. Modern medicine is nowhere close to a cure. That is not the case, however, with assistive technologies, which have advanced a great deal. By far the most helpful for me has been the technology that tracks my eye movements about an on-screen keyboard for speech, typing, and mousing. The lap-

---

1 "Text of Lou Gehrig's Speech on 75th Anniversary," USA Today, July 4, 2014, http://www.usatoday.com/story/sports/mlb/2014/07/07/text-of-lou-gehrigs-speech-on-75th-anniversary/12174919.

top setup is what I used to write this book—all 80,000 words, typed with only my eyes. For these communication devices, my thanks go to the Gleason Initiative Foundation and the ALS Association, two organizations devoted to improving the lives of ALS sufferers.

After living with the disease for six years, I wonder if I could say the same thing about myself as Gehrig so grandiloquently pronounced in 1939. I don't think so, if only because his sentiment was a little overstated. I have certainly seen and experienced more than my share of natural beauty and wonders, as the stories in this book attest. Like Gehrig, I have also been blessed with kind and loving parents, brothers, and friends. If there is anything good about this disease, it is that its victims get to experience such love, as family members become caregivers. Also, they get plenty of time to reflect on their lives and experiences as they slowly wither away; writing this book essentially forced me to do that. Overall, then, I think my impression is closer to Gehrig's closing statement, which was, "I might have been given a bad break, but I've got an awful lot to live for"—and to look back upon. Moreover, I have been fortunate to experience the best that humanity can give, the unending support of family, friends (especially Lisa Acree, Vicqi Lin, and Paul Baber, who were with me on that awful day when I was diagnosed), and you who are reading this right now. I hope that this book will inspire you to build your own connection to nature, and that you'll be inspired to take action to safeguard nature from the worst of global warming.

Keeping me company on the adventures in this book were many different friends and family members, including (in the order in which they appear): Jim and Jeanne Yochim, my twin Jim Yochim, Ellen Petrick, Daniel Barbir, Mike Tercek, Brian Yochim, Jill Yochim, Ashea Mills, Ivan Kowski, Beth Taylor, Pat Bigelow, Kerry Gunther, Sean Miculka, Eric Compas, Garrett Seal, Carla Polk, Jared White, Jill McMurray, Dave Moser, Cathy Moser, Tom Richards, Tom Yochim, Stacey Gunther, Steve and Denice Swanke, Jim Williams, MacNeil Lyons, Tim Hudson, Mike Stevens, Josh Becker, Tony Britten, Ben Underwood, Christina Mills, and Jim Roche. Not only did you hike and ski and canoe with me, but you made the trips fun, enriched, and memorable, as well as safe.

The rangers of the U.S. Forest Service and National Park Service (specifically mentioned were Brad Ross and Jim McKown, but there are thousands more) deserve our gratitude, for they have defended Yellowstone and its neighboring national forests against threats internal and ex, for almost a century and a half. The NPS has long had its own education branch, whose staff members do their best to give visitors a sense of wonder in Yellowstone, and from there, a desire to preserve the park. Where they leave off, the folks at Yellowstone Forever and Teton Science School step up, offering a wide selection of educational opportunities, from one-day seminars to multi-day backpacking trips, with a similar hope for the Greater Yellowstone Ecosystem's continued protection. And where these two organizations leave off, a variety of conservation organizations and private guides pick up, advocating for the responsible protection and stewardship of that landscape of power. May they all continue to excel in their efforts.

A few friends and colleagues deserve special mention because they helped move this project forward. My parents and caregivers Jim and Jeanne Yochim helped keep the mornings free of distractions so I could focus on writing, addressed my never-ending physical needs, and scanned some of my old photos for publication. Michelle Reynolds Gray plowed through several shoeboxes of photos and slide files searching for the figures that grace these pages. Yellowstone historian Lee Whittlesey and archivist Anne Foster helped track down obscure details of park history. Erik Skindrud generously volunteered to bring the project to completion if ALS made that impossible for me, and read early drafts of the manuscript. Graphics whiz Jim Donovan cleaned up some images for publication. David Kirtley wrote the haiku that start each chapter. Eric Compas created the maps, volunteering to make more if needed. Josh Becker, Brian and Jill Yochim, Sean Miculka, Eric Compas, Ellen Petrick, Jared White, and Jill McMurray all helped fill in the details of some of the outings. All of these people provided ongoing support and encouragement for the project, without which it would probably not have been completed.

Last but certainly not least, Chris Cauble and the staff at Riverbend Publishing in Montana saw the value in a book that is part memoir, part natural and cultural history, and part essay and search for meaning. Thanks for taking a chance on my project and for transforming it from a collection of words to a beautiful storybook. Any errors or lingering misstatements are my own.

References

Archival Collections

National Archives, College Park, Maryland.

National Archives, Yellowstone National Park, Gardiner, Montana.

Yellowstone National Park Research Library, Gardiner, Montana.

Books and Articles

Abbey, Edward. *Desert Solitaire: A Season in the Wilderness.* New York: The McGraw-Hill Companies, 1968.

Allen, M., O. P. Dube, W. Solecki, F. Aragón–Durand, W. Cramer, S. Humphreys, M. Kainuma, J. Kala, N. Mahowald, Y. Mulugetta, R. Perez, M. Wairiu, K. Zickfeld, "Framing and Context." In: *Global warming of 1.5°C. An IPCC Special Report on the impacts of global warming of 1.5°C above pre-industrial levels and related global greenhouse gas emission pathways, in the context of strengthening the global response to the threat of climate change, sustainable development, and efforts to eradicate poverty* [V. Masson-Delmotte, P. Zhai, H. O. Pörtner, D. Roberts, J. Skea, P.R. Shukla, A. Pirani, W. Moufouma-Okia, C. Péan, R. Pidcock, S. Connors, J. B. R. Matthews, Y. Chen, X. Zhou, M. I. Gomis, E. Lonnoy, T. Maycock, M. Tignor, T. Waterfield (eds.)]. In Press, 2018.

Ambler, Marjane. *Yellowstone Has Teeth.* Helena, MT: Riverbend Publishing, 2013.

Bach, Orville E., J. *Reflections from Yellowstone and Beyond: Forty-three Years as a Seasonal Ranger.* Morristown, TN: Blue Willow Press, 2016.

———. *Tracking the Spirit of Yellowstone: Recollections of Thirty-one Years as a Seasonal Ranger as a Seasonal Ranger.* Morristown, TN: Blue Willow Press, 2005.

Bartlett, Richard A. *Yellowstone: A Wilderness Besieged.* Tucson: University of Arizona Press, 1985.

———. *Nature's Yellowstone.* Albuquerque: University of New Mexico Press, 1974.

Becker, Scott A. "Habitat Selection, Condition, and Survival of Shiras Moose in Northwest Wyoming." Master's thesis, University of Wyoming, 2008.

Berry, Evan. *Devoted to Nature: The Religious Roots of American Environmentalism.* Oakland: University of California Press, 2015.

Biel, Alice Wondrak. *Do (Not) Feed the Bears: The Fitful History of Wildlife and Tourists in Yellowstone.* Lawrence: University Press of Kansas, 2006.

Bruggeman, John. "Spatio-Temporal Dynamics of the Central Bison Herd in Yellowstone National Park." Ph.D. Dissertation, Montana State University, 2006.

Farrell, Justin. *The Battle for Yellowstone: Morality and the Sacred Roots of Environmental Conflict.* Princeton: Princeton University Press, 2015.

Ferguson, Gary. *The Carry Home: Lessons from the American Wilderness.* Berkeley, CA: Counterpoint Press, 2014.

———. *Hawks Rest: A Season in the Remote Heart of Yellowstone.* Washington: National Geographic, 2003.

Franke, Mary Ann. *Yellowstone in the Afterglow.* Mammoth Hot Springs, Wyo.: National Park Service, 2000.

———. *To Save the Wild Bison: Life on the Edge in Yellowstone.* Norman: University of Oklahoma Press, 2005.

Fuller, J. A., R. A. Garrott, and P. J. White. "Emigration and Density Dependence in Yellowstone Bison." *Journal of Wildlife Management* 71 (2007): 1924-1933.

Gresswell, Robert E., and Lusha M. Tronstad. "Altered Processes and the

Demise of Yellowstone Cutthroat Trout in Yellowstone Lake." Pp. 209-225 in P. J. White, Robert A. Garrott, and Glenn E. Plumb, eds. *Yellowstone's Wildlife in Transition.* Cambridge, Mass.: Harvard University Press, 2013.

Haines, Aubrey L. *The Yellowstone Story,* rev. ed., 2 vols. Niwot, Colo.: The Yellowstone Association for Natural Science, History, and Education, Inc., in cooperation with the University Press of Colorado, 1996.

Havlick, David G. *No Place Distant: Roads and Motorized Recreation on America's Public Lands.* Washington: Island Press, 2002.

Holte, Peter. Letter to Major John Pitcher, May 21, 1902. Document #4851, Item 20, Letter Box 10, Yellowstone National Park archives, Gardiner, Montana.

Intergovernmental Panel on Climate Change [Core Writing Team, R.K. Pachauri, and L.A. Meyer (eds.)]. *Climate Change 2014: Synthesis Report: Contribution of Working Groups I, II and III to the Fifth Assessment Report of the Intergovernmental Panel on Climate Change.* Geneva, Switzerland: IPCC, 2015.

Leopold, Aldo *A Sand County Almanac: And Sketches Here and There.* New York: Oxford University Press, 1949.

Leopold, A. Starker, S. A. Cain, C. M. Cottam, I. N. Gabrielson, and T. L. Kimball. "Wildlife Management in the National Parks." Reprinted in Lary Dilsaver, ed. *America's National Park System: The Critical Documents.* Lanham, Maryland: Rowman & Littlefield, 1994.

Meagher, Mary. *The Bison of Yellowstone National Park.* Washington, DC: U.S. Government Printing Office, 1973. NPS Scientific Monographs 1 series.

Mernin, Gerald. *Yellowstone Ranger.* Helena, MT: Riverbend Publishing, 2016.

Meyer, Judith L. *The Spirit of Yellowstone: The Cultural Evolution of a National Park.* Lanham, MD: Rowman and Littlefield, 1996.

Murie, Margaret and Olaus. *Wapiti Wilderness.* Boulder: Colorado Associated University Press, 1985.

Nabokov, Peter, and Lawrence Loendorf. *Restoring a Presence: American Indians and Yellowstone National Park.* Norman: University of Oklahoma Press, 2004.

National Park Service. *Yellowstone Science.* Various issues, but especially volumes 23(1), 23(2), 24(1), and 25(1), which were entirely devoted to climate change, grizzly bears, wolves, and native fish conservation, respectively.

Olliff, S. Thomas, Roy A. Renkin, Daniel P. Reinhart, Kristin L. Legg, and Emily M. Wellington. "Exotic Fungus Acts with Natural Disturbance Agents to Alter Whitebark Pine Communities." Pp. 236-251 in P. J. White, Robert A. Garrott, and Glenn E. Plumb, eds. *Yellowstone's Wildlife in Transition.* Cambridge, Mass.: Harvard University Press, 2013.

Peacock, Doug. *The Grizzly Years: In Search of the American Wilderness.* New York: Henry Holt and Co., 1990.

Pritchard, James A. *Preserving Yellowstone's Natural Conditions: Science and the Perception of Nature.* Lincoln: University of Nebraska Press, 1999.

Reynolds, Harry V., Jr. "Thorofare Ski Patrol, February 27 – March 11, 1956." File "Thorofare Patrol Cabin, YELL #HS-0291, LCS #51027," YCR National Register files, NPS, Mammoth Hot Springs, Wyo.

Rogers, Edmund. Memorandum to NPS Director Arno Cammerer, Oct. 5, 1937. File "Yellowstone National Park, Sept. 15, 1937 thru Dec. 31, 1939," box 13, Records of Arno B. Cammerer, 1922-40, Record Group 79, National Archives, College Park, Maryland.

Romme, William. "Fire and landscape diversity in subalpine forests of Yellowstone National Park." *Ecological Monographs* 52 (1982): 199-221.

Romme, William, and Don Despain. "Historical Perspective on the Yellowstone Fires of 1988." *BioScience* 39 (Nov. 1989): 695-699.

— and —. "The Long History of Fire in the Greater Yellowstone Ecosystem." *Western Wildlands* 15 (Summer 1989): 10-17.

Rubinstein, Paul, Lee H. Whittlesey, and Mike Stevens. *The Guide to Yellowstone Waterfalls and Their Discovery.* Englewood, CO: Westcliffe Publishers, 2000.

Runte, Alfred. *National Parks: The American Experience.* 4th ed. New York: Taylor Trade Publishing, 2010.

Sax, Joseph L. *Mountains Without Handrails: Reflections on the National Parks.* Ann Arbor: University of Michigan Press, 1980.

Schullery, Paul. *Mountain Time: A Yellowstone Memoir.* Albuquerque: University of New Mexico Press, 2005.

——. *Searching for Yellowstone: Ecology and Wonder in the Last Wilderness.* Boston: Houghton Mifflin, 1997.

——. *Yellowstone's Ski Pioneers: Peril and Heroism on the Winter Trail.* Worland, WY: High Plains Publishing Company, 1995.

——. *The Bears of Yellowstone.* Worland, WY: High Plains Publishing Company, 1992.

——, and Lee Whittlesey *Myth and History in the Creation of Yellowstone National Park.* Lincoln: Bison Books, 2011.

Smith, Jordan Fisher. *Engineering Eden: The True Story of a Violent Death, a Trial, and the Fight over Controlling Nature.* New York: Crown, 2016.

Smith, Robert B., and Lee J. Siegel. *Windows into the Earth: The Geologic Story of Yellowstone and Grand Teton National Parks.* New York: Oxford University Press, 2000.

Sellars, Richard West. *Preserving Nature in the National Parks: A History.* New Haven: Yale University Press, 1997.

Smith, Diane. *Letters from Yellowstone.* New York: Viking Penguin, 1999.

Smith, Douglas W., and Gary Ferguson. *Decade of the Wolf: Returning the Wild to Yellowstone* (Guilford, Conn.: The Lyons Press, 2005).

Stegner, Wallace. *The Sound of Mountain Water: The Changing American West.* Lincoln: University of Nebraska Press, 1985.

Tweed, William C. *Uncertain Path: A Search for the Future of National Parks.* Berkeley: University of California Press, 2010.

Vale, Thomas R. *The American Wilderness: Reflections on Nature Protection in the United States.* Charlottesville: University of Virginia Press, 2005.

Vale, Thomas R., ed. *Fire, Native Peoples, and the Natural Landscape.* Washington, D.C.: Island Press, 2002.

Wallace, Linda, ed. *After the Fires: The Ecology of Change in Yellowstone National Park.* New Haven: Yale University Press, 2004.

Westerling, Anthony L., H. G. Hidalgo, D. R. Cayan, and T. W. Swetnam. "Warming and Earlier Spring Increase Western US Forest Wildfire Activity." *Science* 313 (2006) 5789: 940–943.

Westerling, Anthony L., Monica G. Turner, Erica A. H. Smithwick, William H. Romme, and Michael G. Ryan. "Continued Warming Could Transform Greater Yellowstone Fire Regimes by mid-21st Century." *Proceedings of the National Academy of Sciences* 108 (August 9, 2011) 32: 13165–13170.

White, P. J., and Kerry A. Gunther. "Population Dynamics: Influence of Resources and Other Factors on Animal Density." Pp. 47-68 in P. J. White, Robert A. Garrott, and Glenn E. Plumb, eds. *Yellowstone's Wildlife in Transition.* Cambridge, Mass.: Harvard University Press, 2013.

Whittlesey, Lee H. *Death in Yellowstone: Accidents and Foolhardiness in the First National Park.* Lanham, MD: Roberts Rinehart Publishing, 2014.

——. *Storytelling in Yellowstone: Horse and Buggy Tour Guides.* Albuquerque: University of New Mexico Press, 2007.

——.*Yellowstone Place Names.* N.p.: Wonderland Publishing Co., 2006. Second edition, revised.

——, and Elizabeth A. Watry, eds. *Ho! For Wonderland: Travelers' Accounts of Yellowstone, 1872-1914.* Albuquerque: University of New Mexico Press, 2009.

Williams, Florence. *The Nature Fix: Why Nature Makes Us Happier, Healthier, and More Creative* (New York: Norton, 2017).

Yochim, Michael J. *A Week in Yellowstone's Thorofare: A Journey Through the Remotest Place.* Corvallis: Oregon State University Press, 2016.

——. *Protecting Yellowstone: Science and the Politics of National Park Management.* Albuquerque: University of New Mexico Press, 2013.

——. "Yellowstone City Park: The Dominating Influence of Politicians in National Park Service Policymaking." *Journal of Policy History* 23 (2011): 381-398.

——. *Yellowstone and the Snowmobile: Locking Horns over National Park Use.* Lawrence: University Press of Kansas, 2009.

——. "Compromising Yellowstone: The Interest Group-National Park Service Relationship in Modern Policy-Making." PhD Dissertation, University of Wisconsin-Madison, 2004.

——. "Beauty and the Beet: The Dam Battles of Yellowstone." *Montana the Magazine of Western History* 53 (Spring 2003): 14-27.

Websites

Peak Bagger. "Most Remote Spots in USA Wilderness Complexes," www.peakbagger.com.

National Park Service, Yellowstone National Park. Numerous webpages, www.nps.gov/yell.

Wikipedia. "Cougar," "Gray Wolf," and "History of Wolves in Yellowstone," www.wikipedia.org.